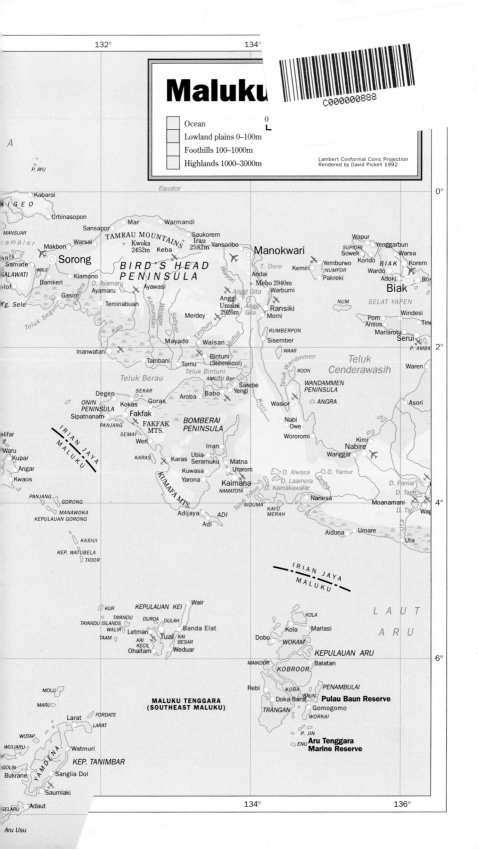

MALUKU

INDONESIAN
SPICE ISLANDS

Text and photographs by
KAL MULLER

Edited by David Pickell

PERIPLUS
EDITIONS

Maluku

This book is organized into
the following four sections

CENTRAL MALUKU

BANDA ISLANDS

NORTH MALUKU

SOUTHEAST MALUKU

© 1997 by Periplus Editions (HK) Ltd.

Third edition
ALL RIGHTS RESERVED
Printed in the Republic of Singapore
ISBN 962-593-176-7

Publisher: Eric Oey
Designer: David Pickell
Cartography: David Pickell

We welcome comments and additions from
readers. Please address all correspondence to:
Periplus (Singapore) Pte. Ltd.
5 Little Road #08-01
Singapore 536983.

International Distributors:
The Netherlands: Nilsson & Lamm BV,
Postbus 195, 1380 AD Weesp
Germany: Brettschneider Fernreisebedarf,
Feldkirchner Strasse 2, D-85551 Heimstetten
Indonesia: PT. Wira Mandala Pustaka
(Java Books - Indonesia), Jl. Kelapa Gading
Kirana, Blok A14 No. 17, Jakarta 14240
Japan: Tuttle Shokai Inc., 21-13, Seki 1-Chome,
Tama-ku, Kawasaki, Kanagawa 214
Singapore and Malaysia: Berkeley Books Pte.
Ltd., 5 Little Rd, #08-01, Singapore 536983
U.K.: GeoCenter U.K. Ltd., The Viables Centre,
Harrow Way, Basingstoke, Hampshire RG22 4BJ
U.S.A.: NTC/Contemporary Publishing Company
(Passport Guides), 4255 W. Touhy Avenue,
Lincolnwood [Chicago], Illinois 60646-1975

The Periplus Adventure Guides Series

BALI

JAVA

SUMATRA

KALIMANTAN *Indonesian Borneo*

SULAWESI *The Celebes*

EAST OF BALI *From Lombok to Timor*

MALUKU *Indonesian Spice Islands*

IRIAN JAYA *Indonesian New Guinea*

DIVING INDONESIA

SURFING INDONESIA

BIRDING INDONESIA

TREKKING INDONESIA *(1998)*

WEST MALAYSIA *and Singapore*

EAST MALAYSIA *and Brunei*

While we try to ensure all the information in our
guides is accurate and up-to-date, the authors
and publisher accept no liability for any
inconvenience, injury or loss sustained by any
person using this book.

Cover: A man from the Tanimbar Islands.
Pages 4-5: The islands around Ternate.
Pages 6-7: A fisherman off Ambon.
Frontispiece: A Naulu woman from Seram.
All photographs in this volume, unless
otherwise noted, are by Kal Muller.

Contents

PAGE 49

PAGE 19

PAGE 87

PART III: Banda Islands

PART IV: North Maluku

PAGE 118

PAGE 150

PART V: *Southeast Maluku*

Practicalities

Area Practicalities

AUTHOR'S DEDICATION

To Don Jorge Alvarez Castillo
with appreciation and deep respect

With special thanks to: Des Alwi, Banda's perfect host; Tony Tomasoa, who is always helpful; Pak Sumileh, friend and travel companion; The Molucca's Roman Catholic bishop and his excellent library; The Hotel Mutiara, owner and staff, for their generous, friendly hospitality; the local tourism office headed by Pak Oratmangun.

THE AUTHOR

Kal Muller has photographed and written about Indonesia for many years. His work has appeared in dozens of books, as well as in the pages of *National Geographic*, *Geo* and many other magazines.

CONTRIBUTORS

Nico de Jonge is a cultural anthropologist at the Center for Non-Western Studies at the University of Leiden. He is the author of numerous publications on the material culture of various Indonesian ethnic groups.

Sylvia Pessireron is a Dutch-Moluccan journalist who writes on travel and lifestyle for various Dutch newspapers and magazines. She has traveled extensively in Southeast Asia, including several times to Maluku.

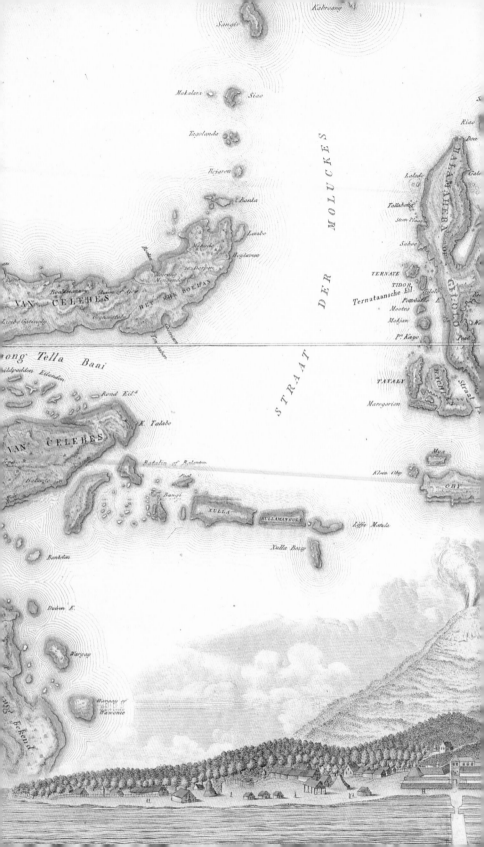

PART I

Introducing Maluku

The Moluccan archipelago, a thousand-odd islands in a vast expanse of blue, lies well beyond Bali and the usual Indonesian tourist circuit. Some of the islands are volcanic, and dressed in luxuriant vegetation. Others are coral atolls, lined with swaying palms. But they are all beautiful. And they are blessed with some of the finest beaches in the world: oases of soft sand and impossibly blue water.

Today, a mere 1.85 million people—of a nation of 197 million—live here in scattered, usually small, villages. Only Ambon, the provincial capital of the Moluccas, now called Maluku, is of sufficient size to be called a city.

Maluku's Spice Islands have a rich, though not particularly savory, history. Tiny islands here—Ternate and Tidore, Ambon, the Bandas—supplied Europe with precious cloves, nutmeg and mace. The search for the source of these spices, the 15th century's great mystery, fueled the Age of Exploration.

In successive waves, beginning in the 16th century, the Portuguese, Spanish, Dutch and British overran the islands, each claiming an exclusive on the lucrative trade. Only the Dutch, through sometimes brutal suppression of indigenous sovereignty, were able to make the monopoly stick.

Like most of Indonesia off the beaten path, the islands of Maluku provide an endless series of attractions for those with a true spirit of adventure. The possibilities range from tough inland trekking into jungle-clad mountains to basking on white sand beaches a short distance from a comfortable hotel.

Of the nine or more still-smoking volcanoes here, two are easy to reach. Gunung Api ("Fire Mountain") in the middle of the tiny Banda archipelago, is a perfect cone reaching 656 meters above the surface of the Banda Sea. This volcano erupted as recently as 1988, devastating crops and forcing the thousands of people who lived on Gunung Api's lower slopes to evacuate. Gamalama Volcano, crowning tiny Ternate, tops 1700 meters.

On the old Spice Islands, clove and nutmeg groves recall the days of European exploration. Today, all the clove production is used within Indonesia, as the chopped spice is rolled with tobacco in fragrant *kretek* cigarets. Centuries-old Portuguese and Dutch forts, sometimes crumbling and overrun with vegetation, stand as reminders that the European trade monopolies were established here by force.

In the interiors of some of the larger islands, like Buru, Halmahera, Seram and the Sulas, people live in a way more or less uninfluenced by the outside world. And on several of the islands, including Ambon, traces of ancient and poorly understood megalithic civilizations remain in stone altars and thrones, and old style costumes, dances and rituals.

Most Moluccans live a stone's throw from the water, and these clear tropical seas are teeming with life. Maluku is near the center of species diversity for the entire Indo-Pacific region, and has more species of fish and invertebrates than just about anywhere in the world. Most of the reefs are pristine, and ideal for snorkeling, scuba diving or fishing.

Life in Maluku has interesting rhythms of its own. Sago palm trunks are processed into flour to provide an island staple. Tie-dyed thread is woven into Indonesia's famous *ikat* cloth, and strips of fiber are worked into baskets and sleeping mats. Hunters seek wild pigs and deer, and fisherman snare their quarry from outrigger canoes.

To earn a little cash, cloves and nutmeg, and coconuts (for copra) are extensively cultivated. Divers plunge for pearls, mother-of-pearl oysters and *trepang*—a sea cucumber that is dried and made by the Chinese into a delicious soup.

Overleaf: *An old Dutch map of the Moluccas. In the foreground is Ternate.* **Opposite:** *A secluded beach on the Kei Islands in Southeastern Maluku.*

GEOGRAPHY

Islands of Coral and Islands of Fire

Those islands…you couldn't see them in a lifetime. Not in two lives. Some are great countries and some are three coconuts, and the ocean is full of them. They are like stars in the sky. There's thousands of them.
— C. M. Thomlinson, *Tidemarks*

Maluku's thousand-odd islands (one count claims 999; another 1,029) extend across an area of some 851,000 square kilometers, only 10 percent of which is land. Geologically, biologically and culturally, these islands form a fascinating zone of transition between the Sunda Islands to the west and the Sahul zone to the east.

In geological terms, the Moluccan island chain is an infant, no more than a few million years old. Still, it is amazingly complex. Three of the earth's great tectonic plates meet in the Moluccas. The plates collide directly, scrape

past each other, force another plate up or down, or fragment, producing a variety of geological effects. The result is the great, 6,000-kilometer-long Indonesian Ring of Fire. One end is marked by the Nicobar and Andaman islands; the other, the arc leading up through Maluku and into the Philippines.

Split island chain

Through Maluku, this island arc is split. In the south, the outer arc is formed of contorted, mostly calcareous mudstones, limestones and a some rare intrusive rock. (See map below.) This outer arc marks the northern boundary of the shallow Arafura Sea. It begins in the west with the barren, uplifted coral reefs of the Leti and Babar islands, and continuing counterclockwise, includes the forested, slightly larger Tanimbars, the Kei, Watubela and Gorong groups, and finally hooks sharply back to include large, almost inaccessibly mountainous, Seram and Buru. Somewhat east of this outer arc is the Aru group, built of raised coral reefs cut through with narrow, mangrove-lined channels.

The inner arc is geologically quite different. A continuation of a chain that includes Sumatra, Java and Bali, here are the volcanic islands, beginning with large Wetar in the west, and extending northeast through the Damar group to include tiny Gunung Api in Banda. These islands mark a plate boundary, where molten rock has worked up through fissures in the earth's crust.

North of Seram, the double line of islands becomes less clear. The strangely shaped island of Halmahera (like Sulawesi, formed by the slow collision of two narrow islands) is marked on its western side by a line of young, active volcanoes, including Ternate. The rest of Halmahera is made up of older volcanic rock, calcareous sediments, and ultrabasic materials forced up from beneath the ocean.

Taliabu and Mangole Islands are anomalous, having been formed when granitic fragments of the earth's crust were torn from the land mass of Irian Jaya and carried several hundred kilometers away by currents of magma. These islands disrupt the symmetry of the double chain.

Farming and economics

With the lucrative spice trade a thing of the past, the economy of Maluku has now settled into a more mundane pattern of subsistence

Geology of Maluku

☐ Raised coral limestone
☐ Volcanic
☐ New Guinea granites

PACIFIC OCEAN

P. Morotai

Note: The eastern half of Halmahera is made of limestone, old volcanic rock, and ultrabasic sediments.

P. Ternate
P. Tidore
Pulau Halmahera

LAUT MALUKU

LAUT HALMAHERA

Kepulauan Sula
P. Bacan
Pulau Obi

Irian Jaya (New Guinea)

P. Seram
P. Buru
Kepulauan Lease
P. Ambon

Kepulauan Banda

Kepulauan Kei

LAUT BANDA

Kepulauan Aru

P. Wetar
Kepulauan Babar
P. Leti
Kepulauan Tanimbar

Timor

Opposite: *An atoll north of the Tanimbar islands, only a tiny bit of which is still land.*

agriculture. Zanzibar, in the Indian Ocean off the coast of Tanzania, and other islands in Indonesia (e.g. Sumatra) now produce more cloves; Grenada and other Indonesian islands provide the lion's share of the world's nutmeg. Neither spice commands the fabulous price it did in the 18th century and before.

In Maluku, the staples today are mostly root crops such as manioc (also called cassava, the source of tapioca), taro and sweet potatoes, supplemented by beans and other vegetables. The sago palm also provides prodigious quantities of staple starch. In the few favored alluvial plains, wetland rice is cultivated. Bananas are ubiquitous. Fishing provides the bulk of the protein in the local diet, although wild pigs and other game are hunted in some areas.

The biggest cash crop is copra, dried coconut meat. Cloves, cacao (for chocolate), nutmeg and coffee are also exported from the region. Cacao, a relatively new introduction, is grown mainly in the Tobelo district of Halmahera, in Bacan, and on Taliabu and Mangole in the Sula archipelago. Nutmeg comes from Banda, while cloves are produced principally in Seram and the neighboring Lease islands. Commercial fishermen export a variety of fish, especially tuna, as well as shrimp. Smaller operations yield *trepang* (sea cucumbers), mother-of-pearl, seaweed for medicines and cosmetics, squid and sharks' fin. The Japanese skim off the best, paying top yen for the tuna and shrimp. Chinese gastronomes buy the *trepang* and sharks' fin, for soups.

Many of the larger islands hold large timber resources, which provide thousands of jobs. In a few areas, rattan is harvested for furniture (about 500 tons a year) and on a few islands, damar or gum copal, used in varnishes, is harvested (about 165 tons per year). Other valuable tree products include massoi bark, which produces an aromatic oil used in folk medicine to cure rheumatism and other ills. On Buru Island, the cineole rich leaves of a type of tropical myrtle are harvesting, yielding the renowned "kayu putih" medicinal oil used in a variety of remedies.

So far, mineral wealth from the subsoil has been disappointing, although exploration is still going on and holds hope of future finds. Gold has recently been discovered on Wetar Island and the nickel mines on Gebe Island have for several years produced ore, most of which is shipped to Japan.

In addition to these legitimate products, other high-priced exotica still reach the markets illegally, including bird of paradise skins and feathers, live cockatoos and parrots, and untaxed ambergris and pearls—usually white, but with an occasional black beauty. Fine old ancestral carvings and traditional gold jewelry are also being sold off to finance a new outboard motor or a TV set.

—with assistance from David Wall

FLORA AND FAUNA

A Mix of Australian and Asian Species

The plants and animals of the Moluccas are much like those present on Hollywood tropical islands. Overhead are exotic clove and nutmeg trees, coconut palms, bananas, and trees sprouting strange and fragrant tropical fruits. A great variety of birds—pigeons, sunbirds, lories, cockatoos and kingfishers—fly and screech overhead. Just offshore, the coral-filled seas teem with bright fish, anemones, and sponges. Even scientists are moved to grandiloquence.

"The forests of the Moluccas offer to the naturalist a very striking example of the luxuriance and beauty of animal life in the tropics," writes British naturalist Sir Alfred Russel Wallace in *The Malay Archipelago*. "The glorious birds and insects render the Moluccas a classic ground in the eyes of the naturalist, and characterize its fauna as one of the most remarkable and beautiful upon the globe."

From the biologist's point of view, Maluku—except for Aru—falls into a large area called Wallacea, named after Wallace, who spent eight years here during the 1850s.

In an 1863 paper Wallace had drawn a red line on the map of the Indies west of Sulawesi and Lombok, dividing Asian and Australian faunas. T. H. Huxley later called it "Wallace's Line." (See map opposite.) As evidence grew, more lines were proposed, but scientists now think of a transition zone rather than a line.

Wallacea is the island region between the Sunda and Sahul continental shelves. During the great Ice Ages, with much of the world's water tied up in ice, much of the South China Sea was dry land, and Sumatra, Borneo, Java and Bali were all connected to the Asian mainland. At the same time, New Guinea was connected to Australia by a land bridge. When the Ice Ages receded, the seas rose and the western land mass became the islands of today. New Guinea and the Arus separated at the same time from Australia.

The Moluccas therefore form a transitional zone between the two very different types of plant and animal species—those characteristic of Asia (e.g., placental mammals), and those characteristic of Australia (e.g., marsupials). As a result of selective migrations of species and their ensuing isolation on these islands, many unique hybrids and evolutionary holdovers found nowhere else in the world flourish in the Moluccas.

Moluccan wildlife

As one might expect of an island region, where dispersal required the ability to fly or swim, the wildlife of the Moluccas is marked by a scarcity of land mammals and a profusion of birds, insects and fish. The animal world can be characterized as having an impoverished Asian fauna, supplemented by scattered Moluccan endemics and some representatives of the Australian sphere.

During his years of exploration, Wallace found only 10 species of land mammals, several of which were likely to have been introduced by man. The "baboon monkey" (the Sulawesi crested macaque, *Macaca nigra*), which he found only on Bacan, the civet cat, the babirusa (only on Buru), deer and a small shrew were brought in as domestic animals or pets, according to the eminent naturalist.

Except for the wild pig, the indigenous species are all marsupials. These include a

Left: *The Moluccas' white-bellied sea eagle feeds on fish, snared in shallow water.*

small, flying opossum and the cuscus, a cat-sized, tree-dwelling creature with a long, prehensile tail, a small head, large eyes and woolly fur. The cuscus is a cute little bugger, but unfortunately makes good eating. When sighted, these slow-moving animals are captured by climbing the trees and just grabbing them. Maluku also hosts 25 species of bats.

Moluccan waters harbor an unusual marine mammal as well, the sluggish and gentle dugong. A relative of the freshwater manatee, it is the only marine mammal that is an herbivore. This poor beast is now endangered, thanks to poachers, who eat the 400–600 kilo animals and make cigaret holders out of their tusks.

Although he found few mammals, "The fishes," Wallace writes, "are perhaps unrivalled for variety and beauty by those of any one spot on earth." As Wallace notes in 1863, the renowned Dutch ichthyologist Dr. Pieter Bleeker had already identified 780 fish species in Ambon harbor alone, almost as many species as are found in all the rivers and seas of Europe.

In Wallace's treks through the forest he saw numerous insects and brilliant birds. The sheer numbers of birds, he notes, are not as high as, for example, tin he tropical Americas. But among the 265 species he identified were some real beauties. The majority were parrots, pigeons, kingfishers, sunbirds and, in the Arus, the spectacular birds of paradise.

(See "Aru" page 144.) The 25 parrots include red-crested and sulfur-crested cockatoos, red parrots and crimson lories.

Some of the islands host the bush turkeys or megapodes, primitive birds that lay their eggs in a nest consisting of a huge pile of vegetation or sand, sometimes reaching eight meters in diameter and two meters in height. These birds are evolutionary throwbacks and do not incubate their eggs, but bury them like reptiles. The warm sand or decomposing vegetation provides the heat necessary to hatch the eggs. The chicks, which gestate for a remarkably long two months, spring from their shells quite well-developed and require no further maternal assistance. Unfortunately for the megapodes (the word means "big-footed"), man finds their flesh quite tasty, and if the prominent nests are found, steals the eggs too.

The large, extraordinary cassowary, found in Maluku only on the Aru Islands and Seram, also ends up in the natives' pots. These birds are hunted carefully, as the flightless, ostrich-like cassowaries have disemboweled men with their sharp claws and tough feet. The birds stand up to a meter and a half tall, and their large bodies are covered with hair-like feathers—these are used in headdresses and other ornamentation. Instead of wings, cassowaries sprout a group of horny black spines, something like blunt porcupine quills. The birds feed on fallen

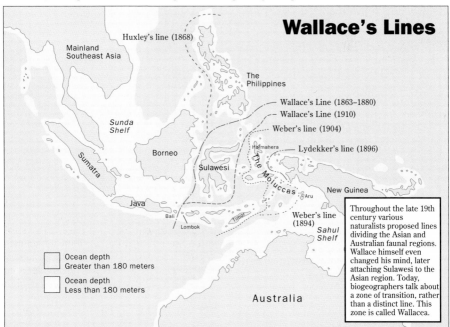

Wallace's Lines

Huxley's line (1868)

Mainland Southeast Asia

The Philippines

Wallace's Line (1863–1880)
Wallace's Line (1910)
Weber's line (1904)
Lydekker's line (1896)

Sunda Shelf

Sumatra

Borneo

Sulawesi

Halmahera

The Moluccas

Aru

New Guinea

Java

Bali

Lombok

Timor

Weber's line (1894)

Sahul Shelf

Ocean depth Greater than 180 meters

Ocean depth Less than 180 meters

Australia

Throughout the late 19th century various naturalists proposed lines dividing the Asian and Australian faunal regions. Wallace himself even changed his mind, later attaching Sulawesi to the Asian region. Today, biogeographers talk about a zone of transition, rather than a distinct line. This zone is called Wallacea.

fruit, insects and crustaceans. The species found on Seram is called the helmeted cassowary (*Casuarius galeatus*) because of the horny casque or helmet that adorns its head. The bare skin on the neck of this species is conspicuous with bright blue and red colors.

"There is, perhaps, no island in the world so small as Amboyna [Ambon] where so many grand insects are to be found," Wallace writes. The most dramatic is the grand bird-winged butterfly (*Ornithoptera poseidon*), whose brilliant blue-green wings, 20 centimeters across, gracefully carry its golden, crimson-breasted body. In addition to the colorful butterflies, Wallace found endless joy in the many strange beetles he found.

Cloves and nutmeg

Maluku is most famous for two trees: the nutmeg and the clove. At one time, the Banda Islands were the nutmeg garden of the world. Few cultivated plants are more beautiful than nutmeg trees (*Myristica fragrans*), which thrive on Banda's moist air and light volcanic soils. The hard, aromatic "nut" or seed of this tree is ground into the familiar spice. Even more valuable however, is mace, a spice prepared from the bright red, waxy aril that covers this nut. Nutmeg trees are somewhat sensitive, like coffee, and are cultivated in groves protected by tall *kanari* trees. (Ironically, nutmeg prices have fallen so much that the rich, oily *kanari* nuts planted to protect the nutmeg now produce a crop that is more valuable.)

Cloves were the most valuable of Maluku's spices. Until the Dutch intruded, all of the world's cloves came from five small islands off the west coast of Halmahera: Ternate, Tidore, Moti, Makian and Bacan. Wild cloves, native to these islands, possessed little flavor, and were tended by man to produce fragrant, spice grade cloves.

The spice comes from the flower buds, which cluster at the ends of the twigs of a moderate-sized tropical evergreen tree called *Eugenia aromatica*. These nail-shaped buds (the English word "clove" comes from the French *clou,* or "nail") are dried and used whole or ground. An average tree yields a few kilos of cloves per year, gathered from June through December with June–September being the peak harvest.

There are relatively few flowering plants in Maluku, and trees are chief among the islands' plant species. The coconut tree provides nourishment and sustains an export market in copra, dried coconut meat which is used in cooking and is pressed to yield oil for

cooking and cosmetics. Fruit trees are not uncommon in the islands, but there are fewer than in mainland Asia. Bananas are everywhere and many families plant papaya trees. Less common are *rambutan*s and the universally appreciated mangosteen.

One of the region's most famous fruits is the durian. Foreigners are often repelled by this incomparable fruit's strong smell, but according to one 17th century account, "the natives give it honourable titles and make verses on it." Wallace, for his part, considered that it was worth a trip to the East just to eat durian. He first says the flavor cannot be described, then characterizes it as "a rich butter-like custard highly flavoured with almonds...intermingled with wafts of flavour that call to mind cream cheese, onion sauce, brown cherry, and other ingredients...the more you eat of it, the less you feel inclined to stop." The strong flavor of the durian inspires either love or hate. And it takes strong, knowledgeable hands—and a heavy knife—to open the spiny husk of this pineapple-sized fruit and get at the creamy pulp.

Wallace waxes only slightly less eloquent when writing of the breadfruit: "a luxury I have never met with before or since [coming to Ambon]." Baked on hot embers, he compares the taste to Yorkshire pudding. "With meat and gravy, it is a vegetable superior to any I know, either in temperate or tropical countries. With sugar, milk, butter, or treacle

it is a delicious pudding."

Taro and yams were brought from the Asian mainland by the early inhabitants of the Moluccas and, along with rice and millet, were the staples of the Moluccan diet. Since the introduction of sweet potatoes from the New World (perhaps as early as the 5th century A.D., or much later by the Portuguese) this vegetable has become popular. The basic farming method in the Moluccas is swidden agriculture (slash-and-burn).

Manioc was also brought from the New

World by the Portuguese, and today is the most frequently planted root crop in Maluku. Manioc (also called cassava) yields more than either taro or the native yams, and with less work. Corn from the Americas is now thoroughly integrated into the diet. On the arid islands between Timor and Tanimbar only corn can be grown. Even corn cannot survive seasonal drought, and in the dry Southwestern Islands, January and February are called the "hunger season."

The productive sago palm

An important non-swidden crop, the sago palm (*Metroxylon* spp.) sustains life in the central and northern islands. In the past, sago was precious, because it could be stored almost indefinitely and carried long distances without spoiling. And no other crop produces so many calories for so little work. The density of trees can be anywhere from less than a dozen to 330 per hectare, making it an economical land user.

Working sago provides up to three times more calories per man-hour than the cultivation of domesticated tubers or grains, and the palms suffer little damage from wild animals, pests or an abnormal season.

Ten man-days of work harvesting sago can produce enough food for a year's supply of food for an adult—280 kilos of sago cakes. "Without sago," writes Shirley Deane in her excellent *Ambon: Island of Spices*, "Ambon

would cease to function." Sago's only disadvantage is that its ease of harvest often discourages the planting of other crops, which are needed to balance out a diet based on sago's satisfying, though relatively non-nutritious, starch.

Sago starch comes from the pith of a large palm tree. It is harvested after the tree is about 15 years old, and is just about to flower (after which it dies). The trunk-like stem is cut and then the bark is stripped off, revealing the pithy starch that makes up the bulk of the tree. This pith is laced with woody fibers that must be broken down using a special club-like tool which has a sharp piece of stone or metal embedded into the business end.

Once broken up, the narrow strips of fiber are cut away, and the remaining starchy matter is strained through leaf mats to remove the stringy fiber. The sago is then boiled, and baked into little cakes, which allows it to keep almost indefinitely.

Many westerners consider sago bland, but Wallace, ever the optimist, writes that hot sago cakes "are very nice with butter, and when made with the addition of a little sugar and grated coconut, are quite a delicacy."

Shirley Deane notes that sago is not just a foodstuff, but a building material as well:

"[E]very scrap of the sago palm is used for making something. The outer walls of houses are made from its tough bark.... The roofs, like the ceilings inside, are made of sago leaves.... They don't look too secure, but they survive the high winds and obliterating downpours of the rainy season, without too much damage or leaking."

Opposite: *Picking cloves requires tedious hand labor.* **Above, left:** *Nutmegs, just harvested, with the fruit (like a small, hard peach) already removed. The scarlet aril will be removed and shipped separately as mace.* **Above, right:** *Cloves, just picked. The spice comes from the unopened flower buds of* Eugenia aromatica.

Sea Crossings and Stone Monuments

Not much is known about the earliest population of the Moluccas. It is assumed that the first inhabitants came on foot from the Asian mainland during the most recent period of low sea levels. By some estimates, these people reached Australia 40,000 years ago, so they would have made it to Maluku even earlier. At that time the South China Sea lay dry and the western half of the Indonesian archipelago formed a whole with the continent.

As the last Ice Age came to a close, about 10,000 years ago, meltwater had caused the sea level to rise to the point that the land bridges were submerged. The inhabitants of the area became isolated on numerous islands, some of which now form Maluku.

Skeletons excavated in Sumatra indicate that the appearance of the first island inhabitants was much like that of the current Papuans of New Guinea. Traces of these aboriginal people can still be found in the Moluccas today, in language and genes.

It is assumed that the first Moluccans lived on hunting and fishing. Agriculture is believed to have not yet been known.

The Austronesian expansion

We are more familiar with the immigrants who assimilated into the earliest population of the islands in the Neolithic Period, the late Stone Age, about 5,000 years ago. These were the so-called Austronesians, speakers of Austronesian languages. These are the ancestors of today's Malays. It is generally assumed that, starting at the beginning of the third millennium B.C., they spread out over the Indonesian archipelago and the islands of the Pacific coming from the Asiatic mainland in seaworthy boats with outriggers.

Right: The decorated prow of a stone ship in the village center of Sanglia Dol in the Tanimbar islands. **Opposite:** The ship is thought to have brought to Sanglia Dol the village's founders.

Linguistic research has shown that nearly all languages spoken in the Moluccas belong to the Austronesian Ambon–Timor language category, even the languages from Aru, which geologically and biologically belongs to New Guinea. Only a few ethnic groups in or near North Halmahera, like the Tobelo and Sahu, speak a non-Austronesian language, as do some of the inhabitants of Kisar, in the southwestern islands.

As far as appearance is concerned, the Austronesian migrants were related to contemporary Indonesians. They introduced the breeding of pigs and chickens, the cultivation of tubers and bananas and they were skilled potters. An important Austronesian tool was a special kind of adze with a stone blade, the so-called quadrangular adze, ground into a rectangular cross-section. Examples of this artifact have been found at many archaeological sites in Indonesia, and it is now considered to be a "guide fossil" of the Neolithic Period.

The Dongson culture

The Austronesian immigrants who displaced the earlier hunters and gatherers in the archipelago, were soon influenced by a bronze and iron culture, which is called the Dongson culture, after an archaeological site in what is now Vietnam. The Bronze and Iron Age probably penetrated Indonesia around the middle of the first millennium B.C. In various areas

of life new attainments were adopted. The cultivation of rice on artificially irrigated fields was introduced, the technique of weaving was established, the water buffalo was domesticated, and—of course—the working of bronze and iron was started.

Chickens were introduced somewhat later, as were betel chewing, the increased utilization of breadfruit, yams, taro and new techniques to work the sago palm.

An important result of all this was an increasing specialization of labor, which led to more differentiated social organization. Instead of a more or less egalitarian society, a hierarchically structured one arose. The status of the leaders was confirmed by ritual festivals with a competitive character and the erection of megaliths as lasting signs of prestige. On various islands there was a complete hierarchy of these festivals and stone raisings. Many of the most famous traditional groups in Indonesia, for example the Batak of Sumatra, the Toraja of Sulawesi and the Dayak of Kalimantan, are still known for their megalithic ceremonies.

On Ambon Island one still finds sacred grounds with stone slabs and throne-like seats. Despite the age-long influence of Islam and Christianity these traces of the Dongson culture are still perceptible.

In the Tanimbar islands the influences of the Dongson tradition are apparent in the decorations on stones which lie, grouped in the form of a ship, in various village centers. It is said that these large "stone ships" symbolize the vessels in which the village's founders came from the west. In earlier days the stone ships served as a meeting place or ceremonial dance location, and rituals for the deities and ancestors were performed here.

The finely worked prows of the stone ships are conspicuous. The ornamentation of the applied decorations is typified by a play of forms of bent lines, in which spiral motifs are predominant. These are the characteristic artforms of the Dongson culture, with which we are reasonably familiar because of the excavations of numerous bronze objects from the last centuries B.C.

Insight into the Dongson artforms has been gained through the study of bronze kettle drums—big, sometimes man-sized, musical instruments. It is believed that the patterns were first modeled in clay, and afterwards the drums usually cast in stone molds. The kettle drums have achieved a special meaning because of the exceedingly fine decorations with which they are covered from top to bottom.

The basic patterns, often spirals from which new spirals spring, are also found in the artforms of many traditional Indonesian cultures. In the Tanimbar islands this is not only found in the prows of the "stone ships," but also in the wooden, beautifully cut prows of the real, seagoing boats.

THE SPICE TRADE

Spices and the Age of Exploration

In Medieval Europe, cloves, nutmeg and mace were literally worth their weight in gold. When Magellan's round-the-world expedition—with five fully outfitted ships and 230 men—finally limped home after three years with just over one ton of cloves, it was still enough not only to pay back the Spanish king's huge investment, but to make the survivors rich for life. The spices were highly coveted, not only to make badly preserved meat palatable, but also as medicines and the ingredients in magic potions—which, at the time, were thought to be able to cure anything from the plague to a lover's anguish.

The islands that held the promise of such great wealth and fueled Europe's Age of Discovery are barely visible on any world map. Yet the tiny Banda islands produced the entire world's supply of nutmeg and mace; and Ternate and Tidore, and a few other nearby specks off western Halmahera, were the source of every clove that flavored every roast served in the castles of Europe.

During the Middle Ages, well-organized and armed Arab traders kept a stranglehold on the spice trade to Europe. They kept the supply to their Venetian partners to a steady trickle, and the Europeans were forced to pay any price that was asked. But Europe was busy with the crusades, and the overland route to the East was blocked by the Muslims. Then history took a fateful turn, and in 1453, Constantinople fell to the Turks—quashing any hopes of a direct overland route to the Spice Isles.

The Portuguese initiative

Tiny Portugal was the first to act on a large scale. Her dynamic neighbor, Spain, was succeeding in pushing back the Moors and was on her way to dominating the whole Iberian peninsula. Portugal had to expand or be swallowed up into Spain.

Triggered by the foresight and fortunes of Prince Henry the Navigator (1394–1460),

Portuguese sailors began a series of epic voyages down the coast of Africa, and in 1498 Vasco da Gama rounded the Cape of Good Hope and made his landfall in India. Under Alfonso de Albuquerque, the Portuguese captured Malacca, the key spice entrepôt of the spice trade, in 1511.

Although heroics played a part, Portugal's victory in the spice race was basically a result of technological advantage: ships, navigational instruments and—most of all—ship-mounted cannon. Asia had never seen anything like the Portuguese carrack, which was fast, stable and bristled with cannon.

In Malacca, Albuquerque learned the route to the Spice Isles. Within a year, in 1512, Antonio de Abreu led a flotilla of three small vessels of 50 tons each and a total of 120 men to the Banda Islands. On the return to Malacca, one of the ships, captained by Francisco Serrão, grounded on a reef off an uninhabited islet, Nusa Telu, near West Ambon. (Some accounts locate the wreck in the Lucipara Islands.) The survivors commandeered a passing local boat and made their way to North Ambon Island.

Hearing of a new breed of men, Sultan Al Manshur of Ternate sent *kora-kora* war canoes to fetch them. Serrão became the sultan's trusted advisor, especially in military affairs, until his death in 1521. Eight months later, the sad remains of Ferdinand Magellan's Spanish financed round-the-world team reached Ternate. From east and west, the Iberians had found the Moluccas.

Early references to the Spice Isles

The earliest record of the Spice Isles was penned by the Chinese. It is possible that northern China acquired cloves through the Yüeh merchants who bartered for the spice in the Philippines. The Early Han Dynasty (206 B.C.–A.D. 200) annals state that the officers of the court were required to put cloves in their mouths before addressing the emperor. It is perhaps the corruption of the Chinese *xiang ding*—"fragrant nails"—that led to the contemporary Indonesian word for cloves, *cenkeh*. A later Chinese source mentions Tanyu—Ternate?—as the source for cloves (today called *ding xiang,* "nail incense").

A logical deduction, taking into account geography, wind patterns, naval craft, navigational technology and history, would con-

Opposite: *A* kora-kora, *the traditional warship of the Moluccas. The Dutch used them in vicious raids to enforce their clove monopoly.*

clude that cloves were first introduced to Java, then to India and later to China. There had been contacts for many centuries between the Moluccas and islands to the west. Banggai—as well as Buton and Selayar—had provided the Moluccas with iron axes, swords and knives.

Pre-Muslim Arab sailors and overland caravans brought cloves to the Roman Empire where they fetched one hundred times their value in India. An apocryphal reference from Pliny the Elder's A.D. 79 *Historia Naturalis* might pass for the first European reference to cloves, but the earliest unquestioned mention of this spice in the Roman Empire surfaces in a law digest of A.D. 176. After this, cloves and nutmeg were always referred to as the most prized of commodities arriving from India. The Romans used cloves in cooking, and most importantly, to scent the air in their temples and during funerals.

From the law digest, we learn that cloves were imported through Alexandria by Eastern merchants who would accept only hard metal cash in exchange. As many a trader was subsequently to discover, European goods were not wanted in Asia (except for Venetian glass). Later, the Spanish had to fill the *Manila* galleon with American silver to obtain Far East luxuries.

Our next reference to this part of the world, from the T'ang Dynasty (A.D. 618–906), calls the clove-producing islands "Mi Li Ku," pretty close to the current "Maluku." Other sources attribute "Maluku" to "Jaziratul Jabal Malik," a term derived from the Arabic expression for the lands or islands of kings; still others suggest it comes from "Maloko Kirana," meaning "area of mountainous islands," referring to Ternate, Tidore, Makian and either Bacan or Halmahera.

Cloves appear in the Arab tales of Sinbad the Sailor in A.D. 1001—together with less than accurate descriptions by the Islamic geographers Masudi and the usually knowledgeable Ibn Batuta. During his sojourn in Sumatra, Marco Polo also mentions the clove trade, but prudently refrains from a distorted description of the region.

The arrival of Islam

During the 13th century, the Sriwijaya Empire of Sumatra was already in the clove business, probably obtaining the spice through various north Javanese ports. By the early 14th century, many Javanese and Arabs had sailed to the Moluccas to trade rice, cloth and luxuries for cloves. Later in the same century, when the spice trade had picked up thanks to European demand, the Javanese chronicle of the Majapahit Empire lists the spice islands as a "dependency"—but this was probably just wishful thinking.

By this time, there was a long history of Javanese and Arab traders in Ternate. They introduced ship-building techniques and the

cursive, phonetic writing of Islam. But the Ternateans never developed high-sided cargo vessels of their own—in all of the Moluccas, only the Bandanese built such ships.

An early account gives the name of the first ruler of Ternate as the most unlikely "Chicho," who began his reign in 1257. More likely, the first king of Ternate to adopt the Islamic faith was Zainalabdin (a 19th century account calls him Mahum, and locals today call him Awal), who took the title of sultan for himself and his descendants. Local histories state that the ruler converted to Islam in the 13th century, while Portuguese sources insist on a date some two centuries later.

Portuguese trade begins

Fra Odoric, a wandering Italian monk who stopped in Java and Sumatra in the 13th century, mentions in his writings that cloves come from somewhere to the east of Java. Another Italian, Ludovico di Varthema, supposedly visited the Moluccas in 1506 and described the clove trees. He would be the first European to have set foot on these islands—if his account could be substantiated. But the best and earliest description of the islands east of Java flows from the quill of Tome Pires, a Portuguese official who lived in Malacca from 1512 to 1515.

Pires' *Suma Oriental,* written after extensive interviews with Javanese and Arab merchants, gives a remarkably accurate geographical description of Ternate, Tidore and three other nearby clove-producing islands. Together, Pires writes, the islands exported 5,000 to 7,000 *bahars* (a *bahar* was 450–660 pounds) of cloves a year. The account includes a description of the ongoing war between the Sultan of Ternate and his father-in-law, the king of Tidore. It was this sultan—called, variously, Sayan Nasirullah, Al Manshur or Ben Acorala—who had sent for Serrão and his mates, shipwrecked during de Abreu's pioneer voyage. Pires throws in such eye-opening details as a description of the sultan's 400-woman harem and his collection of precious Venetian beads.

In 1513, Captain Antonio de Miranda Azevedo led the first commercial Portuguese fleet to the Moluccas. He opened small trading posts on Ternate and Bacan and left behind a few merchants-in-residence. (A conflicting account states it was in 1515, three years after de Abreu reached the Bandas, that the first Portuguese ships, under Alvaro Coelho, reached Ternate.) Azevedo loaded up with cloves and parrots from Morotai for the first successful European round-trip from Malacca to the Moluccas.

By this time, legal disputes were brewing over Portugal's "right" to the Spice Isles. Spain, having finally expelled the Muslims from the Iberian peninsula, itched to take part in explorations. Genoan Christopher Columbus, sailing for the Spanish queen, was

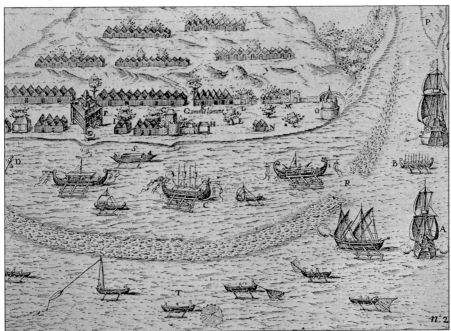

looking for these islands when he happened to discover Hispaniola in 1492. Then Portugal claimed easternmost South America.

To avoid conflicting claims between the two Holy Roman Empire powers, the 1494 Treaty of Tordesillas drew an imaginary line at longitude 47° W. The Portuguese sphere of influence was to begin at this line, which passes through Brazil, and extends halfway around the world to the east, including Africa; Spain's sphere would go halfway around the world to the west, which included the bulk of the Americas. The problem with the Spice Islands was that, according to the current estimation, they were just about halfway around the world from 47° W. The question of who "owned" the Spice Isles led to Ferdinand Magellan's epic circumnavigation.

Magellan's odyssey

Portuguese navigator Fernão Magalhães, the same man as the Spaniards' Magallanes and our Magellan, had fought for Portugal in Africa and during the conquest of Malacca. His future brother-in-law, writer Duarte Barbosa, interviewed members of de Abreu's expedition and penned an accurate description of the Moluccas. Armed with this information and a burning desire for fortune and fame, Magellan returned to Portugal and tried to obtain funding for a trip. He was spurned by the royal court.

Magellan's wounded pride led him to Spain, where he convinced the crown to finance his trip—in order to prove that the Moluccas were on Spain's side of the treaty line. Magellan was in fact confident that this was the case, based on Serrão's celestial observations. (Hindsight shows the clove-producing islands lie between 127° E and 128° E, well within the Portuguese sphere.)

The Spanish-financed jaunt left with five ships and 230 men. Magellan was killed by natives of the Philippines, and the fleet's two remaining ships, the *Victoria* and the *Trinidad,* reached Tidore on November 8, 1521—2 years, 2 months and 28 days after triumphantly sailing out of Seville. The Spanish team was wined and dined in Ternate, and the island was renamed Castigliana (after Castille) and claimed for the Spanish crown. Four traders were left behind. As the two ships departed, the rotting *Trinidad* promptly sank, but her crew of 49 was rescued and piled on the *Victoria* for the journey home. Most died on the way. Still, the four *bahars* of cloves (a bit over a ton) they brought back repaid the Spanish crown's expenses for the trip and made the 18 survivors wealthy men.

Opposite: *Portuguese warships off Ternate, the clove center of the Moluccas until the Dutch concentrated their monopoly on Ambon Island.*
Below: *The first Dutch trading post at Banda Neira, where Bandanese nutmeg growers brought their spices to be sold to the Dutch.*

THE DUTCH MONOPOLY

Holland Seizes the Spice Trade

Though not the first European power to participate in the spice trade, the Dutch were the most successful. For some 200 years they held a monopoly in the precious trade of the Indies. And it was not sailing or marketing prowess that allowed this, but the exercise of sheer, unflinching power.

By the early 17th century, under the determined leadership of Jan Pieterszoon Coen, the Dutch would stop at nothing to maintain their exclusive control of the spices. They fought the Portuguese and Spanish, tortured and executed representatives of their British "allies," murdered tens of thousands of Moluccans, and destroyed all clove trees that they could not control.

The Iberians

In 1522, one year after Magellan had claimed Ternate for Spain, the Portuguese sent a

"governor," Antonio de Brito, to Ternate, and the sultan gave him a plot of land at the edge of the royal town of Gamalama. He erected a fort, officially named Nostra Senhora do Rosario (Our Lady of the Rosary), but usually just called Fort Gamalama. The Portuguese behaved abominably. The least of it was a condescension toward the Ternateans and aggressive Roman Catholic proselytizing. The worst was rape, murder (especially by poison) and countless intrigues designed to fan the existing conflict between Ternate (the Portuguese) and Tidore (the Spanish).

In 1527, the few Spaniards who had settled in Ternate were expelled by the Portuguese. The defeated Spanish settled a short distance away in the rival sultanate of Tidore. The problem was (somewhat) resolved in 1529 when the King Joao II of Portugal, paid 350,000 gold ducats (cruzados) to Spanish Emperor Charles V for the (not quite) undisputed right to the Moluccas. Spain retained the Philippines.

From 1536–1540 Antonio da Galvão, by all accounts a man of integrity and justice, governed Ternate, ending for a while the schemes and murders. Galvão rebuilt the run-down castle, improved the harbor and port facilities, revived agriculture and industry and supported a program of exploration to the east. He established a Portuguese outpost on Ambon which was to come in most handy a few decades later. During his tenure, agricultural products from Brazil and the rest of the Americas made their way to the islands: sweet potatoes, corn, manioc, tomatoes, pineapple, papaya, tobacco, watercress, lettuce and chili peppers.

In 1547, a few years after Galvão left his post, the energetic Francis Xavier, one of Ignatius Loyola's first Jesuits and destined for sainthood, passed through Ternate in an energetic search for souls. Although missionary activities took a leap forward on St. Francis' wings, saving souls—alas—soon took a back seat to another round of intrigue.

A son's revenge

Sultan Hairun, generally considered the second-greatest of the Ternatean rulers, probably enjoyed a most cordial relationship with

Left: V.O.C. head Jan Pieterszoon Coen was responsible for the murderously harsh policies of the Dutch. Opposite: A mid-19th century print of Dutch officers being entertained in Ternate. The dancers' costumes are strictly a product of the European artist's imagination.

Francis Xavier. Historical records are not specific but some suggest that Hairun might have received part of his education from the Jesuits at Goa (a Portuguese enclave in India). But the goodwill between St. Francis and Hairun did not prevent the Portuguese from throwing the sultan into prison for refusing to give his lands to the Portuguese. While in prison, the Portuguese tried to poison the sultan, but he escaped because his ring, equipped with a magical stone, changed colors and warned him not to eat the food. Eventually—the most ill-advised in a long series of venal blunders—the Portuguese succeeded in murdering Hairun.

The murder touched off an infuriated backlash from the Ternateans who, led by the new Sultan Baabullah, Hairun's son, laid siege to the Portuguese fort. It took five years, but in 1574 the Portuguese were forced to make a hasty and ignominious exit.

Baabullah, the greatest leader the Moluccas have known, ruled Ternate from 1570 to 1583, a golden age of prosperity and expansion. Ternatean warriors, carried in swift longboats called *kora-kora,* harassed the Spaniards in the southern Philippines and strengthened ties with the Muslim communities in Mindanao.

The foreign relations highlight of Baab's rule came in 1579 when energetic, adventurous and resourceful Francis Drake (some just call him a pirate) stopped at Ternate on his round-the-world jaunt, the second after Magellan's. Baab and Drake hit it off right away. Both hated the Iberians, and their personalities met in what one historian calls an "electric attraction of elective affinities." Baab entertained Drake most splendidly and placed himself and his possessions under Queen Elizabeth.

Drake loaded up on knowledge of the region and filled the hold of his *Golden Hind* with spices. He was an embodiment of England at the time—small, but tough and confident, ready to challenge the Iberians. In 1580, Portugal was absorbed by the Spanish crown—this would last for 60 years. Just eight years later, in 1588, England delivered a crushing defeat to the huge, "invincible" Spanish Armada.

The Dutch stir

By the late 16th century, Lisbon had become the spice center of the West, and Antwerp was the center of Spain's northern distribution network. Today's Holland and Belgium were then Spanish possessions. But the territories were becoming restless, stirred up by Philip's repression of the Calvinists, and the region rebelled against Spain in 1572, forming the United Provinces in 1579. The independent United Provinces, later to become Holland, stayed at war with Spain until 1648. With the Lisbon spice market closed to her, Holland decided to send her own ships to

fetch the precious cargo.

All the carefully concealed secrets of the spice trade were revealed in 1592 when Jan Huyghen Van Linschoten published his famous *Itinerary*. He had been working as a "factor" in Goa for the capitalist clans of the Fuggers and Welsers of Augsburg. (The old term "factor" comes from "factory," meaning a warehouse, a merchant's residence, or a trading post.) Linschoten had kept his eyes and ears open while working in India. He not only provided a description of the clove islands and the safest sailing routes, but also revealed the hitherto unknown state of the Portuguese empire: corrupt, understaffed and moribund.

Cornelis de Houtman pioneered the Dutch route to the Spice Isles in 1596. Other well-financed ships followed, until the merchants realized that competition among themselves undermined their profit margin. The Dutch burghers who had backed the spice expeditions, eminently practical, united in 1602 to form the Vereenigde Oostindische Compagnie, better known in English as the V.O.C. or the East Indies Company.

But outside competition was not far behind. The period from 1599 to 1606 was to to be the most momentous in north Moluccan history. The Portuguese were still firing resentful cannon and musket when an English translation of Linschoten's book appeared, leading to the formation of the British East Indies Company. England's ships were as swift and sturdy as Holland's and the company as determined, at least initially. The first trip from the Thames, under James Leicester, returned from Banten on the north coast of Java with a valuable load of pepper. The second voyage, under Henry Middleton, reached the Moluccas. While there, the British rescued the Sultan of Ternate from the forces of Tidore and were rewarded with trade rights, and a valuable cargo of cloves.

Portuguese power and glory were fading fast in the Moluccas, but Spain, financed by gold and silver taken from the Americas, could still afford a military presence — its influence in Tidore persisted until 1663.

Since Protestant Holland and England were ostensibly allied against the Catholic Iberians, competition between them for spices was in theory to have been a gentlemanly affair. Both countries were to split the expenses of fighting against the Papists and the rewards: the Moluccas' 1,300 odd ton yearly output of cloves. Things did not work out so smoothly.

From her base in Ambon, built around Portuguese forts captured in 1605 and renamed Victoria, Holland set about eliminating her English competitors. The Dutch were cutting costs by paying half the going rate for cloves, and the British were picking up a sizable share of the trade by paying higher prices. In 1623, accusing the English warehouse team in Ambon of conspiracy to seize the Dutch fort, the British were tortured and executed. England objected, but the bold act put an end to British enterprise in the region (see "History of Ambon," page 42).

The financial backers of the British effort, self-described "Gentlemen Adventurers," were distracted by investment opportunities in India. Nevertheless, the East India Company lay claim to the nutmeg island of Run in the Bandas until the peace treaty of Breda in 1667. (In exchange for which the British received New Amsterdam, better known as Manhattan.)

The dour, financially conservative Dutch, thanks to the prodding of their ruthlessly energetic Governor-General, Jan Pieterszoon Coen, did not flag in their sense of purpose. The V.O.C. board of directors supplied — often reluctantly — the ships, cannon and men required to crush the opposition. The men who ran the V.O.C., the Heeren XVII ("Gentlemen Seventeen"), may have suffered moments of conscience, but in the end Coen got what he demanded.

In 1621, Coen secured the tiny Banda Islands, the nutmeg- and mace-growing center of the Moluccas. Within weeks, he had rounded up and murdered most of the islands' 15,000 inhabitants who couldn't flee, and then turned the islands into Dutch plantations (See "History of the Bandas," page 86). After crushing a 1650 uprising against the unpopular Mandar Syah, installed as Sultan of Ternate by the Dutch, the V.O.C. decreed that clove-growing was not longer allowed outside of Ambon.

A pension of £3,000 was paid to the Sultan of Ternate and £550 to the Sultan of Tidore as consolation. Carrying out a ruthless tree-cutting program, Holland achieved her cherished dream of monopoly by 1681. Periodic *hongi* expeditions, traditional tribute-gathering war parties, were sent out from Ambon to uproot any fledgling trees and murder any "illegal" traders. Since the natives of the clove islands lived in an export economy, where

Opposite: *Quayside at Banda Neira, lined by Dutch trading houses and government offices.*

cloves were exchanged for staple foodstuffs, hunger and misery resulted from this policy.

Even during the 16th century heyday of Portuguese control, the volume of cloves the Iberians shipped to Europe was an insignificant part of the overall trade. One ship a year, carrying maybe 80 tons of cloves, arrived in Lisbon. At the time, 1,300 tons a year were being handled by Asian merchants, the lion's share of which ended up in Europe through the old Arab network. By the 17th century, an increase in demand for cloves brought total production to 2,500 tons in an average year, and 4,500 tons in a bumper year.

But the wars and Holland's extermination policy led to a drastic drop of clove production. During the 17th century, the once-splendid sultanates became backwaters. The Dutch market eventually required only 900–1,000 tons of cloves a year. The rest was either burned or dumped into the sea.

End of Dutch control

As Ternate, Tidore and the nearby former clove-producing islands lost their importance, the world forgot about them—until the Napoleonic wars. From 1796, the British took over the Dutch holdings, returning them after the Treaty of Amiens in 1802.

And in 1810, as a result of the French–Dutch alliance, a British Naval Squadron captured Ternate and other key points in the Moluccas. The British continued the monopoly, but in a more relaxed style. The *hongi* expeditions ended and the British paid in Indian rupees, much more valuable than the inflated Dutch paper. But once Napoleon was safely ensconced on St. Helena, the Moluccas were returned to the Dutch.

But by the second decade of the 19th century, clove seedlings—smuggled out as early as 1770, and those exported "legally" by the British during their takeover—had begun to produce, effectively ending the Dutch monopoly. One of the first to acquire these was the enterprising governor of the Mauritius Islands, Frenchman Pierre Poivre. The seedlings he filched ended up in various parts of the Indian Ocean—including the little islands of Zanzibar and Pemba, just off the coast of Tanzania.

It is one of history's minor ironies that Indonesia is today both the world's biggest producer and its biggest importer of cloves, all but a tiny fraction of which go up in smoke in the popular *kretek* cigarets. Up to 50 percent chopped cloves by weight, *kreteks* are smoked by Indonesians at the rate of 100 million a day. Clove growing is still a big business in Indonesia, but the nation cannot begin to meet its own demand.

The bulk of Indonesia's imported cloves come from—of all places—Zanzibar and Pemba. Sumatra and North Sulawesi contribute most of Indonesia's domestic cloves. The Moluccan contribution is negligible.

DUTCH MOLUCCANS

Expatriate Moluccans in Holland

Caught in the middle of Indonesia's rocky transition from a Dutch colony to an independent republic, the story of Holland's 40,000 expatriate Moluccans is a poignant one. These are the old colonial soldiers and their wives, daughters, sons and grandchildren—whose dream of an independent homeland was crushed by political realities more than 30 years ago.

Dutch Moluccans have clung stubbornly to their hope of repatriation to an independent "Republik Maluku Selatan" (RMS), or South Moluccan Republic, for decades—resisting assimilation into Dutch society and, in some cases, remaining in the ramshackle camps in which they were first housed in the 1950s. In the 1970s, 20 years of resentment and frustration suddenly erupted in violence.

On the cold morning of December 2, 1975, a Moluccan boy pulled the safety brake of a commuter train, which screeched to a halt near the north Holland village of Wijster. For the next 12 days the passengers were held hostage by a group of young Moluccans.

On May 23, 1977, another train was stopped by Moluccans on the same track. Simultaneously, Moluccan terrorists took a primary school in Boven Smilde. The hostages were held for almost two weeks.

The hijackings and the school take-over focused international attention on the South Moluccan cause. As a result, the Dutch government finally began to take steps to heal a community wracked by unemployment, drug addiction and broken dreams.

The Royal Dutch Army

The story begins with the founding of the Koninklijk Nederlands Indisch Leger (KNIL), or Royal Dutch Army, in 1830. The Dutch created the KNIL to enforce their control of the sprawling colony. The force consisted entirely of island soldiers, mostly Moluccans from Ambon and other islands in Central and South Maluku. They were stationed all over the archipelago.

The Moluccan soldiers enjoyed a special relationship with their Dutch employers. They became known for their bravery and loyalty, and these qualities were rewarded with special privileges. The Moluccan soldiers received higher pay and better rations than their fellow soldiers. They prided them-

selves on their loyalty and discipline. They identified with the Dutch, and were comfortable with their colonial masters. The Javanese called them "anjing-anjing Belanda"—the dogs of the Dutch.

Indonesian independence

At the beginning of the 20th century, Dutch power in the Indies was challenged by a growing independence movement. The Dutch refused to discuss reforms that would allow the Indonesians any degree of self rule, but the situation changed dramatically when Japanese soldiers swept through the archipelago in 1942. As the war turned against them, the Japanese sponsored meetings of the former independence leaders in order to lay plans for an independent post-war Indonesia.

Sukarno and Hatta, two early anti-colonialists, later the first President and Vice-President of Indonesia, were at such a meeting when the Japanese capitulated to the Allies, on August 13th, 1945. They flew back to Indonesia and, four days after the surrender, proclaimed the independent Republic of Indonesia on August 17, 1945.

Opposite: *Soldiers of the Dutch colonial army arrive in Holland in 1951, supposedly for a six-month stay. Most of them never left Holland.*
Above: *Ambonese soldiers and their families preparing to disembark from a troop transport ship in Rotterdam harbor.*

At first the Dutch tried to deny the legitimacy of the new state, but the United States pressured Holland to recognize the Republic and to begin the process of decolonization. If the Netherlands refused, the United States threatened to cut off Marshall Plan funds, which were desperately needed to reconstruct Holland after World War II.

So the Dutch settled at the Conference of Malino, and transferred their colony to a Federated States of Indonesia, which included a semi-independent Negara Indonesia Timur (East Indonesian Nation).

Sukarno soon abandoned the federal structure and claimed all of the archipelago for the new Republic. However, resistance cropped up in the Celebes (now Sulawesi) and the Moluccas. Although his advisors Soumokil, Manusama and Manuhutu (all Moluccans) pressed for independence for their home islands, Sukarno would not grant special status to the Moluccas.

After parts of the Celebes and the North Moluccas seceded, Manuhutu proclaimed an independent "Republik Maluku Selatan" (South Moluccan Republic) on April 25, 1950. The inhabitants of the Moluccas were again thrust in the midst of a war. Some villages, destroyed in the fighting between RMS supporters and Indonesian troops, were the same that had been leveled in battles between the Indonesians and the Dutch, and before that, between the Dutch and the Japanese.

Caught in the middle

For most KNIL soldiers, still stationed all over the archipelago, the proclamation of the RMS came as a complete surprise. They asked to be transferred to West New Guinea (at the time still held by the Dutch) to organize against Sukarno's army. Hoping to maintain some military influence over the situation, the Dutch at first agreed to their proposal. But, again facing U.S. pressure, Holland recognized Indonesia and agreed to dismantle the colonial army. The soldiers were offered little choice: join the Indonesian Army, or demobilize.

The soldiers sent a delegation to the Netherlands and brought a lawsuit against the state. The Dutch government was found responsible for the soldiers, and they were to be brought to Holland, together with their families, for a period of six months. Included in this was a promise, explicit or implicit, that the soldiers would return, with full Dutch support, to fight for an independent South Moluccan Republic.

During the transfer, the soldiers were told (in Dutch, a language few of them understood well) that they had lost their military status and that all uniforms, guns and ammunition—one soldier carried a box of hand grenades all the way to Holland—were to be surrendered. When the ship arrived in Rotterdam in 1951, the South Moluccans were taken to Dutch army headquarters in Amersfoort where they were required to sign letters of resignation from the KNIL.

Though puzzled, the Moluccans still had great trust in the Dutch authorities, and without protest the 35,000 soldiers, wives and children were settle in various temporary quarters: former concentration camps, labor camps, army barracks and cloisters.

The soldiers entered a world that was new and foreign to them. They knew the Dutch as managers and officers, not as peasants and street cleaners. And never did the Moluccans imagine that there were so many of them. This country was very strange—they didn't even celebrate Queen Wilhelmina's birthday, which was the occasion for a grand parade in their colonial army days.

Stripped of their former status, the ex-soldiers and their families had to survive on three guilders per adult a week and some clothing vouchers. Their only comfort was the knowledge that they would be sailing for the Moluccas again in six months' time. Conditions were lousy. Heavy, bland Dutch food was prepared in the central kitchens.

As time passed, the children attended school, the wives cooked Moluccan food and tried to make the best of the situation, and the husbands just waited. Slowly their confidence in the Dutch began to erode, although they still didn't express displeasure.

After six months, the ship that was to

carry the soldiers in triumph back to the Moluccas failed to materialize. To add insult to injury, the Dutch cut off their stipends. The Moluccans were now supposed to fend for themselves in a post-war Dutch economy afflicted with unemployment and spiraling inflation. This stirred up racism, resentment and fierce trade union opposition. To many Moluccans the final indignity came when they discovered that for the privilege of being taken from their native land, interned in concentration camps and thrust among a hostile populace, they were to pay 60 percent of what little income they could earn to the Dutch government in taxes.

For most Moluccans this was the limit. They refused to pay taxes and protested that the Dutch hadn't kept their promise—where was the RMS? The protests began peacefully, but tensions escalated in 1966 when the Indonesian government executed RMS leader Soumokil. His followers in Holland angrily set fire to the Indonesian embassy in The Hague. Moluccan youngsters blamed both Holland and Indonesia for the harm done to their parents. Then radical young Moluccans hijacked the second train and took the school.

On Saturday, June 5, 1977, Dutch commandos stormed the train stopped two weeks before by Moluccan radicals and several Moluccans and a hostage died in the maneuver. Emotions flared—the Dutch public was outraged over the death of innocent people; the Moluccans, though they may not have condoned the violence, blamed the government for its neglect and broken promises.

Opposite: *The soldiers and their families were housed in former barracks and even concentration camps, like this one in Westerbork.* **Above:** *Two South Moluccan radicals keep a lookout from the Dutch train in which they held 50 passengers hostage in 1977.* **Right:** *A former KNIL soldier and his son spend their first winter in Holland.*

Although the Dutch public and the Moluccan community were shocked by the hijackings, it was the violence that brought the government to the point of action. The Hague has responded with "orientation trips" to the Moluccas, a bi-cultural education program, a drug counseling center, a Moluccan Historical Museum in Utrecht and a Moluccan advisory council. The latest step is a "1,000 job project" for unemployed Moluccans.

Going home

Since they have had the opportunity to return to the Moluccas, an increasing number of Dutch Moluccans have visited their homeland. Most still remember the island and *kampung* of their birth, and they stay with relatives they haven't seen for 30 years. Moluccan aunts and uncles meet nieces and nephews they have only heard about and seen in letters and photographs.

Young Dutch Moluccans who go "home" in search of their identity are left in confusion. While they are considered "dole-drawing Moluccans" in Holland, once in Maluku they become wealthy Dutchmen. Those who bring up the Republik Maluku Selatan quickly realize that the only RMS sympathies left are in Holland. Despite the inward conflict that a trip to Maluku causes, a lot of young Moluccans spent their holidays on the islands. But only a very few remain behind.

—Sylvia Pessireron

PART II

Ambon and Central Maluku

Ambon is the capital of Maluku province and serves as the area's communications hub. From here, jets fly to and from Jakarta, Bali, Ujung Pandang, and Irian Jaya. Smaller planes fan out from Ambon to the many tiny, out-of-the-way islands in the Moluccan group. Mixed passenger and freighter ships make their slow way along convoluted loops that reach the far corners of the archipelago.

Ambon became the center of the Dutch clove monopoly, and the headquarters of Dutch presence in the eastern part of the archipelago. At the height of the East India Company's wealth and power, Ambon was referred to as "The Queen of the East."

Ambon Town today holds few physical charms: it was bombed to the ground during World War II and the post-war buildings are drab modern structures with no aesthetically redeeming features. But the city's nondescript architecture and non-stop traffic is saved by its spectacular setting: it lies between a sparkling, deep-water bay and lush, steep-sided hills. And the friendly, exuberant Ambonese enliven all human contact.

The modernity of Ambon can be a balm to the weary traveler. Here there are many comfortable, modern hotels, plenty of banks, and lots of stores to stock up on essentials for a trip to the outer islands, or to spoil oneself on the way back. The restaurants in Ambon are inexpensive, and of good quality. If you dig around a bit, you can even find a place serving the local specialty: black dog.

The Ambonese are mostly Christians in the south, with a few Muslim outposts in the north, but in all cases the old mystical ancestral religion still occasionally surfaces: in marriage rituals, in seasonal rites and in local costumes and dances. In one village just a short hop from town, sacred eels are pampered and fed chicken eggs in a crystal clear pool. The physical well-being of Waai's eels ensures the spiritual well-being of the village. Although the bay and beaches close to

Ambon City have suffered from the city's development, the northern Hitu Peninsula harbors some excellent beaches and unsullied reefs. For a real treat, catch a ferry to one of the neighboring Lease Islands—Haruku, Saparua, Nusa Laut—little paradises with perfect beaches, swaying coconut trees and beautiful coral reefs.

Seram is the *nusa ina,* the "mother island" of Ambon. There is something mysterious and brooding about mountainous Seram, the largest of all the Moluccan islands. The Ambonese hold the island in high regard—considering it the birthplace of their culture—and attribute a variety of supernatural powers to the indigenous Alfur peoples of Seramese interior.

Seram is a gold mine of lumber, and the infrastructure laid down as a result of the lumber industry—together with the convenient location of the district capital, Masohi—insure frequent communications with Ambon. Already a rudimentary road network covers the southwestern part of Seram, and the dirt road across the central highlands to the north coast should soon be finished.

Seram is close enough to Ambon that boats can take the traveler quickly to any of a number of points on Seram's southern shore. From there, crazy minibus rides over rutted but scenic dirt roads lead to quiet little coastal villages. From these, one can trek inland in the hopes of meeting some of the mysterious Alfur people.

The tiny Seram Laut islands, on the far eastern tip of Seram, are former pirate dens and historical trade emporiums through which black market spices, slaves and all the exotic products of the east passed.

Overleaf: *The island of Ambon, former center of the Dutch clove monopoly, now offers balmy weather and transparent waters to the visitor.*
Opposite: *An Ambonese girl poses in front of some whimsical decorations.*

HISTORY OF AMBON

'Queen of the East' and Her Lively Past

Before the Europeans ever reached Ambon, the village of Hitu on the north coast was already important as a watering hole for passing Arab spice traders. They stopped here to wait out unfavorable weather or for the seasonal onset of steady monsoon winds. Islam was introduced to Hitu by the traders who plied the route between North Java and Ternate, two early centers of Muslim influence in the archipelago.

While Hitu and its vicinity saw increasing trade traffic, and became even more open to the Islamic world, most of the islanders still clung to their traditions and ancestral religion. Even earlier, scattered immigrants from Java had influenced some local leaders to assume the Hindu title "raja" and incorporate elements of the Hindu-mystic religion prevalent on Java during the Majapahit period.

The Portuguese arrive

The first European faces seen by the Ambonese were those of de Abreu's motley, shipwrecked crew, which included eight men and their hapless leader. (See "The Spice Trade," page 26.) They landed at Hitu and promptly endeared themselves to their hosts by helping out in a war with Luhu, the principal settlement on Seram's Hoamoal Peninsula, a short distance from Hitu.

But hearing of the strange foreigners, the area's strong man, the Sultan of Ternate, had them brought to his headquarters for an audience. Other sailors arrived, and the Portuguese were allowed to establish a trading post. In 1522, they erected a small fort on the north coast of the Hitu Peninsula, at the mouth of a small river that emptied into the sea between Hitu town and Mamala.

The Portuguese were horrible guests, hatching intrigues against the Spanish—who had also reached the Spice Isles—and their Moluccan allies. The Portuguese were finally expelled, but regrouped on the peninsula's south coast, building a fort at Hative, near the present village of Rumah Tiga. Until 1569, this would be the center of Portuguese presence in Ambon.

Ambonese villages seeking allies against Muslim expansion from Hitu accepted and encouraged the Portuguese presence in their area. Efforts to convert the north coast Muslims had made no headway, but Catholicism received a favorable response among the animists of the South. The first three villages embraced Christianity in 1538. By 1565, after a visit from Francis Xavier (later Saint Francis), Catholics claimed some 10,000 souls on Ambon. Thirty years later, this number would rise to 20,000. Elements of Portuguese Catholic culture remain to this day on the island, visible in clothing styles,

romantic *keroncong* ballads, family names and Portuguese loan-words.

Although the Portuguese (and their Ambonese allies) made some effort to regain the north coast, the Hitu Muslims were supported by a noble named Leiliato who arrived from Ternate with a strong force in 1558. The Portuguese pulled back to the vicinity of the Batu Merah villages, and in 1575 constructed a fort called Nuestra Senhora da Anunciada, where the town of Ambon is today.

When the Dutch arrived at the very end of the 16th century, a history of Iberian abuses led the Muslims of Ambon's north coast to back Holland. In 1599, Dutch ships seeking spices under Wijbrand van Waerwijk, Jacob van Heemskerck and Admiral Jacob van Neck found the Ambonese in arms against the Portuguese, who were trying to impose a trading monopoly. The Dutch aided the Ambonese, but could not drive the Iberians from their forts. A few years later, in 1605, the Dutch returned under Admiral van der Hagen and captured the Fort Anunciada with only a show of force. After the Dutch victory, the name of the Portuguese stronghold was changed to New Victoria.

The Dutch desecrated the Catholic churches and deported both "white" (European) and "black" (mestizo) Portuguese. Still, traces of Catholicism remained: the Portuguese-Malay patois, Portuguese baptismal names and modified Portuguese manners, customs and modes of living.

Dutch supremacy

The Dutch based much of their legitimacy in Ambon—and the rest of the archipelago—on the "Het Eeuwig Verbond" (The Eternal Compact) signed by local rulers who could not know that it would lead to their subjugation. With the Portuguese driven out and the Ambonese bound to their service (on paper anyway), the Dutch faced only one real competitor in the region—England.

The English, ostensibly allied with the Dutch against the papists, had been running a trading post in Ambon since 1621. In 1623, charging (falsely) that the British merchants had been conspiring to overthrow the Dutch government, the Dutch tortured and beheaded 18 British subjects. John Dryden later wrote a play about the incident entitled, *Amboyna or the Cruelties of the Dutch to the English Merchants.*

The consolidation of Dutch power in the Moluccas between 1614 and 1656 finally led to the sought-after spice monopoly. (See "The Dutch Monopoly," page 30.) By controlling clove, nutmeg and mace production at the source, the East India Company, or V.O.C., could set the prices in Europe and Asia. The company decreed that clove trees would be concentrated in Ambon, which the V.O.C. controlled, and systematically destroyed them elsewhere. For 200 years thereafter, Ambon was the center of world clove production.

The key to the Dutch success was a ruthless, scorched-earth war with the Muslims of North Ambon and the Hoamoal Peninsula on Seram. After five years (1641–1646), Hitu was destroyed; after a later four-year conflict with Hoamoal, the V.O.C. finally won in 1656. The Dutch could never compete in the tra-

ditional Asian barter trade, wherein rice and fabrics were swapped for cloves. Thus, at saber or musket point, they paid ridiculously low prices for the cloves and charged ridiculously high prices for unwanted Dutch goods.

As early as 1622, Dutch accountants saw that Ambon and Seram alone were producing twice the world clove consumption. In those circumstances, it was impossible to maintain high prices. So in 1625, the first of the "*hongi tochten*" or duty rounds, made up of 60 to 70 armed native vessels, began their annual extirpation sweep. Over the years, hundreds of thousands of clove trees were destroyed to hold down the supply. When the clove crop reaching Europe still exceeded demand, the V.O.C. paid out dividends in spices.

RETRATO: DE: Micer: Francisco: Xavier DA: Ordem: DA: Comp. De: Iesv. *Anno.* 1542.

From 1677 to 1744, the monopoly managed to keep prices more or less fixed. But when production declined more than anticipated—too many trees cut, storm damage, tree pests—the reduced supplies drove prices up, leading to a drop in demand, which didn't always bounce back the next year when supply rose again. So the monopoly controls sometimes inadvertently worked to the detriment of profits.

Opposite: *A Portuguese carrack. The Portuguese were the first Europeans to reach the eastern islands, at the beginning of the 16th century.*
Above: *The indefatigable Francis Xavier—later Saint Francis—visited Ambon in 1565.*

During the early V.O.C. years, the Moluccas accounted for over one-half of the company gross, some $1.6 billion. This supported 7,500 military and civil employees. The Dutch policy of buying cheap and selling dear yielded 1,000 percent profits for a while, but the scheme was undermined by high overheads (including building and maintaining garrisons) and a great deal of smuggling, some by corrupt V.O.C. personnel.

In retrospect, it's hard to blame the V.O.C. employees, who were underpaid and suffered an extremely high mortality rate. During the company's early years, scarcely more than one in ten of its employees made it back to Europe. And those who did were seldom healthy or wealthy. Understandably, the service was quite unpopular. Those who successfully acclimated to the region found their terms being stretched out indefinitely—the company preferred to keep them on rather than bring in a newcomer who was likely to die of tropical disease.

'Queen of the East'

The Dutch who were stuck in Ambon made the best of it, trying to amass fortunes and to lead as pleasant a life as possible under the circumstances. In the mid-17th century, "Amboyna" was a bustling little town, with a well-developed merchant sector. The population of Ambon almost tripled during the 1600s from 2,500 to 7,000. (In the same period, as a result of Dutch policies in the region, the population of the Moluccas dwindled—due to wars, famine, and emigration—from 100,000 to less than 50,000.)

Holland ruled Ambon through the local aristocracy, the *orang kaya* (rich men). But the real power was in the hands of high company officials. A representative council of sorts, the first in the Indies, included *orang kaya* as well as V.O.C. officials. The Ambonraad, as this council was called, later expanded to include the Muslim representation in the form of their leader, called by the title "Captain Hitu."

All the *orang kaya* were invited to the Dutch celebrations, where they could show off their European finery and manners. These occasions were excuses for dazzling costumes, feasting and drinking. The booze was a heady mix of French and Persian wines, beer, local *arak* palm brandy and, of course, gin. The feasting featured Westphalia hams and Dutch cheeses and confitures. Nonstop music and dance sometimes included the local *cakalélé* war dances.

According to one account, the *orang kaya* once played a trick on their Dutch hosts by scheduling a very authentic dance by tribal warriors. The event was a success until the gentlemen saw that the Dutch women were fainting. The ladies had noticed that, under the brilliant paint-and-feathers outfits, the warriors were stark naked. Contemporary

accounts note that the Ambonese were extremely fond of European dances. The night shows featured massive and elaborate displays of fireworks.

During Ambon's Dutch colonial heyday, near the end of the 17th century, it is said that she fully justified her title—Queen of the East. At this time, accounts state, the city outshone Batavia (Jakarta), Malacca and Manila. But in the 18th century Ambon lost much of its former importance. By 1735, textiles had overtaken spices in the V.O.C. profit column, and the tea, sugar and coffee plantations being started in Java would dominate the Indies' economy in the next century. By the 19th century, the Moluccas were a financial drain, an "expensive relic of past glory." By the 20th century, Ambon was basically a forgotten backwater.

World War II

The Japanese landed on Ambon on January 31, 1942. The outnumbered Gull Force of the Royal Australian Army put up a tough fight from nearby Laha airfield, but within 24 hours the Japanese held the island. (Of its 1,170 man force, the Australians counted just 121 survivors.) Dutch resistance evaporated on February 1.

The Moluccas had been a top strategic priority for the Japanese, and once in control of Ambon, the Laha airfield was enlarged and work proceeded on the largest Japanese installation in the archipelago outside of Java. Ambon was administered by the Japanese navy from its headquarters in Makassar (now Ujung Pandang).

The crushing defeat of the Dutch had a traumatic impact on the Christian community of Ambon, which had long identified with Holland. "The collapse of the colonial army was particularly poignant for the Christian Ambonese," writes historian Richard Chauvel, "as their soldier compatriots failed to live up to their reputations for military prowess either in defense of their homeland or elsewhere in the archipelago."

Life under the Japanese was not pleasant. Food and goods were in short supply, and the Japanese expected their 25,000 troops to be fed first. The residents of Ambon town feared constant air attacks, since by early 1943 Ambon was near the front line of military

Opposite: *An illustration from John Dryden's sensationalist book on the "Ambon massacre." The caption reads: "The Torments Inflicted by the Dutch on the English in Amboyna."*

activity. In August 1944, an Allied bombing raid destroyed most of the town.

The Japanese, with good reason, held the Christian Ambonese under deep suspicion. The new masters reversed the Dutch practice, favoring Islamic organizations and the Muslim one-third of the population. The Japanese also nurtured local nationalist leaders, encouraging them to plan for the eventual independence of Indonesia (of course, under Japanese control). The leader of the local pro-independence organization, Serikat Ambon, was then E.U. Pupella, a Christian.

Indonesian independence

After World War II, Indonesian nationalists fought a tough guerilla war on Java (in which the Ambonese fought on the side of the Dutch) and the fighting, world opinion and finally, U.S. pressure, forced the Dutch to grant independence to Indonesia in 1949. The Dutch tried to retain some control in the Moluccas but eventually bowed to the inevitable. The first provincial governor under the Republic of Indonesia was Latuharhary, a former head of the Serikat Ambon independence group.

But the Christian Ambonese, who for so many years identified with the Dutch, tried to set up an independent nation—Republik Maluku Selatan (South Moluccas Republic)—which would have included Seram, Ambon and the Lease islands. Many of the colonial army's former Ambonese soldiers fought a nasty guerilla war with Indonesian forces, retreating to the mountains of Seram after they were defeated on Ambon. RMS President Chris Soumokil was captured in 1956 and executed ten years later. Still, intermittent skirmishes continued for several years.

One of the group's leaders, Manusama, escaped from Seram to set up a government-in-exile in Holland. One of the many sad ironies in the situation is that it was Dutch ships that transported the Indonesian invasion force to Ambon in 1950.

After their defeat on Ambon, thousands of ex-colonial army members and their families fled to Holland, where they were settled into temporary barracks while nursing their dreams of returning home. Somehow they believed that Holland would help them to "regain" their homeland. Even today, many of the 40,000 expatriate Ambonese, most of whom were born in Holland and have never seen their ancestral homeland, have resisted assimilation in the Netherlands. (See "Dutch Moluccans," page 34.)

AMBONESE CULTURE

Christianity, Islam and Ambon's Adat

Although about half the population of the Central Moluccas are Protestant Christians, and the other half are Muslims, many aspects of life here still depend on the Ambonese *adat,* sacred customary belief handed down by the ancestors.

In Central Maluku people live *menurut agama dan menurut adat*—"according to religion and according to *adat.*" This continues despite many changes, including the loss of the indigenous Ambonese language and the introduction of a secular political system.

Ambonese adat

Ambonese social structure is founded on localized patrilineal clan groups called the *fam* or *mata rumah* ("eye of the house"), according to Dr. Frank Cooley, whose *Ambonese Adat* gives an excellent summary of Ambonese customary practice. And several

of these united clan groups aggregated into a larger political unit called *soa.* One or more *soa* formed a village, called *negeri,* led by a small-time chief. The chiefs assumed the grandiose title of "raja" only after contact with the cultures of Western Indonesia made the term fashionable.

Certain clans traditionally provided the candidates for village leadership, while others provided those for the traditional animist priesthood, called the *mauwang.* The village assembly, made up of all the heads of households, elected the raja from the proper clan's short slate of candidates. The raja was assisted by a central committee of elders, called *saniri negeri.*

Land title was held by the *dati,* a corporation of patrilineally related kinsmen. Each of these lineages also owned a sacred spring or a sacred stone, and with the *dati*-lands came an honorific title.

One lineage (occasionally more) is considered to be the direct descendant of the man who first cleared the land. The *adat* traditions, surrounded by an "aura of awe and fear," Cooley writes, represent the will of the village founders and other ancestors.

The founders' success in establishing a new society was the de facto evidence of their wisdom and prowess. When the ancestors laid down the *adat* laws, they knew what was good for society both in their own time and in the future. So *adat* functions as both a gift and a command. Neglecting *adat* triggers the anger of the ancestral spirits, those unseen supervisors who guarantee the unwritten laws' fulfillment.

Disease and death are the usual punishments for neglecting or transgressing *adat.* Dr. Cooley gives the example (circa 1960) of a man who failed to pay the customary bride price. Eleven of his 12 children died and the last was ill in the hospital before he finally payed his aging wife's bride price. Once he did, the last child quickly recovered.

In the past, and continuing until Dutch times, head-hunting was a crucial part of traditional marriage ceremonies, the erection of new buildings and the observance of other, specific rites.

Most Ambonese (as well as the inhabitants of the other Lease Islands) recognize that their ancestors either hail from West

Left: *A fine traditional ancestral woodcarving from Tanimbar, on display in Ambon's Siwalima Museum.* **Opposite:** *The inside of Fort Victoria in Ambon, from a late 19th century Dutch print.*

Seram or at least spent enough time there to adopt its language and customs. The different circumstances of founding the villages as well as the groups' different backgrounds led to variations of *adat*.

The division of villages into several kinds of federations, usually called *uli,* is an example of this. The literal sense of *uli* is "brotherhood." In the past, villages near each other often joined for political reasons. Federations thus created were distinguished as *uli teru, uli lima, uli hitu* and *uli siwa,* that is, combinations of 3, 5, 7, and 9 villages. The most common federations were 5- and 7-village groupings.

Outside religions arrive

After about 1450, Ambon fell under the influence of the twin spice sultanates of Ternate and Tidore. This included the tentative introduction of Islam, the prohibition of head-hunting, and the use of foreign items such as gongs, porcelain, cloth and metal knives.

In some cases, entire villages fled to new locations to avoid religious and political subjugation. Shortly after the arrival of Islam, the Catholic Portuguese brought further disruptions. Francis Xavier (later sainted), stormed through the Moluccas in 1574, baptizing many in Ambon, Ternate and Halmahera.

In the early 17th century, the Dutch expelled the Portuguese from Ambon and shortly thereafter set up a clove-growing monopoly on the island. From Ambon's centrally located, well-protected harbor, the Dutch sent *kora-kora* war canoes on expeditions to enforce the monopoly by tearing out trees, murdering offenders and generally instilling terror.

Ambonese men were pressed into service on these *hongi* expeditions as rowers. The more men a village provided, the more land it was allowed by the Dutch, thus upsetting the traditional system of land tenure.

The Dutch also enforced the ban on head-hunting, which played a crucial role in *adat* rites. The island's new rulers broke up the political aspects of the Patasiwa and the Patalima, appointing new rajas who were not necessarily of the proper hereditary clan.

The Dutch introduced new items such as foreign booze, cloth and European knick-knacks, which replaced heads as part of the bride price. Elopement was—and still is—practiced, but even in these cases the bride price eventually has to be paid. The Calvinist Dutch Reformed Church did not begin its proselytizing efforts until the 19th century, and then with less vigor than the Portuguese Catholics.

The *mauwen,* the traditional animist village priest, continued for a long time to peacefully coexist with the local Muslim or Christian religious leaders. The *mauwen* continued to placate the founding ancestors, obtaining their help in the agricultural cycle

and to cure illness.

Before the arrival of the Europeans, the "rajas" or local chieftains ruled with limited control over small areas. Even after Islam became accepted, the head of the villages kept the title "raja" instead of switching to the Muslim "sultan."

Religious vs. political power

The *mauwen* had always functioned as a semi-independent group under the rajas. The priests conceded just enough to Islam, then Catholicism or Calvinism, to maintain their function as intermediaries to the spirit world.

As the Dutch imposed their control over Ambon, they targeted the rajas as the local elites for inclusion in the colonial administration. The rajas delivered a labor force when required by the Dutch, such as when necessary for the clove harvest, and generally maintained law and order among their subjects. For example, it was they who quelled the constant discontent over the low fixed price offered by the Dutch for cloves.

In return, the Dutch offered the rajas approval, titles and income from the colonial government. All was going smoothly for the rajas and the *mauwen,* who were protected by the legitimacy extended by the Dutch to the rajas, until the middle of the l9th century.

Then the problems began. With the 1863 abolition of the clove monopoly, the rajas' resources declined drastically. Then, recent converts to the Dutch Reformed Church tended to fanaticism, tormenting and challenging the old *adat* structures and leaders. Whenever possible, they threw the sacred stones into the sea, destroyed the magic heirlooms and prohibited *adat* rituals connected with funerals and burials.

Muslim areas were spared this upheaval as Islam and the traditional religion had worked out a modus vivendi with the traditional rulers. The Muslims, to a greater degree than their Christian counterparts, respected the the rajas, thanks to the supernatural powers attributed to them. Muslim leaders also maintained stronger unity thanks to dynastic marriages, neglected by the Christian leaders.

More trouble brewed when the Protestant Church of the Moluccas was granted its independence in 1935 by the Queen of Holland. As more Moluccan ministers—but outsiders to the local village structure—came to preach and live alongside the rajas, conflicts over power and status developed. The *mauwen* prudently kept to the background, but generally supported the rajas against the outsiders.

The new Protestant ministers, as well as the rajas, tried to "rule" the villages, competing for the highest local stature. A government decree giving villages legal possession of their church building and property favored the rajas. Things soon boiled down as to who had the stronger personality, raja or minister.

Whoever won this clash of wills and popularity ended up with the prestige.

Identification with the Dutch

Unlike their Muslim and Portuguese predecessors, the Dutch did not combine trade with proselytizing fervor. The V.O.C. spice monopoly was interested in profits, not in souls. Nevertheless, the first Protestant vicar preached in Ambon city in 1614, both in Dutch and Malay.

Not much later a school system was developed, which would become the backbone of Ambonese Protestantism. Every village got a school with an Ambonese teacher, whose primary task was religious instruction. In this way, the number of Protestants increased steadily during the next centuries.

Protestant missionaries arrived during the latter of the two brief periods during the Napoleonic Wars when England controlled the Moluccas. An English Baptist missionary arrived in Ambon in 1814; he was followed by a Dutch Calvinist in 1815. As the century wore on, the pace of conversions accelerated.

Something curious happened during the latter part of the 1800s, perhaps triggered by the official abolition of the clove monopoly in 1863. Ambon had lost most its clove-based importance and no other export products were discovered that could prod the economy back into high gear. Up to this time, European travel accounts usually heaped scorn on the Ambonese. British naturalist Sir Alfred Russel Wallace, in his mid-19th century account, calls the Ambonese living in town, "strange, half-civilized, half-savage, lazy people"—an unusual outburst from a normally even-handed observer, and one not usually given to racist invective.

But Christianity was slowly bringing the Ambonese new status in the eyes of the Dutch. Christian Ambonese imitated their Dutch masters in dress and conduct—as far as possible. They even dubbed their first political organization "Ambonese Wilhelmina Society," in honor of the Dutch queen. The Christian Ambonese were quite happy being called "Belanda Hitam" (Black Dutch), even though it was meant by their fellow countrymen as an insult. (They were less happy with terms such as "dogs" or "monkeys" of the Dutch, however)

In 1871, schools and other institutions were finally secularized, and Ambon was soon blessed with the best educational system in the archipelago. But the Muslim population still refused to send their children to school because, in their estimation, the schools were closely allied with Christianity.

Education and employment provided for

Opposite: *Mosques are common in the island's north coast villages.* **Below:** *Guitar players add excitement to a Sunday service. Ambon has produced many of Indonesia's finest singers.*

the rise of the Ambonese Christians. These opportunities were hard to come by elsewhere in the archipelago, except among the Javanese aristocracy and the Christians of Manado in North Sulawesi. As the profit-oriented and aloof Dutch began to suffer pangs of conscience about their treatment of the people of the East Indies, many Ambonese Christians threw in their lot with their colonial masters, even to the point of learning the Dutch language.

From the 1880s on, thousands among the cream of the educated Ambonese became soldiers, clerks and minor professionals, most of them working for the Dutch administration. Improved medical and educational services led to the emergence of a sophisticated elite. By 1930, more than 10 percent of the Ambonese population had emigrated from their island for employment elsewhere in the East Indies.

The most important segment of the Ambonese exodus joined the Dutch colonial army which, prior to World War II, had integrated thousands of Ambonese soldiers. The islanders had always been famous for their martial skills.

Legendary was Captain Jonker, a full-blooded Moluccan who did much of the dirty work for the Dutch between 1651 and 1689, including fighting under Admiral Speelman at the Battle of Makassar in South Sulawesi. (Note: Despite this service, he was later murdered by V.O.C. troops under suspicion of treason.) Ambonese also staffed the vicious *hongi* expeditions to enforce the spice monopoly and fought with the Dutch in the bloody 1675-1682 Java wars.

The Ambonese in the Dutch colonial army formed a class to themselves, fathers followed by sons. They made ideal soldiers: smart, brave, tough, obedient and respectful. During the early part of the 20th century, Ambonese—who made up half of the colonial army—were crucial to the military expeditions that brought many semi-independent areas under Dutch control. Some of the Christian Ambonese identified so closely with the Dutch that they referred to their island as the 12th province of the Netherlands.

Adat today

In spite of all the changes and influences pouring into the island, contemporary Ambon retains a strong sense of the traditional beliefs. There is widespread reverence for the powers of ancestral spirits, and an aura of magic power surrounds certain places and objects. Everyone respects the *baileo,* the communal meeting place where village affairs are discussed, which retains some of its former sacred character. To one side of the *baileo,* some villages retain a "taboo" or sacred chunk of stone, called *batu pamali,* vested with supernatural powers. The rituals of *adat* are still seen in traditional marriages, the ceremony connected with installing a new village ruler, and village purifications.

A complicated set of inter-village alliances called *pela* represents one of the strongest surviving features of Ambonese *adat.* These pacts, usually between two villages, are the basis for Ambonese identity, transcending religion and locality. The *pela* unite villages—sometimes far apart—in West Seram, Ambon, Haruku, Saparua and Nusa Laut. The origins of *pela* probably go back to the headhunting days, when mutual protection was essential for survival. *Pela* partners exchanged a binding oath and drank each other's blood from a vessel into which weapons had been dipped. Intermarriage was considered incestuous between *pela* villages.

These ties were reinforced from the 15th century onward by the search for stability in the face of the chaos created by the influx of Islam, Christianity, and the Portuguese and Dutch. Plenty of mutual assistance was needed to face powerfully armed foreigners and their conflicting ideologies.

Through the centuries, the *pela* helped the villages face famine and other crises, as well as providing shelter during war, labor for community construction projects, and security in a unified Ambonese society. Today, a Christian village may contribute funds, materials and labor to help build its *pela* partner's mosque, receiving the same assistance to renovate its church when needed.

As the Indonesian government assumed control over Ambon in 1950, the judicial functions of the rajas and their councils were terminated. Still, many rajas retain the deference of the villagers, due to a lasting respect for *adat* traditions—and perhaps partially for their imputed supernatural powers.

Today, most Ambonese work in the civil service or other white collar jobs, thanks to their educational level. The exuberance of the Ambonese is famous throughout Indonesia, and their ranks have produced the country's best singers and boxers.

Opposite: *A statue of St. Francis Xavier, an early Jesuit and Ambon's most celebrated missionary, in front of the city's cathedral.*

AMBON CITY

The Bustling Hub of the Moluccas

Ambon, an architecturally plain city of 275,000, is the bustling commercial and administrative hub of the Moluccas. Unfortunately, World War II bombs destroyed all the old colonial buildings, but the city still offers beautiful weather, a stunning bay, and bustling shops, markets and wharves.

Born as a tiny Portuguese trading outpost more than 400 years ago, Ambon soon grew to become the center of the clove trade under the Dutch. Once their spice monopoly was broken, however, it settled into a somewhat more idyllic role as the decadent "Queen of the East." During the post-war period the city has grown by leaps and bounds as the capital of Indonesia's far-flung Maluku Province.

Soon after the first Portuguese traders arrived in the area, Muslims in Hitu forced them from an outpost on the island's north coast, and they fled to the south of the island.

At first they settled at Poka, on the south coast of the Hitu Peninsula, but a few years later moved across the bay to a better site deeded to them by the Raja of Soya. In 1575, a fortress and a church marked the beginnings of Ambon Town on the northern shore of the the island's Leitimor Peninsula.

'The most salubrious of towns'

Portuguese language, religion and bloodlines blended with local Ambonese culture to create a new mestizo mix on the island. But soon the Dutch arrived in Ambon, attracted by the strategic site. In 1605, a Dutch fleet under Stephen van der Hagen laid siege to the town. Two days later Portuguese captain Gaspar de Mello surrendered, without so much as putting up a fight against the better prepared Dutch. (See "History of Ambon," page 42.)

Under the iron hand of the V.O.C., the town grew slowly. But when the company went bankrupt in 1799, the little town between hills and harbor quickly began to expand. Open trade had been introduced during the brief interregnum of British rule during the Napoleonic Wars, and by the end of the 19th century, the population of Ambon, then called Amboyna, had reached 7,500— including 750 Dutch and 250 Chinese.

"Amboina is the most salubrious of towns," writes Anna Forbes in the 1880s. "It is situated on a long, river-like arm of the sea, and commands a fine prospect over the water

to the mountains beyond, while it is encircled by verdure-clad slopes, to which shady, arbour-like roads lead from the centre of town." Forbes was surprised to learn that the most elegant mansions in the little entrepôt belonged not to the Dutch, but to wealthy Arab and Chinese merchants.

In the 20th century, Ambon continued to grow, and by the time of the Japanese occupation had some 17,000 inhabitants. But the real growth occurred after Ambon's incorporation into the Republic of Indonesia. By the early 1970s, the population had reached 86,000 and today some 150,000 people crowd the city, including many migrants from various parts of Indonesia. (The island itself has 275,000 inhabitants.)

With only four square kilometers of flat land between hills and sea, the desperate search for space has caused builders to find ever more creative solutions. Houses now cling to the steep hillsides and reclamation pushes back the edge of Yos Sudarso harbor. A 17th century description of Ambon is still very apt: "alive and crowdy."

Island Patriots

Anyone spending a few hours in Ambon will notice the absolutely awful statue at one end of the city's sports field. Meet Thomas Matulessy, a.k.a. **Pattimura**, a 19th century Moluccan patriot. Pattimura led a ragtag army and occupied Fort Duurstede on Saparua Island in 1817. The rebel was the leader of a short-lived independence movement that cropped up after the Napoleonic Wars, during which the islanders experienced a taste of "enlightened" British colonialism.

When the Dutch returned, some Moluccan leaders and their followers took up arms. Prince Diponegoro was harassing the Dutch on Java, and Pattimura, a former sergeant major in the British Army, represented a serious threat in the Spice Isles until he and his followers were betrayed and delivered to the Dutch.

The rebels were executed in Ambon in December 1817, where the monument now stands. Pattimura's last words are said to have been: *"Selamat tinggal tuan-tuan."* A droll, "Have a pleasant stay here gentlemen." The statue depicts an angry, aging pirate with cutoff pants, brandishing a cutlass.

One account suggests he looked much better in real life, with his thick wavy hair crowned by a tiara of gold and diamonds, and even tipped with bird of paradise feathers. The yearly Pattimura celebration starts on May 14 on Saparua Island, culminating the next day in Ambon.

Another Moluccan patriot, Martha Christina Tiahahu, gazes out heroically over Ambon Bay armed with a spear from the top of

Opposite: *The city of Ambon, capital of Maluku, faces a large, sheltered bay.*

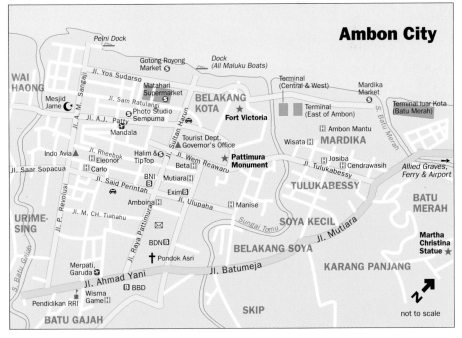

Karang Panjang Hill, two kilometers in back of town. Caught up in the same rebellious era as Pattimura, her father was executed by the Dutch and Tiahahu kept up the fight among her people on Nusa Laut, a lovely little circular island next to Saparua. Eventually captured, she was pressed for information about rebel movements but refused to cooperate with the Dutch, and starved herself to death on the way to exile in Java. Tiahahu was buried at sea.

Every year on January 2, a ceremony for the heroine takes place at the picturesque site of her statue, where yellow, green and red coconuts brighten the hilltop. The event concludes with the symbolic scattering of flowers on her grave, the sea.

From hills to docks

The architecture of Ambon is undistinguished. Unfortunately, the charming historical buildings were all destroyed in a massive bombing raid on August 28 and 29, 1944, as the Allies knocked out the Japanese base. The architecture today is post-war practical, mainly of concrete block construction.

A paved but narrow road leads to the top of 700 meter **Gunung Nona**, easily identified by the bright red television broadcast tower on its upper slope, which offers the best panorama over the bay and most of the city. There is no public transportation to Nona, but a taxi will take you there, and you can even walk if you're not in a hurry. Late afternoon light is the best for photography.

Another overlook, three kilometers from town, is from the **Siwalima Museum** (see below), which faces out over the bay from the Taman Makmur Hills. The road to the museum is a steep, winding half-kilometer that leads past the old Japanese shore batteries. One of the reinforced concrete bunkers still squints maliciously out over the harbor. Clinging to the steep slope above the museum, rather unexpectedly, is a full-fledged Balinese temple.

Ambon's urban landscape is full of churches, and there is a famous statue of the energetic **Saint Francis Xavier** (locally called Fransiscus Xaverius) in front of the Catholic Church on Jalan Raya Pattimura. The saint stands cross upraised, boldly defying the forces of heathenism. At the statue's base, a crab "hands" Saint Francis a Bible. This illustrates one of the many legends circulating about Saint Francis, in this case that The Book, which he had dropped into the sea while calming a raging storm on the way from Ambon to Seram, was later returned to him by a crab.

Just after the stores end on Jalan A.Y. Patty stand two mosques, right next to each other. This is a unique arrangement and when the stylish new **Al Fatah Mosque** was recently completed, the old one, should have been destroyed, according to Islamic tradition. But the elderly servants of Allah loved the ambience of the old **Jame Mosque** and put up such a fuss that it still stands. The Jame Mosque has character under its new green paint, a relief from the dull modern architecture of Ambon.

The bustling, patch-quilt **Gotong Royong** market around Jalan Yos Sudarso provides a teeming antidote to the city's persistant drabness. Here, sellers of sundries, fruit, fish, squawking birds and all manner of odds and ends overrun the old quarter of town between Jalan Ratulangi and the old docks, still used by the small inter-island ships. Unfortunately much of this interesting slice of Ambonese life is scheduled to be moved further up the bay, into an orderly group of recently constructed buildings.

Undoubtedly more hygienic and efficient, the new site promises to be far less colorful. And no doubt the market will cease to be, as one 19th century traveler described it, "exceedingly picturesque."

Some shops have already moved into the low, white rectangular buildings which, streaked with black by the heavy rains, looked worn out before they even opened in 1988. The new complex, called **Pasar Mardika**, includes the bemo-taxi terminal, with one parking lot for local and one for out-of-town traffic.

In the new market, the chaos is more ordered, although it is not completely charmless. Billiard rooms, *warungs* and small restaurants are moving into the area, gracing it with a bit of local flavor. A bridge crosses the Batu Merah Creek to the north of the complex, and more concrete sheds are being built there.

Some of the original walls from the old Dutch **Fort Victoria** are still standing in the back of a park, on the harbor front near Pasar Mardika. The rest of the walls wander in and out of a site that is now an Indonesian army camp—a testament to early efforts at South Moluccan independence—and a letter from Jakarta is required for photography. The walls remain in surprisingly good shape, considering that the fort began as Fort Nuestra Senhora da Anunciado, built years ago, by the Portuguese in 1575.

The Dutch took over Fort Anunciado in 1605, naming it New Victoria, and rebuilt it in 1775. The only really interesting part of the fort is the old gate, which is inscribed with the reconstruction date and features a carved sailing ship set into an oval relief. Some of the original color still clings to the rock. Alas, even this seemingly harmless object is protected by the army officials as if it were a state secret—absolutely no photographs are allowed.

While visiting the Gotong Royong market, it's worth a look at the **old docks**. Here are the cheap seats to the nearby islands. There is an office with posted ships and departures, and the ships go to lots of out-of-the-way places, like Wetar in the far southwest Moluccas and Aru in the far southeast. Find out when the boat returns before hopping on. The prices are negligible, but so are the services, so know what you are getting into.

The main docks, where the Pelni line ships call, are southwest of the old market. If you feel the kind of wanderlust than can only be cured by hopping a slow boat through the tropics, then this might be your jumping off point. These huge liners carry 1,500 to 2,000 passengers in five classes. You can ride Pelni to Irian or Sulawesi—or Jakarta. The *Pan Marine II* shuttles back and forth between Ambon and Manado, Sulawesi, stopping at Ternate and the Sula Islands, including Dofa on Mangole Island, and Sanana, on Sulabesi.

A mixed passenger/freighter is perhaps the most romantic solution. Accommodations are deck passage only (although you can probably talk a crew member out of his bunk for a fee) but the ships ply the Indonesian trade routes, stopping at all the tiny out-of-the way Moluccan ports.

The island's ties with Australia are reinforced every year in the **Darwin to Ambon yacht race**, which brings plenty of color and excitement to Ambon. Usually held in late July, over 40 racing yachts cover the 600 or so nautical miles in three to five days. So far, the record stands at an even 72 hours. Aside from the Aussies, participants have included yachts from New Zealand, France, the United States, Britain, Canada and even a lone entry from the Virgin Islands. The crews sometimes stick around for the festivities of Indonesia's Independence Day, August 17, Ambon's biggest yearly bash.

Clove ships and ikat

Ambon's main street is Jalan Raya Pattimura, named for the patriot, which is lined with banks, hotels, the telephone and telegraph office and the Catholic bishop's office. The shopping strip is on **Jalan A. Y. Patty**, where there are stores selling pearls, mother-of-pearl, trinkets made of cloves, and fabrics.

On Jalan Pattimura, between the post office and the Catholic Church, in back of the priests' living quarters, the bishop's library holds a treasure trove of Moluccan source material. The library is not open to the public, but if you are really interested, the bishop will show you his collection, painstakingly built up over a 30-years service in the Moluccas.

Although most of the books are in Dutch or Indonesian, many are in English (as well as some in German and French) and cover all topics—history, anthropology and linguistics. Like many Catholic missionaries, the bishop is highly educated and widely read. When not too busy, this renaissance man can provide delightful and instructive conversation.

The shops on Jalan Patty offer unique **Moluccan souvenirs**: mother-of-pearl montage "paintings," crafted of thin slices of the iridescent material (about $20); fragrant model ships, intricate creations of cloves and

Opposite: *The statue of Martha Christina Tiahahu, of Nusa Laut island, an Ambonese patriot who fought against the Dutch in the early 19th century. She eventually starved herself on the way to exile in Java.*

wire, complete with miniature sailors ($10 to $35); handwoven *ikat*—tie-dyed strand cloth—from Tanimbar ($10 to $60); handsome tortoise-shell fans and the embroidered "*baju kurung*" traditional shirts.

The mother-of-pearl pieces are cut, polished and fitted at a dozen family workshops in Ambon's **Batu Merah** suburb. The artists have been practicing their craft for generations, using mother-of-pearl oysters from the Aru archipelago. Visitors are welcome to watch. The artisans usually produce a few popular designs, mostly flowers, but special orders will be entertained.

The **Siwalima Museum**, on the slope of Gunung Nona above the city, displays fine, ancestral woodcarvings from southern Maluku, mock-ups of traditional Moluccan material culture, displays of natural history, fine porcelain, weapons and more. The museum is well worth a visit, and many of the captions to the exhibits are in English. The museum's terrace looks out over the panorama of Batu Capeo. The museum shop sells various ethnographic-type souvenirs, including *ikat* from the Tanimbars. The Siwalima's hours, at last check, are: Tuesday-Thursday 9 a.m.–2 p.m., Friday 9 a.m.–11:30 a.m., Saturday 9 a.m.–1:30 p.m. and Sundays 10 a.m.–3 p.m.; closed on either Monday or Tuesday, and Fridays. (Before heading out to the museum, however, ask your hotel to check that it is open.)

Reminders of World War II

The war in Ambon was brutal. The Ambonese suffered greatly under the Japanese, an outnumbered Australian defense battalion was literally wiped out, and three-quarters of the Allied prisoners brought in to build the Japanese airfield at Liang died of the horrible conditions in the internment camp.

The **Dolan Memorial**, on Jalan Kayadou in the Kudamati (Dead Horse) district near the hospital, is a simple, elegant homage to the Australian soldier who died while covering his compatriots' retreat during the Japanese invasion of Ambon in February 1942. While called the Dolan memorial ("Tugu Dolan"), the plaque on the simple rectangular store block commemorates a 1967 visit by former members of the Australian Gull Force (See "History of Ambon," page 42). The plaque mentions the Aussie soldiers, sailors and servicemen who died on Ambon.

There is, unfortunately, no mention of the brave Ambonese who, defying Japanese orders, stole away Dolan's corpse and buried it under the tree where the monument now stands. Nor is there mention of the Ambonese who secretly aided the Allied prisoners of war on Ambon, most of whom were to die of Japanese maltreatment.

The **Australian War Cemetery** is located about 5 kilometers out of town, but already part of the urban sprawl, in the suburb of

Tantui, on the main highway to the airport. It's just across from the national tourism office, where you can get help to locate the cemetery's gate-keeper.

The faithful keeper, thanks to his Australian salary, is often away, but one of his seven assistants is always around to show you the guestbook and to tend the graves and meticulously trimmed lawns. The graveyard is a superbly kept tropical garden, with bright green lawns, hundreds of shrubs and huge, majestic trees overlooking the blue waters of

Ambon Bay.

More than 2,000 servicemen from Australia, Holland, India and New Zealand find eternal rest here. They died during World War II in the Moluccas and Sulawesi. All the graves have a similar bronze plaque, giving the deceased's name, branch of service and an inscription, either from the Bible or a few words from their families. The 30 Indian soldiers—Muslim and Hindu—are buried in a separate section of the cemetery. Almost all the men who died were in their early 20s, a testament to the tragedy of war. The cemetery also contains the remains of prisoners of war who died. Only one in four of the 1,000 men survived their 18-month ordeal of imprisonment.

Next to the Allied Cemetery, another holds the remains of the *pahlawan* or Indonesian heroes who gave their lives during the Ambon rebellion which lasted from 1950 to 1956.

A (once) beautiful bay

For experienced **scuba divers**, the very best spots in the Ambon area are off Tanjung Setan (Satan's Cape) on the northwest coast of the Hitu Peninsula, around the Pulau Tiga (Ela, Hatalala and Lain), or off Tanjung Sial, the far southern tip of Seram. The best months for diving are September through April, but although the weather is usually clear, February is known for some uncomfortably high seas. Serious divers should bring their own basic gear, including regulators and buoyancy compensators, and an international certification card. Count only on finding basic tanks and weights.

There is a diving club in Ambon, but their outings usually only lead on weekends to two easy places: Latuhalat and Seri, both on the southern coast of the Leitimor. The governor's tourism office provides equipment for rent, but it may take a while to get things organized there.

The best bet for setting up a diving jaunt is Pata Dayal Tour and Travel. They can arrange everything—boat, food, guides—and have their own compressors, tanks and weight belts, all reasonably priced. (See "Ambon Practicalities," page 186.)

The construction boom that has doubled Ambon's population in the last 20 years has also destroyed her bay. Using coral as fill and dredging for the building boom has wrecked and killed much of the reefs, and garbage has spoiled what remains in accessible places.

Gone are the days when British naturalist Sir Alfred Russel Wallace could write, "There is perhaps no spot in the world richer in marine productions, corals, shells and fishes, than the harbour of Amboyna." Wallace wrote in the mid-19th century, but the damage, alas, has been done just in the last two decades.

But not all has been destroyed. In the early 1970s, Shirley Deane can still write, in *Ambon: Island of Spices,* "The coral world, which I glided over with my mask and snorkel, was—like the sunsets—a constant shift of color and movement. There was the coral itself blossoming up from the seabed in the subtlest shades of mauve and pink and green."

Opposite: *A craftsman delicately constructs a collage "painting" of mother-of-pearl shells.* **Above, left:** *A grave marker at the Australian war cemetery.* **Above, right:** *Diving off Ambon.*

AMBON ISLAND

Crystal Water, Sacred Eels and Odd Tales

Ambon Island is the best known, and most developed island in the Moluccas. Good paved roads reach most of the important villages, and they unfold beautiful panoramas: steep mountains, curved bays and deep blue seas. The island provides fascinating cultural spectacles as well: sacred eels, a supernatural kidnapper who inhabits a mountain village, and the yearly *sapulidi* ritual in the Muslim villages of the north, where young men beat each other until their blood runs.

The rugged island of Ambon is made up of two peninsulas, joined together by a tiny spit of land. In fact, geologists speculate that the two peninsulas were once separate islands, until the force of the sea built up the tiny spit of land that now connects them. In the past, Ambon Bay to the southwest and Baguala Bay to the east would have been a continuous channel separating the islands.

Ambon's 761 square kilometers are mountainous, and the rise from the sea to 1,038-meter Mount Salahutu is steep. Where it is not too rough to farm, Ambon's soil is rich. Numerous volcanic eruptions were reported on the west side of the island up until the end of the 17th century. Things quieted down, and no live volcano has been seen here since 1824, when the last crater was formed. Today, only hot springs, sulphur beds and the occasional earthquake testify to the still unstable crust under Ambon.

Ambon is blessed with many beaches of clean sand, lapped by warm tropical waters. The spots closest to town are crowded on weekends, but on weekdays these same beaches are almost deserted. Diving off Ambon's coasts can be disappointing, as much of the coral has been destroyed to make cement or building blocks for the city's building boom. Today, the biggest threat to coral reefs around this island is fish bombing, in which small powder charges or sticks of dynamite are used to stun and kill fish.

East Hitu: beaches and sacred eels

One of the most popular beaches on the island is **Natsepa**, at Baguala, a short 17 kilometers from Ambon city, just past Passo on Hitu's southeast coast. (See map opposite.) The main highway leads right past the beach. There are vendors here to cater to bathers' whims, and places to stay—the Losmen Linda

and the Miranda Beach losmen have 10 rooms each. Natsepa is a favorite family picnic spot, and parents find the gentle slope of the sandy bottom and the calm seas to be an ideal environment for their little charges.

The main road forks just past Natsepa and the right branch passes through Suli village before twisting for 8 kilometers along the coast to **Tengah-Tengah**, a Muslim fishing village on a lovely cove. The pebble beach is too uncomfortable for tanning, but you can hire an outrigger to take you to any of a number of fine swimming spots.

Past Tengah-Tengah, the coast road leads to **Tulehu**, the ferry landing for Saparua, Haruku, Seram and the other Lease Islands to Ambon's east. A more direct route to Tulehu, just 24 kilometers from Ambon city, is the highway past Natsepa. Just 5 kilometers from Tulehu is the village of **Waai**, the site of one of the island's strangest spectacles—the sacred eels.

A crystal clear stream flows out of a cave into a shallow pool, empty except for some carp. The keeper flicks his fingers on the surface, and at this signal the sacred eels slither out of the cave. He then takes a chicken egg and breaks it underwater, to be gobbled up by the quickest of the eels. The meter-or-more-long fish receive these attentions because they embody ancestral spirits.

Legend has it that the pools were created by a raja's spear. Casting about for a place for his people to relocate, the raja hurled his spear from his mountainside dwelling, proclaiming that wherever it landed would be the suitable place. The great spear carved out quite a divot, and what was left filled with water and became the pools. Locals believe that when the eels and carp (which are also sacred, although they receive no eggs) swim away, a disaster will occur. This portent last occurred in the 1960s, and sure enough, an epidemic struck. Once the villagers made atonement to the ancestral spirits, the eels returned and the disease stopped.

The pools used to be the local raja's bathing pools, though they are now open to the hoi polloi. Clothes washing, however, is allowed only at the downstream end. The traveler will also find here a seashell-and-flute orchestra which, with a few days' notice and $25–$35, can give a private performance.

Pombo Island, a few kilometers off the northeast tip of Hitu, offers good snorkeling in shallow reefs, although fish bombing has ruined much of the deeper coral. A shallow fringing reef circles most of the Pombo atoll. On the east side, opposite the nature conservation cabins, the reef lies about 100 meters from the beach. We found lots of coral sloping 5–6 meters to the sandy bottom of the lagoon.

Opposite: *Fishermen work the rich waters of Ambon's east coast while a passenger boat heads to nearby Haruku and Saparua Islands.*

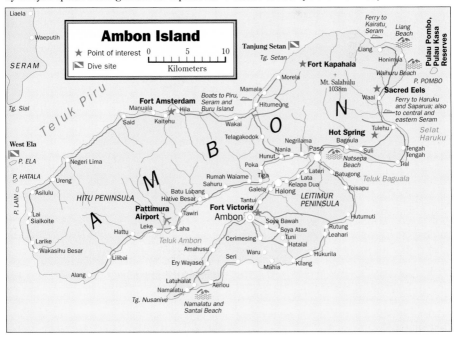

The scenery is just as lovely above the surface, especially at sunset, when flocks of birds (the name Pombo comes from Portuguese for pigeon) take to the air.

The conservation department (PPA) maintains four huts on Pombo and brings in fresh water from the mainland. With prior permission from their office—near the Australian cemetery, just outside of Ambon city—visitors can overnight here.

Honimua, 38 kilometers from Ambon city, on the northeastern tip of Hitu, is the closest point on the mainland from which to catch a speedboat to Pombo. The trip takes a few minutes and costs about $30, round trip. You can also catch a speedboat, for the same price, from the Tulehu ferry terminal, closer to Ambon city but further from Pombo. Still, the trip takes no more than 15 minutes. From Tulehu, outboard-powered canoes can be hired for half of the speedboat price, and if the winds are right and the seas calm, sailboats can make the run. The best months for sailing are September through November.

If you decide to embark from Honimua (a car and passenger ferry from Honimua also runs twice a day to Waipirit on Seram) stop at the beautiful **Liang Beach**. Just before reaching Honimua, the main road forks, and to the left, the long, lonely beach gazes out toward Seram. Some 20 kilometers distant loom Seram's mountains, grand and gray, rising out of the sea.

North Hitu: Muslim stronghold

Before the Europeans arrived in Ambon, the Muslim trading and supply center at **Hitu**, in the middle of the north coast of the Hitu Peninsula, was the most important settlement on the island. Hitu and the other Muslim villages of the North Coast lie about 45 kilometers, on a paved road, from Ambon city.

The longest road trip from Ambon city (public transportation available) reaches the twin villages of Hila and Kaitetu, 45 km away, on Hitu's north-central coast. After rounding the end of Ambon Bay, the road cuts straight across Hitu Peninsula before following the coast to the west. The road passes stands of clove trees, fewer nutmegs, and here and there, sago palms. The first village is Hitu.

Mamala village is just north from Hitu, where the paved road ends. This Muslim enclave is famous for a mystical ritual called *sapulidi*. Once a year, just after Hari Raya Lebaran/Idul Fitri, the village boys gather before a large crowd in the middle of the village, arm themselves with the sharp central spine of a palm frond, and beat each other, savagely, until their naked torsos are lacerated and bloody. After this flagellation, their wounds are salved with coconut oil, and the bleeding stops. Within an hour, it is said, no sign remains of the mutilation.

Opinions as to the meaning and origin of this local festival are varied, as Shirley Deane,

in *Ambon: Island of Spice,* notes: "Sceptical Ambonese (particularly Christians) say that it's a publicity stunt for the sale of the oil, which is much in demand afterwards. Others believe it is magic with an ancient origin, and related to a dance which is still performed on the neighboring island of Haruku, called the Combalélé. Here men are repeatedly stabbed with daggers or spears, but at the end have no scars at all."

Although the exact source of the ritual is not known, it is generally related, as Deane notes, to several famous rituals found elsewhere in the archipelago. The *pukul sapu* or *sapulidi* festival takes place seven days after the Idul Fitri festival; in 1997 it was on February 9. (Recall that the Muslim lunar calendar is an average of 11 days shorter than the Gregorian calendar.)

Fort Kapalaha, mostly in ruins, lies about 5 kilometers and 1.5 hours from Mamala on a path heading slightly inland. Close to Mamala, on the coast to the north, is **Satan's Cape**, said to hold Ambon's best diving. We hired a speedboat from Tulehu, which took a bit over an hour, but were disappointed with the diving. While there were some interesting soft corals and sponges, there were few hard corals and fish were remarkably scarce. Perhaps we did not find the right spot.

West of Mamala, along the coast road, is **Hila**, where there is a lovely colonial church.

Immanuel Church was built by the Dutch Reformed Church in 1780, and is still faithfully attended today. The nearby Tua Wapauwe Mosque, small, but well-proportioned, is Ambon's oldest, originally built in 1414. Just a short stroll from the mosque is **Fort Amsterdam**. The thick, high walls of the fort were built atop Portuguese fortifications.

A magnificent giant banyan tree, which had until recently covered the fort, has been unfortunately cut down. But another tree still manages to hang on, its roots intertwined among the topmost stones. The decaying majesty of the fort is perhaps only palpable to romantics and history buffs. If you need a guide for this area, ask for Atus Lumaela. He speaks passable English and is a pleasant young man.

A couple of kilometers out of Hila and adjoining Kaitetu village, the pleasant, thatch roofed **Manula Beach Hotel** offers cold beer, good meals or rooms for an overnight stay. (See "Ambon Practicalities," page 186.) Following the coast, a half hour or less brings you to Negeri Lima where a small old fort still stands in good condition overlooking the sea (but hidden by vegetation). Negeri Lima is just off the coastal road which ends at Asilulu,

Opposite: *Using a homemade contraption, a local spearfisherman prowls Ambon's clear waters.* **Above:** *Sacred eels that embody ancestral spirits are hand-fed eggs in Waai.*

a Muslim fishing village dominated by a mosque. Three idyllic islands lie offshore, offering snorkeling and good scuba diving. There are no commercial accommodations at Asilulu so you have to rely on local hospitality. If planning on overnighting, see the raja beforehand. He is a very nice elderly gentleman, retired from the navy.

One bus a day (more if the number of passengers warrant it) makes the 2.5–3 hour run to Ambon, $1.40. These are of fairly high axle as after heavy rains, flooded rivers between Hitu and Asilulu prevent minibus crossings.

Leitimur: south of Ambon

The sandy beach at **Amahusu**, 7 kilometers from Ambon city, is the closest place to town for a quick dip. The beach is pleasant, or you can rent an outrigger to view the remains of once magnificent reefs (now bombed out and dead). The Tirtha Kencana Hotel here, favored on weekends by well-to-do locals, has 10 air-conditioned rooms for rent ($30D).

A few kilometers past Amahusu is Eri, 10 kilometers from Ambon along the bay road, which boasts a reef. Bombed-out and polluted, the reef drops off steeply a mere 30 meters from the shore. Skip it.

Namalatu beach, 16 kilometers from town on Leitimur's southern tip, attracts a large weekend crowd. There is a government *losmen* here for overnighters, the Mess Pembda ($4, without meals). Coral forma-

tions jut out of the white sand beach and the shallow water close to shore. The coral is decorated with lovely streamers of plastic garbage bags, thoughtfully contributed by picnickers. The view from the cliff tops above nearby Latuhalat is better, where the little details are less noticeable. The area does offer some nice snorkeling, but further out, near the *losmen*. The best months are September to May.

The strange village of Soya Atas

The most pleasant trip out of Ambon is also the shortest. The village of Soya Atas, perches 400 meters up the flank of 950-meter Gunung Sirimau. A pretty little church sits in Soya Atas' clean village plaza, and it is faced by the raja's house, filled with momentos from the days of past splendor, when this raja controlled the city. But there is something strange about Soya Atas.

In colonial times, Nenek Luhu, the daughter of a raja of Soya Atas, fell in love with a Dutch official. Her father disapproved of the match and the girl drowned herself out of grief. Her spirit, it is said, has never found peace and occasionally returns to this area: to kidnap foreign men, to replace her lost love; or small children, to replace the babies she never had. The kidnappings all follow the same pattern. The victim disappears completely for a few days, then is discovered, sometimes dead. If not dead, he is in shock,

dazed, or in a trance. The "cure" is for the victim to be given a drink of water by the Raja of Soya. Then all is well, except the victim can never recall what happened.

"[Soya's] best documented kidnapping took place just before the Second World War, when Indonesia still belonged to Holland," writes Shirley Deane. "The Dutch Governor-General came to Ambon on an official visit, and stayed with the Dutch Resident in his house above the city. He disappeared, while taking a stroll alone round the well-guarded gardens before dinner. There was, of course, a full-scale, frantic search, with the entire army and police force, and most of the population of Ambon looking for him. He was found in a trance three days later, quite near Soya, in a place which had been thoroughly searched before, by the present Rajah who was then a little boy of nine. The boy's grandfather, Rajah then, brought him round with water from the well—and was rewarded, at his own request,with scholarships for his sons to be educated in Jakarta."

When in Soya, it's best to not think about this too much, and instead, walk past the neat village houses and up a little rise to perhaps the best preserved (and certainly most accessible) *baileo,* or ritual meeting place, on the island. The meeting place includes ancient megaliths and stone seats for dignitaries. The main path next to the *baileo* winds upward to about 700 meters where there is a sacred site at the top of the hill. A stone throne, encircled by croton bushes, faces a splendid panorama—Mount Salahutu, the Lease Islands, Leitimur's southern coast, and sometimes, in the faint distance, Banda's Gunung Api.

The shrine holds a sacred urn, **Tempayan Setan,** or "Devil's Urn," that never empties of water even during the driest parts of the year. The water cures illness, brings prosperity, and can even encourage the affections of the person of your choice.

If you are visiting Soya Atas on the second Friday of December, you can witness the **Cuci Negeri** (Purifying the Village) ritual. An ancient rite preserved despite Christianity, the ceremony rids the area of evil influences, and assures the land's fertility and the people's good health. In addition to the magic, the down-to-earth locals scrub their houses inside and out, wash the streets and clean up all the garbage.

For the ambitious, several paths (you need a guide) lead downward to Leitimur's southern coast from the Soya Atas area. All offer beautiful scenery and the chance to witness traditional Ambonese life, but the path past the isolated villages of Hatalai and Naku is the most interesting.

Opposite: *The Muslim towns of Ambon's north coast have long been a regional trade center.* **Below:** *The beaches and turquoise water off Liang on the Hitu Peninsula's northeast point.*

GEZIGT van CI

KAART
DER
Ambonsche Eilanden.

R A M

Hatoe Alam
Tockoesa
Swaay
Loeloto
Ipapoetok
Inoe Tia
Bocan
Noesacca
Het Strand Sakella
R. Batewike
Het Strand Ninni
R. Aserlla
Het Strand Adepe
Het Strand
Rete Batilpo
Soeuselko
Knop met Dogoerti
Besanery
Heena
Lammia

Werinama
Het Nabelae Bÿ
Batie Mahoe
Het Strand Zelen
Kolla Koek
Canal
Pt. Gofie
Killing
Pt. Gawas
R. Mohiren
Lemwardens Eilᵈ
Pt. Aost
Sinus Navis
Eÿstheep
Ketangaa
Kilen
Ceram Laoet Maor

Goram
Tenimbar
Salormaki
Menabesw

BANDASCHE EILANDEN

Cepal
Pt. Prampon
Pt. Swangi
Pt. Ay
Neira
Nglackie
Pt. Rhum
Goenong Apie
Lonthoir
Rosngyn

THE LEASE ISLANDS

Ambon's Jewel-like Neighbors

From the prow of a motor launch heading east from Ambon, Seram's mountains loom to portside, while starboard the boat passes lonely stretches of beach, swaying coconut palms, and everywhere, the lovely green-blue water. Underwater, the scenery is perhaps even more beautiful: stands of stately staghorn coral, sea fans, and bright fishes, darting like birds.

Three small islands—together with Ambon itself—make up the Lease (Lay-AH-say) group, formerly called the Uliassers. The smaller eastern islands—Haruku, Saparua, and tiny Nusa Laut—offer a more relaxed glimpse of island life than busy Ambon, and the reefs off their shores have not suffered the intense fish-bombing and dredging that have destroyed those on Ambon.

Haruku Island, a short hop from Ambon, is best known for its medicinal hot springs and crumbling Dutch forts. Fort Nieuw Zeeland and Fort Nieuw Hoorn are both in Pelau village on the island's north coast. Haruku's population of some 25,000 is evenly divided between Christians and Muslims.

Haruku Island

Haruku was the site of a small Japanese airstrip in World War II. Three hundred Japanese troops were stationed here, and the British, Australian and Dutch prisoners of war from Singapore, once they finished Ambon's Liang airfield, were brought over to build Haruku's strip.

Every three years, the people of **Pelau** on Haruku's north coast perform a little-known ritual called Tari Maa Tenu. Information on this event is somewhere between scarce and non-existent, but the three-day-long ceremony is described as including *cakalélé* war dances, a special dance performed by weavers, and a great deal of ritual activity. The ceremony is also said to serve as a reception of guests into an extended family called the Hatuhaha.

The ceremony is said to be held just after Maulud of the Islamic calendar, although other sources mention the months Rabiulawal and Rabiulakhir. We can offer no guarantees, but ask about it.

Two bank reefs off Haruku's north coast, not too far from Pelau, are said to be an excellent spot for diving. The slope off the

atolls is dramatic, increasing to nearly vertical by about 30 meters out. Much of the coral here has been blasted, but the atolls' almost vertical walls rising out of the depths attract a number of interesting open-water fish to the area. The pelagic species include sharks and giant groupers.

Waeriang beach, just west of the ferry terminal at Pelau, is an unconfirmed nesting ground for the strange megapode or *maleo* birds. Like reptiles, these birds bury their eggs in a heap of vegetation, allowing the heat of decomposition to incubate the eggs.

Saparua Island

Next to Ambon, Saparua is the most populous of the Lease Islands, with 45,000 people. The island boasts a network of paved roads, plied regularly by minibuses, radiating outward from the ferry terminal at Haria. The ferries dock about 5 kilometers from Saparua Town, which is approximately in the center of the H-shaped island. Just east of town is beautiful **Waisisil beach,** a long stretch of white sand.

There are clove and nutmeg plantations within easy reach of Saparua Town, as well as stands of sago palm. The clove harvest takes place from August to December, and it is worth watching this painstaking process. Disputed trees were the source of frequent and bloody feuding in the past, but today these conflicts are restricted to fistfights, with an occasional torching of an enemy's thatch

roof. Since the government helped to resettle several hundred families on nearby Seram, tensions have cooled.

On market days, Wednesday and Saturday, the usually sleepy town of **Saparua** bustles with activity. Sellers begin arriving early in the morning, but activities don't peak until 10 or 11 a.m. By early afternoon, the show is over. Much of the produce is truly strange, but you will recognize 5–10 kilo cones of sago paste, red palm sugar, and a bewildering variety of delicious smoked fish. The best of the latter, which make a great snack, are the *komo,* a small tuna, the *lalosi,* a herring, and *sakuda,* a snapper. Most of the selling takes place at curbside on one of Saparua's main streets, but there's also a large covered area, much sought-after on rainy days.

The island's pottery-making center is in **Ouw village**, 9 kilometers southeast of Saparua town. The utilitarian clay pieces are not thrown on a wheel, but built up by hand. Wads of clay are pressed and worked gradually into a recognizable bowl or other piece of kitchenware. The craftsmen can be seen at their trade every day except Wednesday and Saturday, when they are at the market along with the rest of the island. The clay work is

Opposite: *Saparua Island offers excellent swimming, snorkeling and diving together with cozy accommodations and services.*

fired twice a week, on Tuesdays and Fridays, just before going to market.

There is a landmark at Ouw, a curious old, moss-covered building. The locals call it *benteng* Portuges ("Portuguese fort"), but the accuracy of this is doubtful.

A real fortress, the recently restored Dutch **Fort Duurstede**, points its iron cannons over a clear, peaceful bay, just outside of Saparua Town. And the war paraphernalia of local hero Pattimura, aka Thomas Matulessy, who temporarily conquered the Dutch fort in 1817, is lovingly cared for by an elder in nearby Haria village. (See "Ambon City," page 52.) Pattimura's accouterments have remained in good shape for over 170 years, and they have thus acquired a magical, and vaguely sacred character.

The story is locally told of how Thomas Matulessy got his name. Matulessy led a rebellion against the Dutch after having gotten a taste of British rule during the Napoleonic wars (when Britain took over administration of the Moluccas). Apparently, Matulessy captured a whole contingent of Dutch soldiers during his rebellion. At sunset, he slaughtered all but one—he spared the son of the enemy commander. Because of this act of mercy, he was given the name "Pattimura," meaning "Generous-hearted one." The Generous-hearted one's rebel band included more than 1,000 Alfur head-hunters.

The rebellion did not last, however, as the Dutch rounded up their own 1,000 Alfur headhunters, with an extra 500 for good luck, and Pattimura met his match. Eventually, he and his men were turned in, and he was executed by the Dutch.

Even at the end, he didn't lose what must have been a fine and ironic sense of humor—his last words: "Have a pleasant stay here gentlemen." The yearly Pattimura celebration starts on Saparua Island on May 14, making its way to Ambon on the next day.

Fish bombing has unfortunately ruined the best diving spots along the northern section of the island, but just off **Booi village** in the southwest, 4 kilometers from the ferry dock, are shallow reefs with abundant tropical fish and unbombed coral. Though not for serious scuba divers, the snorkeling here is excellent.

The northwest shore of **Molana**, a little sliver of coral island southwest of Saparua, also makes a beautiful spot for snorkeling. Avid scuba divers will head for Molana's southernmost point, where the deep waters bring large, pelagic fish.

Nusa Laut

The tiniest of the Lease Islands, Nusa Laut is a jewel. The 24 kilometers of coastline are fringed with shallow reefs, teeming with marine life and unsullied by bombing and dredging. The sandy bottoms, particularly near **Ameth** village, are a treasure trove for shell hunters, and some fine specimens are sold in the village. Divers can see lobsters, moray eels, sharks, and a variety of reef fish. Fishermen snag grouper, tuna and mackerel.

Ameth, in fact, offered the finest diving we found in the area. The small bay in front of this village offers a very healthy reef, with very good numbers and varieties of reef fishes, including occasional large pelagics. Remember to ask permission of the village head before diving. Akon village, south of Ameth, is also said to offer good diving.

Nusa Laut's 14,000 inhabitants live in seven villages. The island itself is split in half by a low stone wall—all the people on one side are Patalima; on the other, all are Patasiwa.

The pretty island has two early 19th century churches, the Ebenezer and the Ameth, and the neglected remains of the Dutch East Indies Company's Fort Beverwijk.

Right: *Fort Duurstede on Saparua Island has been restored to its original condition, including the re-mounting of its old cannon.*

SERAM

The Mystical Mother Island of Ambon

Even at this late date, the Moluccas' largest island is shrouded in mystery. With a forbidding interior marked by a chain of huge peaks, Seram is as much a place in the imagination as a physical island of rock, jungle and sand. The Seramese are reported to possess strange faculties, allowing them to disappear at will, or transport their bodies hundreds of kilometers away. And these are not parlor games—the indigenous peoples, generically called Alfur, have a history of settling scores with enemy heads.

The Ambonese refer to their large, mountainous neighbor with a mixture of respect and awe. They call Seram the Nusa Ina, or "Mother Island." To the Ambonese, Seram is the source of *adat* customary practice, which is central to village life, particularly the *pela* system of village alliances. Legend even places the beginnings of agriculture on Seram. A beautiful princess, it is told, after being spurned in a love affair, ordered herself killed, cut into pieces and buried. The different limbs of the poor girl then grew into the various root crops (yams, taro, manioc) that now provide the region's staple diet.

Seram is the largest island in Maluku, and covers 18,410 square kilometers, about half the size of the Netherlands. The island stretches 340 kilometers east to west. The tallest peak in the chain of high mountains is Gunung Binaija, which reaches 3,055 meters. Much of the island is densely wooded, mountainous, but not volcanic. Seram's eastern point is less mountainous, and is dominated by spreading lowlands and swamps. There are three great bays evenly spaced along the island's south coast, and one in the middle of the north shore.

About 200,000 people live on Seram, with the population concentrated in the west and almost entirely along the coasts. When the island became important as a trade center, waves of immigration pushed the indigenous Seramese inland. But a counter-tendency has been created by forced relocation of tribal peoples, beginning in the colonial period and continuing until today, which has gradually emptied out the interior. The fierce Bati and Moro people were easier to control when they were out in the open on the coast.

The result today is that even the coastal areas are ethnically mixed. Still, even govern-

ment statistics admit at least several thousand unregenerate animists in the island's mountainous center. And the eastern half of the island, far from the trade and growth of the west, still harbors thousands of Bonfia, a peaceful and retiring people.

An imaginary line running from Selaman Bay on the north coast to Teluti Bay on the south divides the island in half for the purposes of *adat*. The people living east of this line are affiliated with the Patalima branch, and their ritual activities are marked by the importance of the number five; to the west of the demarcation, the people are Patasiwa, where nine is the key magic number.

The Alfur and their magic powers

In colonial times, the dark-skinned peoples of Seram and other Moluccan islands were called Alfur, from the Portuguese *alifuro*. The unflattering appellation was synonymous with "savage," as the members of these tribes were head-hunters and warriors, and generally conducted themselves in a way of which the Europeans did not approve. Today, the term Alfur has taken on an almost honorific connotation, perhaps because the Seramese people are known as being the source of much of Ambon's *adat*.

The Alfurs are ethnically distinct from the Austronesian (Malay) people who make up most of Indonesia's population today. Ethnically they are of Papuan stock, the abo-

riginal inhabitants of the region. The west and east Seramese are racially somewhat different, with the people from West Seram belonging to the same race as the ethnic Ambonese and other Lease Islanders.

According to colonial accounts, the peoples of Seram varied from fierce head-hunters to peaceful farmers. The most trouble for the Europeans came from the warlike Patasiwa Hitam, who lived in the mountainous interior. A 19th century report notes that, like the Dayaks of Borneo, the Alfurs require a head be chopped off to consecrate a marriage. A pre-World War II account calls the Patasiwa Hitam "among the most feared head-hunters in the Indies…giving the Dutch much trouble." The same account says the "central districts are inhabited by mixed Alfur tribes, of a more peaceable disposition: the Patasiwa Putih, Patalima and Seti." The hills and marshes of eastern Seram shelter a Papuan people, the Bonfia, who are shy, unwarlike and culturally distinct from the Alfurs.

Even today, the inhabitants of Seram's interior are credited with a plethora of magical powers, including the ability to kill an adversary with magic, to render themselves invisible, and to "fly" on sago palm leaves, this last apparently requiring that someone first be murdered with a metal object. Well-

Opposite: *Storm clouds gather over Seram, home of people with reputed magic powers.*

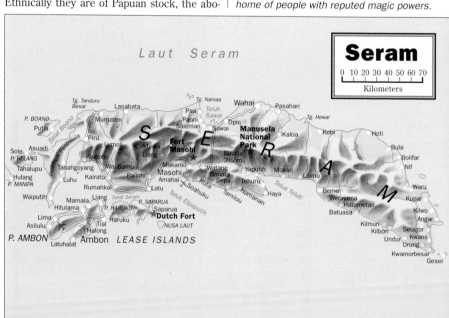

educated Christian Ambonese recount these abilities with curious precision. For instance, one informant said, these gifted Seramese men can hop from Seram to Ambon, pick up a cold beer, and be back in less than a minute.

The most feared of these are the Bati shaman-warriors, who not only can fly through the air and render themselves invisible, but also possess notorious homicidal tendencies. With the Bati, these powers will be turned against perpetrators (breaking a taboo, failing an *adat* obligation, even slighting a warrior) to bring swift and supernatural justice. Some of the Bati tribe send their children to school. But the kids have learned enough magic before leaving home. When they need money, it is said, a rice-winnowing tray, offerings of tobacco and mantras are all that is needed to produce the cash.

Few outsiders—and no anthropologists so far—have had contact with the Seram supermen. One account does mention a Seramese group called the Kakehan as harboring the only secret men's society in Indonesia. Even though many people from the interior have now moved to the coast, according to one recent account they still maintain the *suane,* the village ritual house where sacred valuables are stored, in their old mountain villages near the spirits.

A trade emporium

Only recently, with the 1910 oil strike near Bula, did the "mainland" of east Seram become of economic importance. But even before the Europeans arrived in the Moluccas, a tiny string of islands off Seram's easternmost tip—Geser, Kilai, Keffing and Gorom—was a booming trade emporium.

Of all the islands, collectively known as Seram Laut, only Gorom has some size to it. The others are exposed, low-lying atolls, vulnerable to high tides, and subject to frequent flooding and hurricanes. There is no land for cultivation and the available drinking water tastes distinctly brackish. But from the 17th through the 19th centuries, these tiny islands saw a volume of trade that rivaled Ambon.

The earliest Portuguese sources describe a booming commerce in *trepang* (dried sea cucumbers), *massoi* bark and bird of paradise feathers on Seram Laut. The area was known for textile exports since at least the beginning of the 17th century. And the Sultan of Tidore, who claimed authority here, had no real control. The islands in Seram Laut provided primary anchorages for Malay, Makassarese and Javanese trading vessels.

After the Dutch massacre in the Banda Islands in 1621, many Bandanese fled to Keffing and nearby Guli-Guli Island. Period maps call the little island "Banda-Keffing" due to the influx. Some Bandanese also settled on Gorom Island where, as might be expected, they tended nutmeg groves. (See "History of the Bandas," page 86.)

The Dutch had fought long and hard for the monopoly on Banda, and decided the competition on Gorom had to go. The Europeans organized a small-scale attack in 1624, but were repelled. The Dutch may have underestimated Gorom, which was the principal power in the area at the time. The little island could mobilize 50 *kora-kora* war canoes on short notice, a force definitely to be reckoned with. By 1633, the Dutch launched their first *hongi* raid—backed up with Ambonese muscle—against "illegal" spice growers and merchants in Seram Laut. The effects of the raids were mitigated, however, by the ease of escape to other islands or, where possible, by moving settlements further inland.

The center of political power and commerce continued to shift from island to island in the Seram Laut group, but the volume of trade in high-value commodities such as *massoi* bark and bird of paradise feathers remained surprisingly stable over the centuries. During the 18th century, in response to the reopened Chinese market, trade in maritime products such as *agar-agar,* pearls, *trepang* and shark fins grew dramatically.

In the middle of the 19th century, a commentator described Geser, the current trade center, as "one of the busiest and most curious marts in the extreme East." Bird skins, pearls, tortoise-shell, nutmeg, damar pitch (for varnish), beeswax, and *trepang* poured into the tiny entrepôt. These goods were exchanged for scarlet, blue and white cottons and calicos from Dutch and English looms, yellow-handled hoop-iron knives (the region's universal small change), beads, glass balls, knobs of amber, and old keys and scraps of metal. The trade was conducted by Malay and Chinese traders from Makassar (now Ujung Pandang), Singapore, and Ternate.

By this time, the Dutch were beginning to recognize the importance of Geser. Vague plans for a fort in the region had been lying around for at least a century. But in the mid-1800s, the colonial masters of the region built a coaling station and an administrative post

Opposite: *The Naulu, even those now living on the coast, are famous for their hunting skills.*

on Geser. At this time, skilled labor from Seram Laut was making its way all over the region. Carpenters and bricklayers from Geser were working in West Irian and the Raja Empat islands; the other islands produced ironsmiths, goldsmiths, carpenters, potters and boat builders.

Other than punishing the Seramese with periodic *hongi* raids, the Dutch pretty much ignored the island during the heyday of the V.O.C. monopoly. In 1654, the Dutch punished settlements on the Hoamoal Peninsula for growing cloves by destroying the region's sago trees, bringing starvation and ruin to the tribes. There is also said to have been a small fort on Kambello on the west coast of Seram, probably to control shipping.

But by the 19th century, accounts refer to a rebellion on Seram, which created headaches for the Dutch before it could be crushed. In 1882, Holland formally took over administration of the island, including tenuous control of the island's central region. A military garrison was stationed at Wahai, on the north-central coast, at the head of Selaman Bay, to man the "pacification" efforts. By 1910, when pacification was more or less complete, the troops were withdrawn.

Seram today

The administrative capital of the Kabupaten Maluku Tengah (Central Moluccan District) is at Amahai (Masohi district) on Seram's south coast, on the shore of Elpaputih Bay. Since there is no great population concentration anywhere in the area, Masohi, with some 40,000 inhabitants, was probably chosen for its central location and proximity to Ambon.

The area of Elpaputih Bay, relatively flat and fertile, has seen its sparse population increase dramatically in the past decade. Resettlement programs have moved tribal groups out of the inaccessible interior of Seram itself to the coast, and people have been brought here from the crowded islands of Ambon, Haruku, Saparua and Nusa Laut.

Further, all previous inhabitants of the volcanic islands Teun, Nila and Serua now live here. The permanent danger of volcanic eruptions on these islands, near Damar in the Maluku Tenggara district, caused the government to organize a total migration. Now years have passed, with no eruption having occurred, and the island people ask for nothing more than to be returned to their original homes. The government approval for this, however, seems further away than ever.

Oil was discovered around 1910 near Bula on the northeast coast and the field was soon tapped and into production. Small-scale pumping has continued ever since. During World War II, when the Japanese had 18,000 troops on Seram, the wells produced about 1,500 barrels a day, or 40,000 tons per year. But things have slowed down, and the wells are today rated at 300 barrels a day.

THE NAULU

Seram's Traditional Alfur People

The people who possess the most unusual magical powers are said to live inaccessibly deep in the mountains of eastern Seram. They are not easy to visit—guests are by invitation only. When these people want to see someone, their visitor is flown in, gratis, on the wings of the tribe's mystical powers.

But this does not mean it is impossible to visit the island's Alfurs. The villages of the Naulu (formerly called the Patakai), a traditional, animist people who live in central Seram, require no supernatural assistance to visit. The Naulu village of Bonara is just a short *bemo* hop from the Seramese port of Soahuku, near the island's largest city and the capital of the region, Masohai.

The Naulu, who wear a trademark red headband, make offerings to the spirits, conduct initiation rites, and can perform a rousing war dance for visitors.

The more traditional villages are deeper in the mountainous interior, but the several-day trek through the 100,000-hectare Manusela Reserve is an adventure in itself. The reserve is famous for huge butterflies, including the beautiful blue *Papilio ulysses,* as well as perhaps the widest variety of bird life in the Moluccas: hornbills, kingfishers, cockatoos, lories, parrots, honey-eaters, and oddities like the megapode and cassowary.

Naulu traditions

In times of trouble, the Dutch recruited Alfur auxiliaries, including Naulu, as did nationalist hero Pattimura in his war against Holland. The Naulu were were proud of their deserved reputation as fierce warriors and headhunters. The raja of the south Seram coastal town of Sepa requested the help of the Naulu in defending his people against the periodic, raids from western New Guinea. According to tradition, the Naulu finally gave the Irianese forces such a trouncing that they never returned. The Naulu who came to Sepa's aid, formed several small settlements around the village, where they still live today.

Although recently the government of Indonesia has become more sensitive to the practice of animism among its citizens, in the past this was not always the case. They were suppressed, as it was thought that such beliefs would stand in the way of national unification. In the 1970s, the native religion of the Naulu was brought under the umbrella of Hinduism, an approved religion, as a section of Hindu Dharma.

When a youth is thought ready to become a man, around age 15, he is taken for five days into the mountains where he must bring down both a deer and a wild pig with his spear. He must also bring down a cuscus with one arrow—or climb up the tree to get the animal. After these feats, the young man returns to the village, where a day-long ritual welcomes him to adulthood. The party includes the *cakalélé* war dance and another performance called the *maku-maku.*

The girl's initiation is a more private, and less exciting affair. When she begins her first menstruation, the girl is taken to a little shed where, naked and smeared with ashes, the young woman is taught the lore surrounding what the Naulu and many other traditional societies consider an unclean period. While she is in the hut, the girl can only eat boiled food—sago, manioc and bananas. When her period is over, she is taken to a river for cleaning. Returning to the village, she is dressed in finery and feted as a woman ready to marry.

As in much of the Moluccas, the Naulu staple foods are sago starch and tubers such as manioc. Protein comes from fish or game. The little cash which finds its way into the local economy comes from copra, cloves and nutmeg. Unlike their coastal neighbors, the Naulu make periodic forays into the mountainous interior, their former home. Small groups of men take their spears and hunting dogs into the mountains, and after anywhere from a week to a month, return with large quantities of smoke-cured venison and boar, as well as damar (used to make varnish) to bring a little cash to the village.

The present pattern of village distribution on Seram is largely a result of Dutch efforts to establish adminstrative control. The Naulu are split into two groups, one on the north coast and one on the south, the two populations separated from each other by the mountainous spine of the island. Before the Dutch

Opposite: With an actor's expressive face, a Naulu village elder recounts the group's history.

intervened, the Naulu lived together in the island's interior.

Bonara village

Bonara is a neat little village of some ten families. The houses, some of which are raised on a little forest of low stilts, are all of wood and bamboo, with thatch roofing. A large, open-sided building, towards the back of the village, is the meeting place and center of the village's ritual activity. The building, called *suane,* has three entrances: one on the west side, for high government officials; another on the east, for traditional Naulu leaders; and finally one on the north, for ordinary folks.

The red headband is the special mark of the Naulu, first worn after initiation rituals at the age of 15 or so, and it distinguishes them from their Muslim or Christian neighbors. Red, the color of blood, reminds the men of their ancestors' prowess as warriors. In the old days, the Naulu fought constantly to acquire heads. These were necessary offerings to consecrate a new house, when "cleaning" a village of evil influences, and as part of the bride price. Today, antique red porcelain plates from China suffice to acquire a wife.

To reach the village, hop on an early morning passenger boat from Tulehu in West Ambon and, after a three-hour voyage, your ship will dock at Soahuku, on Seram's south-central coast. Minibuses wait to whisk off clients. Take one of the buses to Bonara (on the Sepa village route).

On arrival in Bonara, find the *kepala kampung,* the village head. This good-natured man can speak Indonesian, one of the few in the village of his generation who can. Many of the older Naulu do not speak the national language because their parents, afraid that their children would become "corrupted" away from the traditional way of life, would not send them to the missionaries' schools. Now that the government runs the schools, this reluctance is vanishing.

If you can afford it, ask the *kepala kampung* to arrange for a *cakalélé* war dance. The fee will be $60–$100, depending on the number of men participating, and he will need a day to arrange the event. Some 15 to 30 men make up the dance group, wearing traditional accouterments and, occasionally, loincloths. They will use magic to bring both sunshine and a bit of rain on the day the dance is held.

Bonara is largely deserted during the day, as the villagers are out tending their farms. The *kepala kampung* or a child could take you to one of the plots where people farm manioc and other root crops or to the site of a sago harvest. Another Naulu village, **Watane**, is about half a kilometer from Bonara. The Naulu are not sea-oriented, but the nearby pebble beach is a pleasant place for a swim—if the waves are not too high.

Late afternoon brings the people back to the village. There are no formal accommoda-

tions in Bonara, but you can find someone who will put you up overnight. Otherwise, catch a minibus to **Masohi** where there are several losmen. If you intend to spend the night in Masohi, find out when the last minibus heads that way, usually between 4 and 6 p.m. There are some small stores in Soba, about a kilometer down the road, that have food and essentials. Gifts of red cloth, which is used for headbands, and raw tobacco, are most appreciated by the Naulu. These can be purchased in Ambon or Masohi. Bottles of the local booze, called *sopi* ($1.50 in Masohi) also help social intercourse.

Further into Naulu-land

The largest concentration of Naulu, perhaps 250 families, lives deep in the mountains of east-central Seram in and around a village called **Manusela**. Reaching this area requires a ferry from Tulehu to Amahai, the harbor near Masohi, the capital of Maluku Tengah (Central Maluku) district. From here, during the dry season, there are public minibuses to Tehuru, on the coast and at the end of a 54 kilometer road ($3; $75 for charter).

Although it is possible to reach Manusela from the north coast town of Wahai (5 days), the trail is shorter (3 days, but steeper) from the south. The best place to set out from is Tehuru, which is a regular ferry stop from Tulehu on Ambon island ($4). There are ferries to Tehuru from Tulehu ($4) but these run far less frequently than to Amahai. Still, during the rainy season—or often during the dry one—the boat is the best way to get to Tehuru, as several badly built bridges between Masohi and Tehuru have the nasty tendency to wash out.

You must register with the police at Tehuru, and you can overnight in the eight-room *penginapan* ($5–$10 a night). From Tehuru you can start trekking around the westernmost bend of Teluti Bay, cross the Kawa River and cut inland from the coastal village of Saunolu. You could also hire a boat (about $10) from Tehuru to Saunolu or Hatumeto (also spelled Hatumeten), the two suggested points of departure from the south coast to the Manusela Reserve. Perhaps once a week, ferries run to Hatumeto. Even if you made it this far without a guide (assuming that you know basic Indonesian), you will need one from the coast heading inland.

This is a serious trip. Stock up on supplies, as the two to five day trek to the Naulu village of Manusela passes no villages or supplies of any kind. You will hike through swamps full of taro and wind up steep mountains as high as 2,000 meters. The lands you pass through are full of interesting birds and wildlife, including colorful lories and cockatoos.

Below: *A Naulu woman returns from tending fields near Bonara village. The funnel-shaped basket she carries is used throught the region.*

BURU

Rugged Island of Timber and Tradition

Buru has not been blessed with an upbeat reputation. One Dutch official referred to the islanders as "ex-cannibals and consumers of dogs." In more recent times, Buru served as a detention camp for political prisoners rounded up during the Year of Living Dangerously in 1965 and 1966. For years the island was off limits to travelers. Recently things have changed: prisoners, except for those who decided to stay, have been sent back to Java, and the island is now open for tourism. So far, however, the crowds have stayed away (to put it mildly). The infrastructure remains rudimentary, so travel here is only for those adventurous souls willing to rough it out.

Buru covers 9,000 square kilometers, which makes it half again as large as Bali, and the third largest islands in Maluku (after Seram and Halmahera). The interior is mountainous, and the highest peak just tops 2,000 meters. Except for a large plain inland from Kayeli Bay, there is almost no level ground on the island.

The island's economy, communications and history revolve around Kayeli Bay, a 10-kilometer indentation on the northeast corner of Buru. The bay's opening to the sea is flanked by two high capes: Tanjung Kerbau (Water-Buffalo Cape) and Tanjung Waat (named for a local river). The island's principal town, Namlea, is on the bay's north shore, with Kayeli village across it to the south and lots of small villages in between.

The island's capital is Namlea, Buru's only real town. Of the 50,000 Buru Islanders, some one-fourth still follow the ancestral religion, and the rest are evenly split between Muslims and Christian. Over half of the people of Buru live in and around Namlea.

Minyak kayu putih

Although the timber business is booming here, with a large army-owned plywood factory in operation since 1975 at Waiputih, the island is most famous for a trade product. *Minyak kayu putih,* literally "white wood oil," is made from the leaves of a kind of myrtle, (*Melaleuca leucodendron*). All members of the Myrtacea family, of which the eucalypts are best known, have oil glands which, by distillation, can yield valuable medicinal oil. Already by the mid-19th century, Buru had acquired local fame as the producer of this popular medicinal, and it is still appreciated today.

"That oil is still little known in Europe," writes one observer, in the 1920s. "[I]t is used in some patent medicines and occasionally in the perfume industry. In the Indies it is a panacea for all illness, internal and external: a few drops on some sugar will cure a stomach ache, and it is rubbed on the skin against rheumatism or lumbago. The strong smell keeps mosquitos away, and a few drops in a bowl of hot water will loosen a cold."

The medicinal value of *kayu putih* oil—antispasmodic, sudorific (brings on sweating), stimulant, comes from cineole, an etherous substance that smells like camphor and tastes cool and pungent. *Kayu putih* oil lost most of its export value when it was discovered that eucalyptus oil, cheaper and easier to obtain, contained a far higher percentage of cineole. In colonial times, the island produced 200 tons of the oil a year; today that has dropped to 70 tons. The oil is still popular in Indonesia, however, and there are some 100,000 hectares of the trees growing on Buru.

Visiting Buru

A good reason to visit Buru is to trek up to see Lake Rana, (sometimes called Walolo) which sits in the Mala Mountains, near the middle of the island. This will allow you to spend some time with the traditional people, generically called Alfurs, of the interior. The reefs off Buru are said to be excellent, but we didn't have time to check these out.

Lake Rana has several paths leading to it, the best one starting on the north coast at Waiplau and following the valley of the Wai Nibe River. It takes locals about one and a half days, so figure about twice that. The lake is ringed by a dozen hamlets inhabited by the Rana, who follow traditional *adat* custom.

The lake is said to be home to a giant eel. Once a year, it urinates, thus killing all the other eels. These are then gathered by the grateful Rana. The 19th century naturalist Albert Bickmore heard of a plant, growing in the lake, which restored youth. Tell us if you find it, along with the giant eel. (Photos appreciated.) The government has for some time promised an access road from the coast, but this will probably be a long time coming.

Along with the 1,600 Rana, two other ethnic groups on Buru adhere to traditions: the 2,200 strong Wai Apu and two similar groups, the Wai Temu and the Wai Loa (also spelt Lua) with a combined number of around 5,000. Some of these traditionalists have begun to convert, but others live their seminomadic existence in the mountainous region around the south east portion of Buru. They hunt wild pigs with spears and plant beans, taro and bananas.

It seems that the Wai Loa maintain the most traditional lifestyles, wearing their hair long and generally maintaining a wild and woolly appearance. To reach them, take one of the frequent boats from Ambon to Namrole ($5–$7), a small port on the south coast. With a local guide, from there it's about a one day trek into the mountains to reach the Wai Loa. It's said that there are still occasional ritual killings in the area, but the violence is not directed toward outsiders.

Should you want help in arranging a trip to Buru, contact Pak Wim Saliky, a native of Buru, at the Daya Patal Travel Agency in Ambon. You can either fly to Namlea, the only city on the island, or take fairly frequent boats (several a week) to various small ports, with normal passenger fare $5–$7. At Namlea there are a couple of basic *losmen* at $14 a night where meals can be ordered. There are only two motor roads out of Namlea: about 90 kilometers to Waiputih on the north coast and 15 kilometers inland.

History of Buru

The little which is known about the early history of Buru surfaces as footnotes to the better known history of Ambon and Ternate. Early in the 16th century, the sultan of Ternate established enough power on Buru's coast to obtain a small yearly tribute, and to control the clove harvests. The island was partially converted to Christianity under the influence of the Portuguese, and reconverted to Islam by Ternateans in 1558. In the early 1650s, the V.O.C. destroyed all the island's clove plants. A revolt followed the extirpation, and many of the coastal people were forced to move to Kayeli Bay, as one observer puts it, within "range of Dutch cannon."

Naturalist Alfred Russel Wallace stopped in Buru for two months in 1861, during the rainy season. He was somewhat disappointed with Buru, as in his two months he found only 210 kinds of beetles. (In Ambon he collected 300 in just three weeks). Everyone has different criteria for judging a place. He did have better luck with birds, preserving 66 species, of which 17 were new. Based on local informants and one skull, he determined that the strange babirusa were found here, a long way from their Sulawesi home.

American naturalist Bickmore, who stopped here in 1865, mentions in passing that that before the Civil War, American whalers called at Namlea, a "free port" and safe anchorage, with plenty of fresh water and wood available as well as abundant vegetables. A small but well built and maintained fort at Namlea, Fort Defensie, was manned by Javanese and Madurese troops. There were eight Europeans at Namlea, including the commander, a doctor and the *controleur*.

Many of the coastal peoples on Buru, like much of eastern Indonesia in these islands, were Muslim immigrants., but Christianity was not formally introduced until 1885, when the Utrecht Missionary Society began proselytizing on Buru.

Buru island became a huge prison when the political prisoners implicated in the 1965 coup attempt were sent there for had labor and re-education. Some 10,000 former communists lived on Buru from 1969 to 1977. Many of these political detainees were the cream of the Indonesian intelligentsia, including such notable figures as Pramoudya Ananta Toer, the country's foremost—and still-banned—novelist. Toer's novels were conceived in Buru and matured through their being recounted to Toer's fellow inmates.

Rice was introduced with the prisoners in 1969 and they were provided with simple tools for cultivation, along with bare hands to clear shrubs to prepare the rice paddies. Hard work, combined with determination to feed themselves and their families, resulted in the creation of farmland from wild, dry scrub country along the Weapau River, some 40 kilometers inland from Namlea.

When the release of the political prisoners began in 1977, the area was returned to the Moluccan government and the farms were neglected. To stop this trend, in 1980 the central government sent 4,000 Javanese transmigrant families to Buru to settle in the houses of the departed prisoners and on the former rehabilitation area. (The program ended in 1982.) They joined the 100-odd families of former communist intellectuals who had elected to remain in Buru, now living around the hamlet of Savanajaya.

PART III

The Banda Islands

Perhaps the most beautiful of the Moluccan isles are the tiny Bandas, mere specks in the vast Banda Sea. These lush, breezy islands offer little clue today that they once radically changed the course of world history. Vasco da Gama rounded the Horn of Africa, Christopher Columbus landed in the New World, and Ferdinand Magellan's crew became the first to circle the globe—all in an attempt to obtain the spice riches of the East Indies, including Banda's nutmeg. The Age of Exploration realigned Europe as, in turn, the Portuguese, the Spanish, and the Dutch and English became wealthy from the spice trade.

Control of the Bandas was contested up until 1667, when the British traded tiny Run Island for Manhattan, giving the Dutch full control of the archipelago. The result for the Bandanese was already tragic—to monopolize the nutmeg trade, the Dutch in 1621 murdered most of Banda's male population, and divided the islands up into parcels awarded to contract plantation owners. The Dutch *perkeniers*, often no more than criminals and drifters, tended the trees with slaves. The old Dutch Fort Belgica, cannons in place, still dominates the central island of Banda Neira—a silent testament to this sad chapter in Moluccan history.

Situated some 140 kilometers southeast of Ambon, the Bandas cover barely 50 square kilometers of dry land, of which half is taken up by crescent-shaped Lontar Island (also called Banda Besar, "Great Banda"). Lontar's coastline traces the crown of a huge sunken caldera, which also forms tiny Sjahrir, formerly Pisang ("Banana") Island.

Rising out of the sea in the center of the crater are Banda Neira and the perfect cone of Gunung Api ("Fire Mountain") the still smoking snout of a once-huge volcano. A few kilometers east of Lontar is Hatta Island. (See map page 95). West of the Lontar group are three other small islands: Ai, Run, and tiny Neijalakka Island.

Bandaneira, the only town of appreciable size on the islands, boasts several comfortable hotels, guides and facilities for boating, diving, fishing, waterskiing or visiting the outer islands. The town also has several interesting mosques.

Banda is one of the world's finest spots for scuba and skin diving. The reefs surrounding the islands are healthy and lush with fish and colorful invertebrates. Rent a tiny dugout in Bandaneira and paddle out into the protected lagoon to any of a number of fine snorkeling spots for an afternoon spent gliding over water with a visibility to 12 meters.

For the serious diver, the reefs surrounding the outer islands often border on spectacular drop-offs, and this transition between shallow reef and deep water is where the big marine species prowl. Exploring the vertical reef faces, you will meet with inquisitive sharks and giant groupers.

Above water, the Bandas are just as beautiful. On Lontar Island, you can visit fragrant nutmeg groves where these delicate trees are protected by a canopy of towering *kanari* nut trees. The nutmegs are carefully picked with a long pole tipped with a basket. People aren't the only ones who enjoy nutmegs—the Bandas' large fruit pigeon eats the apricot-like fruits as well.

Although a fierce eruption in May 1988 forced the evacuation of Gunung Api's population, some have moved back, learning to live with the occasional tremors and the risk of another eruption in exhange for the island's bounty of rich soil. You can climb Gunung Api in a morning, and the view of the crater and surrounding islands is spectacular.

Overleaf: *This 19th century print illustrates the capture of Dutch Fort Belgica by the British.*
Opposite: *This Bandanese* cakalélé *dancer wears a Portuguese style helmet with a tin bird and bird of paradise plumes. Such haberdashery survives from the 16th century.*

HISTORY OF THE BANDAS

Tiny Islands that Changed the World

From recorded history until the 19th century the tiny Banda Islands were the world's only source of fragrant nutmeg and mace. The spices, used in flavorings, medicines and as preserving agents, were almost priceless. Europeans long suspected that the spices came from somewhere in the Far East, but the Arab traders who sold the spices to the Venetians for exorbitant prices were mum on the exact location of their source.

The secret nutmeg isles

No European was able to divine the exact location of the Spice Isles until Alfonso de Albuquerque conquered Malacca in 1511 for the king of Portugal. Malacca, overlooking the strait between Sumatra and peninsular Malaysia, was the hub of the Asian trade route. Immediately upon establishing control of Malacca, Albuquerque sent a small squadron out to find the fabled Spice Islands.

Three ships, led by Antonio de Abreu, set sail. Malay pilots guided the argonauts east along the Lesser Sundas, then steered them north until they sighted the Bandas. The Portuguese filled their holds with nutmeg, mace and cloves. (In addition to growing nutmeg, the Bandanese conducted a thriving entrepôt trade in cloves.) On the way back, Francisco Serrão, Abreu's second-in-command, was shipwrecked, and ended up in Ternate. (See "The Spice Trade," page 26.)

The first written account of Banda was penned by Tome Pires, a Portuguese merchant and official based in Malacca from 1512 to 1515. Pires interviewed the Portuguese on the first expedition to the Bandas, as well as the much more knowledgeable Malay sailors in Malacca, and produced the well-researched and accurate *Summa Oriental*.

Pires estimates the Bandas' population in the early 16th century at 2,500–3,000. The Bandanese, Pires writes, were part of an archipelago-wide trading network, and Bandanese ships competed with the Javanese ones that took on cargoes of spices at Bandaneira and brought them back to Malacca. The only native long-range traders in the Moluccas, the Bandanese took some of their own nutmeg and mace to Malacca.

Goods that moved through the Bandas included cloves, from Ternate and Tidore to the north, bird of paradise feathers, from the Aru Islands and western New Guinea, *massoi* bark, which was used in traditional medicine, and slaves.

In exchange for these goods and the native spices, the Bandas received mostly rice and cloth: light cotton *batik* from Java, calicoes from India and *ikat* from the Lesser Sundas. In 1603, an average quality, *sarong*-sized cloth traded for 18 kilos of nutmeg. Some of the textiles were then traded again by the Bandanese, ending up on Halmahera and New Guinea. The coarser *ikat* cloth from the Lesser Sundas, was traded for sago from the Kei Islands, Aru and Seram.

Although trading with the Portuguese, the Bandanese never allowed them to build a fort or permanent post in the islands, maintaining an independence which would come to a bloody end after Holland's arrival on the

Right: *The nutmeg harvest. Tall* kanari *nut trees provide shade for the delicate nutmegs.*
Opposite: *A 19th century print showing the main trading settlement on Banda Neira (right) with Gunung Api across the strait (left).*

scene. Ironically, it was because there were no Portuguese forts in the Bandas that the Dutch ships first came to trade at Banda, instead of the clove islands to the north.

The Hollanders arrive

The Dutch disliked the Bandanese from the very beginning. Holland's first merchants complained that the natives reneged on promises to deliver nutmeg and mace at the agreed price, juggled and cheated on weights, and mixed cheaper nutmegs in with the mace. An early Dutch captain writes of the Europeans' exasperation with the Bandanese: "these people are so crooked and brazen that it is almost unbelievable."

The lack of good feelings was mutual. Although the Bandanese welcomed another competitor for their spices, the trade articles the Dutch offered in exchange were usually unsuitable. Heavy Dutch woolens and damasks, and unwanted manufactured goods, could not substitute for the traditional trade items. Though spices were a luxury, the food and cloth the Bandanese received in return were essentials. The Javanese, Arab and Indian traders, and the Portuguese, had brought these indispensable items, along with much esteemed Chinese porcelain, steel knives, copper and medicines.

Although the Dutch may have disliked dealing with the Bandanese, their profits were handsome. The spices sold in Amsterdam for 320 times the purchase price in the Bandas, which fully justified the expense involved in shipping them back. Ringing church bells announced the return of the first ships whose holds were stuffed with the fragrant treasure. "For as long as Holland has been Holland," one contemporary chronicler writes, "there never have been ships as richly laden as these."

In their enthusiasm, the burghers feted the explorers, and plied them with as much wine as they could hold—which must have been considerable after the tedious months at sea. It is even likely that the boom brought on by spice profits helped to finance an artistic renaissance in Holland, supporting painters such as Rembrandt van Rijn.

The phenomenal profits of the first expeditions also awakened the greed of the Dutch merchants who financed the expeditions. As the number of backers willing to fund voyages began to increase, they saw that competition would cut into their astronomical profits, and united to form the Vereenigde Oostindische Compagnie (V.O.C.) or the Dutch East Indies Company.

Eliminating the competition

Early 17th century Bandanese society was ruled, as it had been for a long time, by a group of leading citizens, the *orang kaya,* literally "rich men." Each of these was the political head of a district. The Dutch were able to

lure (or defraud) some of the *orang kaya* into signing a treaty that granted Holland the monopoly on nutmeg and mace purchases.

Although the Bandanese leaders certainly did not understand the full or even partial significance of the Het Eeuwig Verbond ("The Eternal Compact"), they sealed their fate—the Dutch would later use this as the legal basis for bringing in the troops to defend their monopoly. Even though not all the islands' leaders had signed the treaty, the Dutch meant for it to apply to everyone.

Soon the *orang kaya* had grown sick of the low prices the Dutch paid for their spices, the useless Dutch trade goods, the Europeans' ignorance of local etiquette, and the V.O.C.'s tedious insistence on forbidding dealings with any other outside group, including the Javanese. Then, in 1609, the Dutch reinforced Fort Nassau on Banda Neira Island. This was the last straw for the *orang kaya,* who were tired of humoring the absurd barbarians. Luring the Dutch admiral and some 40 of his top men to a secluded spot under the pretext of negotiations, the *orang kaya* ambushed and murdered them all.

The Portuguese and Spanish presence in the region had faded, but the English built trading posts on Ai and Run Islands, which they also fortified. They paid better prices for the nutmeg and mace. In response to this growing threat, Holland built the more commanding Fort Belgica, just above Fort Nassau, in 1611.

Four years later, the growing tensions between the Dutch and British came to a head, and Holland invaded Ai with 900 men. Since this force was almost twice the adult male population of the island, the English discreetly withdrew to Run Island. Quickly regrouping on Run, the British launched a brilliant counter-attack that very night, taking the Dutch by complete surprise, killing 200 soldiers and driving the rest of them back to their ship.

It was a year before the Dutch recovered from their loss, but in 1616, an even mightier Dutch force attacked Ai Island. Even this overqualified invasion force was at first driven back by surprisingly accurate cannonades. But a month later, the inevitable could be kept at bay no longer. When the defenders ran out of ammunition, they were slaughtered. The Dutch strengthened the fort and renamed it Fort Revenge.

With the British out of the way, Jan Pieterszoon Coen, the V.O.C.'s energetic and ruthless governor-general, was free to indulge his impatience with the Bandanese. He wasted no time. In 1621, 2,000 well-armed Dutch soldiers landed on Neira Island; in a few days, Lontar Island fell as well. Then, at musket point, Coen forced on the *orang kaya* a treaty whose terms were impossibly onerous. What Coen wanted in fact was a treaty that would be impossible not to violate, so he

would have an excuse turn his guns on the hated Bandanese. To keep his troops occupied, the governor-general had them build Fort Hollandia on the high central ridge of Lontar Island.

The massacre

Several treaty violations, real or fictitious, were quickly noted and Coen unleashed his men. The result was a bloodbath. Only a tiny fraction of the population survived the carnage. The *orang kaya* received exemplary Dutch justice: Japanese mercenaries hired by the Dutch beheaded and quartered 44 of them, and impaled their heads on bamboo spears for display. Previously, there had been 15,000 Bandanese living on the islands. Even 15 years after the massacre, there were fewer than 600—an inauspicious beginning to the Dutch colonial era.

Some Bandanese were able to flee, and most ended up on the islands of their traditional trading partners. The refugee Bandanese settled on Keffing and Guli-Guli in the Seram Laut chain, as well as in two villages on Kei Besar Island.

After clearing the islands of their people, Coen set about the speedy revival of the spice commerce. The productive land—with perhaps half a million nutmeg trees—was divided into 68 *perken,* parcels of 1.2 hectares each, and handed over to licensed Dutch planters, called *perkeniers.* Of the 68 parcels, 34 were on Lontar, 31 on Ai and 3 on Neira. Since their were no Bandanese to work them, slaves were brought in.

The V.O.C. and the *perkeniers* settled in to enjoy the benefits of a controlled trade in nutmeg and mace. To insure its 300 percent profit margin, the V.O.C. paid the *perkeniers* just 1/122nd of the going price for nutmeg in Holland. Still, the planters did quite well. The merchants who bore the expenses of the Banda War soon began to reap huge profits. Banda, one contemporary account proudly states, was the "brightest star of the V.O.C. constellation."

Tending the bottom line

The Dutch never quite managed to hold an absolute monopoly on cloves, but for two centuries, the entire world bought its nutmeg and mace from the V.O.C. It was a very profitable enterprise.

Because the eastern islands of Run and Ai were less tightly controlled by the Dutch, they exterminated all nutmeg trees there. In the 1667 Treaty of Breda, the formerly British-held island of Run was ceded to the Dutch in exchange for a Dutch-held island on the other side of the globe—Manhattan.

The headquarters of Dutch activities in the Moluccas were on Ambon, and they cut Banda off from its traditional trade network, using the islands solely as a nutmeg and mace plantation. In addition to the valuable spices, the colonialists tried to control all valuable products shipped out of the archipelago: *massoi* bark, pearls, mother-of-pearl, damar, *agar-agar* seaweed and bird of paradise feathers. But the Dutch could not exercise strict control over these resources, and Bugis, Makassarese, Arab and Chinese traders marketed the bulk of them.

The decimated population of the Bandas increased slowly as slaves were brought in from other parts of the archipelago, and as both freemen and slaves arrived from Mozambique, the Middle East, Malaya, China, Japan, Bengal and the Coromandel Coast of India, and the Pegu River district of Burma. In 1638, the Bandas' population was recorded at 3,843, of which only 560 were native Bandanese. At the end of the 17th century, the V.O.C. employed 1,000 people on the islands.

All told, Holland managed to export over a billion guilders worth of nutmeg and mace from the Bandas. In 1621, the V.O.C. estimated its European sales at 450,000 (Dutch) pounds of nutmeg and 180,000 pounds of mace. In 1735, the V.O.C. warehouses were so stuffed with nutmeg that 1.25 million pounds were destroyed to keep sale prices high. The V.O.C. took the lion's share of the profits, but enough was left over for the *perkeniers* to build mansions with polished marble floors, beautiful tiles, crystal chandeliers and European furniture.

These fantastic exports did not come without cost, however. To discourage any thoughts of rebellion by the slaves, the Dutch maintained expensive forts and garrisons in the Bandas. And rampant smuggling by V.O.C. officials, *perkeniers*, soldiers, sailors and even slaves cut into the Dutch margin.

There was a human cost as well. In a five-year period for which there are good records, 1633 to 1638, exports totaled 3,097,209 pounds of nutmeg, and 890,754 pounds of mace. In the same five years there were 25

Opposite: This muscular team competes in the yearly canoe race between Neira and Api. The Dutch enlisted kora-kora war canoes like this modern version to enforce their spice monopoly.

executions. The victims were, variously, burned alive, broken on the wheel, garroted, decapitated or just hanged. One lucky chap was "arquebussed"—presumably shot with one of the heavy, matchlock arquebus guns used at the time. Records also show 52 mutilations and 17 floggings.

Nature had a way of cutting into profits as well. Disease, earthquakes, hurricanes, tidal waves and Gunung Api wreaked constant havoc. During just one shattering hour on April 2, 1778, Gunung Api belched up an especially destructive eruption, accompanied by an earthquake, a tsunami and hurricane-force winds. Half of the nutmeg trees were destroyed, and those that remained were almost completely stripped of fruit. The harvest that year was a mere 4 percent of the previous year's production.

Twilight of the V.O.C.

Toward the end of the 18th century, the V.O.C. could see ominous clouds on the horizon. French ships had smuggled out some nutmeg seedlings which were planted on Ile de France (now Mauritius). The V.O.C. was in the red, headed towards bankruptcy. In 1790s, the great monopoly finally fell, mortally wounded by graft, smuggling, bad management and world events. When it sank, the company was 12 million guilders in debt.

But even when the Dutch thought the Bandas were an unprofitable drain on their resources, accounting showed that the islands still yielded over a million guilders of profit each year. The margins fluctuated, but were always high, at one point reaching 6,000 percent. For a frame of reference, at the time the Dutch were pulling 1 million guilders out of the Bandas, one guilder would buy: 13 pounds of rice, one chicken, 2 1/2 pounds of beef, or 1 pound of (expensive) bread.

Towards the end of the century, the economic importance of the Bandas was fading fast, and the Dutch colonial administration reformed some of the worst of the old V.O.C. practices. The slaves were freed in 1862, and they were replaced by convicts and cheap labor imported from other parts of the archipelago. A decade later, the *perkeniers* were granted the deeds to their nutmeg groves, but poor management and the relatively high cost of labor after emancipation drove most of them deeply into debt. Many were forced to sell out. Three-quarters of the nutmeg plantations ended up in the hands of the Kok family, resident Chinese merchants.

But the local economy was far from moribund. As in times past, and even more recently when the nutmeg harvests failed, the merchants of Banda fell back on entrepôt trade. They brought in goods from Seram and the Kei Islands, the Aru Islands and other points in the eastern archipelago. By the late 19th century, when the bird of paradise plume craze hit Paris, much of the trade was in the

hands of Bin Saleh, a local Arab merchant, who shipped the bird of paradise skins directly from Banda to Paris milliners.

Independence and a son of Banda

Banda was a favorite holding area for troublemakers, and in 1854 almost one-fifth of Banda's 6,000 people were exiles. When the nationalist movement began to take hold in the early 20th century, the Dutch exiled some of the anti-colonialists to Banda.

Mohammed Hatta, later vice-president of independent Indonesia, and Sutan Sjahrir, later the nation's prime minister, arrived on Banda in 1936 from the Dutch prison camp on the Digul River in the malarial swamps of West New Guinea.

While here, the two intellectuals befriended the grandchildren of Seyid Abdullah Baadilla, the patriarch of Banda's Arab community. They tutored and set up a school for the children. Baadilla had earned a small fortune by dealing in pearls from Aru Islands. (Unfortunately, he lost it in the 1920s when, after investing heavily in mother-of-pearl gathering operations, the invention of Bakelite dropped the bottom out of the mother-of-pearl button market.)

Hatta and Sjahrir lived six years in Banda. Only in 1942, when the Japanese were getting uncomfortably close, did the Dutch return the exiles to their native Java. The two politicians were strongly anti-fascist and the Dutch hoped they could help turn the Javanese against the Japanese. When Hatta and Sjahrir left Banda, they took the Baadilla children with them, to continue their education in Java. An American Catalina seaplane took off with the exiles and the children just half an hour before Japanese pursuit planes bombed Bandaneira.

One of the Baadilla children, Des Alwi, was kept behind by his mother. But as soon as she consented, he took a boat to Java and joined his mentors. He was later to become an important force for change and improvement in his tiny archipelago.

As a youthful companion and courier for Hatta and Sjahrir, Des Alwi met the men who were to lead Indonesia to independence, and while at school in England, he met Malaysia's future leaders. After independence, he entered the young nation's diplomatic corps. When discontent with Sukarno's policies led to the Permesta Rebellion in 1956, Alwi was the rebels' overseas spokesmen. After the revolt was crushed back home he was invited to live in Kuala Lumpur by the premier of

Malaysia—an old school friend.

After Sukarno's overthrow in 1967, Des Alwi helped to end the confrontation between Indonesia and Malaysia. With powerful friends in the political world and acute economic skills, Des Alwi did well in the byzantine business world of Jakarta.

After an absence of 25 years, he returned to his homeland, finding the Bandas in a sorry condition. Many nutmeg trees had been cut down to plant subsistence crops during the Japanese occupation. The splendid old *perkenier* mansions had been stripped. Government neglect and shortage of funds left social services in a dismal state.

Des Alwi sought to change this state of affairs. With the help of friends in the government, he obtained a resident doctor for the Bandas, a paved airstrip, and better local government. He has built a vacation home there as well as two hotels and has produced several documentary films on Banda.

But it is perhaps Des Alwi's personal example that will prove most helpful to his native Bandas. He speaks several languages and his children are well educated. He brought Hatta to Banda in 1972, and has since invited many dignitaries from Asia and the West.

Opposite: *Fort Belgica dominates Banda Neira, and offers a perfect view of Gunung Api.*
Above: *If you decide to climb Gunung Api, please stick to the path indicated by your guide.*

VISITING THE BANDAS

The Lush, Green Nutmeg Isles

The first glimpse of the Banda archipelago from the noisy Twin Otter aircraft justifies the effort getting there. The Bandas, a cluster of 10 hilly, volcanic islands, jut out of the depths of the Banda Sea in splendid isolation. Three of the islands, in close proximity, form a lovely lagoon and shelter one of Indonesia's finest harbors. Gunung Api's majestic slopes rise in a perfect cone to the volcano's crater topped by a thin stream of smoke.

A few *prahus,* native launches, glide between the islands. Here and there, thatched or rusting tin-roofed huts cling to the shoreline, crowded by steep slopes. The only concentration of houses visible from the air is on **Banda Neira**, the central island of the group and the only one with enough flat space to allow a small town. Here there are government offices, stores, the wharf and almost half of the archipelago's 14,000 popula-

tion. The twin-prop airplane glides in for a bumpy landing on Banda Neira's paved strip.

The breathtaking scenery continues underwater. The reefs are a kaleidoscope of life, with endlessly varied coral formations and bright tropical fishes. While the lagoon provides safe diving for snorkelers or novices with tanks, experienced scuba enthusiasts will be amazed in the deeper waters. The steep walls sprout hard, soft and leathery corals, sponges and a plethora of other colorful and contorted sessile organisms. Reef residents cling to the sides, and huge pelagic species lurk nearby in the open water.

History buffs will find plenty of reminders of the Bandas' oversized role in world history. The well-restored Fort Belgica, built in 1611, dominates its surroundings on Neira and offers an excellent view, over the old cannon, across the lagoon to Gunung Api. The islands are dotted with forts, and these and the nutmeg plantations attest to the importance of these islands. A small but excellent museum gives an account of the islands' past.

Sights of Banda

The Banda islands are indecently lush with tropical vegetation. Some places are flat and coconut-fringed, while others are steeply hilled and covered by a variety of trees. Naturalist Sir Alfred Russel Wallace first wrote of Banda's large fruit pigeon, *Carpophaga concinna,* with its continuous,

loud booming note. These birds gobble up the apricot-like nutmeg fruits, digesting the meat and the mace but passing the nut. The pigeons are most common on Lontar Island, in the forests and beautiful nutmeg groves.

Often you can see **mace** and **nutmegs** drying in the sun. Ask someone to demonstrate how the nutmegs are harvested. A long pole is used, tipped by two prongs and a small basket. The stalk of the fruit, out of easy reach, is nipped by the two claw-like prongs so the nutmeg fruit drops into basket.

If you are in Banda in April or October, **kora-kora** canoes compete in races on the quiet stretch of water between Neira and Gunung Api. The muscled boatsmen, many of whom paddle all day long as fishermen, send the big boats flying over the water at almost unbelievable speeds.

Your hotel can arrange for you to see the spectacular local dance, called the **cakalélé,** formerly performed to whip up enthusiasm for war. The dance includes some very graceful flowing movements along with lots of shouting and stomping. If you want to see a *cakalélé*, we suggest that you follow all the preparations, including the prayers over the sacred cloths, helmets and other paraphernalia used in the dances. On a more quiet note, night often brings out the musical soul of the Bandanese, with songs accompanied by guitar and ukulele.

Another of Banda's attractions, neglected by most visitors out of ignorance, are her mosques. Visit the gleaming **Hatta-Sjahrir Mosque**, but be sure to follow Muslim etiquette and remove your footwear before entering. You can also observe the faithful at prayer as long as you are decently dressed and show respect.

Fully restored **Fort Belgica** (1611) dominates Neira, with **Fort Nassau** (1609) gracefully crumbling below. On Lontar, **Fort Hollandia** and **Fort Concordia** both offer excellent panoramic views. On Ai Island, **Fort Revenge** (Revingil in Dutch) still has several cannon and a few locals have taken over one corner for homes. The **Rumah Buaya Museum** on Neira is full of antiques and and has some historical paintings. Mohammed Hatta's and Sutan Sjahrir's former home-in-exile has been also converted to a museum.

World-class diving

Just riding a boat around the Bandas to take in the scenery is a wonderful experience. On Neira, you can rent a small dugout in which to try your paddling (and balancing) skills. Although the Bandanese make it look effortless, it is harder than it looks. You see even

Overleaf: *An aerial view of the main islands in the Banda group: Neira, Lontar and Gunung Api.*
Opposite: *The town of Bandaneira, on Neira Island, holds restored Fort Belgica, 12 motor vehicles, and the archipelago's only hotels.*

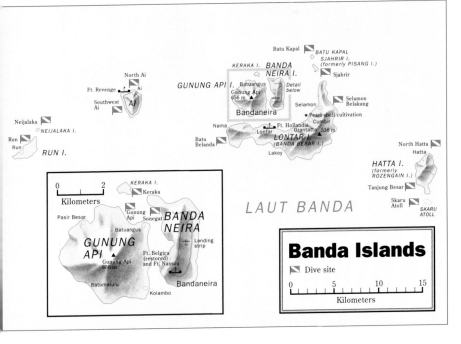

tiny tots confidently guiding their mini-canoes around. If you try it, either obtain a canoe with an outrigger or wear a bathing suit. And remember that white skin sunburns instantly, especially over open water.

There is plenty of serious fishing in the Bandas. Boats and decent tackle and other equipment can be rented from the hotels. From May to September, yellowfin tuna, sailfish, swordfish, Spanish mackerel and other game fish strike regularly. The season for skipjack, bonito and king mackerel runs from March to June, and again from September to mid-January. Barracuda, jacks and medium-sized bottom fish bite year-round in areas close to shore.

Your hotel will cook up the day's triumphant catch, and locals will appreciate whatever you can't eat yourself. Waterskiing is available in the protected waters of the lagoon or Banda Bay. From mid-June to September, and again from January to March, the waters are right for windsurfing, and sailboards are available at Des Alwi's hotels.

Banda is one of the world's very best diving spots. Things haven't changed much since, in mid-19th century, Wallace remarked that "living coral and even the minutest objects are plainly seen on the volcanic sand at a depth of six or seven fathoms." Snorkeling is excellent just off Neira—at Malole Beach, Tanah Rata or just in front of the former V.O.C. palace. Other nearby snorkeling and shallow scuba-diving spots include: Pasir Besar and Kolam Penju off Gunung Api, and near-beach plunges at Wali and Selamon Belakang off Lontar Island. Experienced divers will bring their own regulators, but all the necessary equipment can be rented on Banda.

Great deep dives await those with experience off Sjahrir Island, but the very best are near Hatta, Ai or Run Islands, with dramatic drop-offs and lots of big fish. The hotels provide boats to reach these places as well as a plentiful supply of tanks. In April and May, and again in October and November, you can arrange for the 100-kilometer trip to Manuk Island, famous for its birds, good diving and pristine beaches.

The volcanic centerpiece

The verdant sides of Gunung Api ("Fire Mountain") rise 650 meters above the Banda Sea. Normally dormant, Api is still far from extinct. Between 1910 and 1977, 33 tremors of 5.0 or greater on the Richter scale have been recorded, 20 of them in one year, 1975.

In May 1988, Gunung Api's top blew with great violence, killing three and forcing a mass evacuation of the 2,000 people living on its slopes. Today, its slumber seems peaceful again and many people are back.

The many spectacular and destructive eruptions of Gunung Api often coincided with the visit of a high Dutch official. The best described one occurred on April 18, 1824. Lt. Kolff describes an atmosphere filled with fire and smoke, ejected from a new crater forming on the northwest side with such violence as to cause vivid flashes of lightning and ominous thundering: "this outbreak of nature was indescribably fine and majestic."

Climbing Api is relatively easy if you take a local guide. Start early in the morning, and bring a hat and plenty of water. (See "Climbing Gunung Api," page 99.) The recommended climb starts off at 5:30 a.m., after a boat ride over from your hotel. If the weather is clear, the panorama is absolutely stunning. The way down takes you by the crater and down the north face. From here, you can see the Sambayang cinnamon plantation near the bottom. When you make it down, celebrate with a cool drink of *kelapa muda,* "young coconut." A boat will return you to the hotel on Banda Neira.

Spice production

Nutmeg and mace are still the mainstays of the Bandanese economy, but production of these spices has slipped drastically in recent years, especially compared with the pre-war days. In the 1930s the Bandas still exported 2,000 to 3,000 tons of spices, but harvests in the '80s barely reached one-tenth of that tonnage. The only supplement to spice production in the local economy are the small quan-

Above: Gunung Api volcano, which juts straight out of the ocean. **Opposite:** Lontar, the largest of the Bandas, has several small villages and most of the archipelago's nutmeg groves.

tities of fruits, vegetables, tuna, and salt fish shipped to Ambon.

Banda nutmegs are still ranked by many as the world's best in aroma, flavor and shape. Only small numbers fit the lowest classification BWP: broken, wormy, punky. But oversupply on the world nutmeg markets, mainly from the tiny Caribbean island of Grenada, keeps prices down and discourages efficiency.

The nutmeg trees on Banda still thrive under the giant *kanari* trees, whose roots spring from the trunks in great vertical sheets. These tall trees, which have always provided the essential shade for the delicate nutmeg trees, produce a nut called the "tropical almond."

During the late 1980's, the prices of nutmeg and mace took off again thanks to the age-old practice of price fixing. The Indonesian Nutmeg Association (ASPIN), which supplies 75 percent of the world's nutmeg and mace, joined forces with Grenada, the producer of 23 percent of these two spices, and set production quotas. An old Dutch trading company, Catz International of Rotterdam, handles the yearly quota of 6,000 tons of Indonesian nutmeg and 1,000 tons of mace along with Grenada's 2,500 tons of nutmeg and 200 tons of mace. The United States buys one-fourth of this output, most of which goes into baking and—perhaps—the secret Coca-Cola formula.

This would seem to be good news for nutmeg producers, but now that the spices bring hefty profits, outsiders are trying hard to muscle in on the Bandas' nutmeg groves. North Sulawesi long ago took over as the leading producer of nutmeg, leaving Banda with about 20 percent of the Indonesian output. And world price drops in the past have reduced Banda's nutmeg groves to some 180,000 trees, about one third of their number even as late as the 1950s.

Although as recently as the 1980s, the spices fetched U.S.$7,000 per ton of nutmeg, and $13,500 per ton of mace, because of an oversupply in the early 1990s, nutmeg dropped in price to a ridiculous $1,000 per ton and mace to $2,200. Some Bandanese don't even bother picking their trees. Ironically, the *kanari* trees, planted to provide shade for the nutmeg trees, now produce a nut worth five times more than the nutmeg. If the machinery to press the oil out of the *kanari* nut were available, Banda would gain another valuable export crop.

Eighty percent of Banda's spice plantations are owned by the government, currently operated under a regional company. Although the plantation workers receive half of the crop as payment, they are forced to sell their share to the company—which pays only about 60 percent of the fair market price.

To complicate matters, a new private company in Ambon demands unripened nutmegs,

which it processes in a new nutmeg oil plant. But nutmeg trees are delicate, and stripping off the unripened fruit causes great damage to the tree. These new developments would likely cause grave problems for Banda, but Des Alwi, Banda's most famous citizen (see "History of the Bandas," page 86) has determined to take up the fight in Jakarta for his home islands.

Lore and uses of nutmeg

Nutmegs and mace enter into a bewildering number of preparations in flavoring and medicines. In Europe and the United States, the spices find their way primarily into food and condiments, while in Asia they are used mainly in the production of indigenous medical preparations.

Most of the nutmeg in the West is ground for either industrial purposes (25 to 30 percent) or for domestic culinary preparations (25 to 30 percent). Mace is also used in ground form, but industry finds a use for only 15-20 percent of the production, while 50-60 percent is used in home cooking. Nutmeg and mace flavor processed foods, including bakery products, sauces, pickles, meat products. Of course, nutmeg is crucial for eggnog and hot grogs, and even Chaucer's *The Tales of Canterbury* extoll "nutemuge put in ale." Mace is used to season such savory preparations as pickles and ketchup.

Extracted nutmeg oil imparts a distinctive aroma to foods, soft drinks, liquors and men's perfumes. In aerosol sprays, nutmeg oil is quite good at masking the unpleasant odor of the active ingredient. The oil is used in Western folk remedies such as Vick's Vaporub. Nutmeg butter acts as a mild external stimulant and is blended into scented soaps and shampoos. An ointment from nutmeg butter is touted as a counter-irritant as well as providing relief from rheumatism. Mace oil enters into the complex chemistry of perfumery.

In Asian folk medicine, powdered nutmeg is recommended for overeating, as a carminative for swollen bellies, to stimulate appetite, as a tonic for indigestion and after childbirth, and to alleviate dysentery, rheumatism, malaria, sciatica and leprosy, in its early stages. The spice can even be used as an aphrodisiac and to cure madness. Applied externally, nutmeg ointment is said to relieve all sorts of aches and pains. In Banda, nutmeg is believed to induce sleep when applied to the eyelids or taken internally.

Two chemical compounds of nutmeg, myristicin and elemicin, can be poisonous if taken in large quantities. An excess of nutmeg can lead to liver degeneration and inflammation of the intestine.

Below: *The Bandas' clear waters, such as these off Ai Island, offer great swimming and some of the world's best scuba diving.*

Climbing Gunung Api

Climbing Gunung Api makes a great morning exercise, and leads to one of the most spectacular views in all of Indonesia. Even though the path is well-marked, you should hire a guide ($5.50 a person) who will carry your water and camera. Also, get a good walking stick, as it will make both the climb and the descent a hell of a lot easier.

The guide will take you to the volcanology station, which marks the easiest route to the top. On the regular path, you should reach the summit around 8 a.m., but don't try for a record unless you are in top-notch physical shape. Rest frequently to catch your breath.

Easy beginnings

From shore the climb starts gently, passing manioc gardens as it winds inland across a slightly inclined slope. The serious part begins once you reach a wood and thatch shelter a few minutes from the coast. From here wooden steps make life easy for well over half of the climb.

There are four thatched shelters next to the steps, pleasant rest stops for feeble thighs. We scorned the first three, and within half an hour reached the topmost shelter where the wooden steps unfortunately stop. This last open hut already gives a great panoramic view of a part of Gunung Api, Neira and a section of Banda Besar. A good time to rest, enjoy the scenery and have a smoke to clear out your lungs.

The tough part comes next. While the path is not all that steep (but steep enough), loose volcanic pebbles underfoot often mean a backward slide for each couple of steps forward. Try to keep your forward momentum going and grab whatever vegetation comes within grasping distance. Even if you're a bit overweight or out of shape (or have two-pack-a-day habit) you should make it up to the uppermost reaches of the tree and vegetation line in a half hour from the shelter. From there it's five minutes to the top and the reward of an incredible bird's-eye view of three central Banda Islands—if clouds and fog have not socked you in.

The first two craters are disappointingly shallow with a few fumaroles edged by yellow sulfur and a white precipitate. Rocks offer great variety, with strong hues of several minerals fused in colorful array. Test the ground with a stick before you sit: it could be too hot for comfort.

On to the Caldera

After scenery viewing and rest, you are ready for the main caldera. The path there follows the ridge between the two small craters at the end of the path. A slight climb brings you to the edge of the main caldera, an awesome sight usually reserved for volcanologists.

It was this huge hole that blew up in May 1988, taking its toll in lives and property, and forcing massive evacuation. The powerful, almost vertical sided jagged hole is about 250 meters across and almost equally deep. Hot fumes waft up from several side fissures and the bottom. Great spreads of yellow sulfur mark the most active vents. Green moss-like vegetation somehow survives along a section of the crater's upper lip. Be very careful walking around the rim as it can crumble easily, which would tumble you quite literally into the billowing bowels of the earth.

In the background of the smoldering crater, patterned plantations decorate the volcano's lower slope, and beyond is the deep blue sea, spreading to infinity, its surface giving birth to Ai and Run islands. It's a spectacle worth every strain to get there.

43 minutes to the top

Should you be feeling your oats, during the climb. try to beat the Englishman's record for climbing Gunung Api, 43 minutes (not using the stair) from the water to the peak. Local guide Nyong Rus came in second during the race, organized by the 1987 Operation Raleigh. But don't try the climb with a heart condition. A Dutch competitor suffered a fatal stroke during this attempt.

If you happen to have your own helicopter (as Jacques Cousteau did), fly right down into the crater. But if you do this don't expect the normal certificate proving that you climbed Gunung Api (requires a U.S.$2 donation to the museum) which also makes you an honorary citizen of Banda.

Opposite: *Gunung Api.*

PART IV

North Maluku

Just west of sprawling and four-armed Halmahera Island two volcanoes rise from the Molucca Sea: Ternate and Tidore, the famous clove islands. Three centuries ago, the great kingdoms of Europe fought bitterly for control of these tiny isles and their precious harvest of cloves. Today, Ternate and Tidore have faded from the world's attention, but these lush, breezy islands are just as beautiful as they were when the first Portuguese sailors landed.

The hub of North Maluku, Ternate town is the jumping off point to Halmahera, Morotai, and the chain of beautiful islands stretching south to Bacan, off Halmahera's southwest tip.

Ternate was once the site of a splendid sultanate, and in 1579, the sultan's harems impressed even such a jaded traveler as Sir Francis Drake. Today, the sultan's crown is on display in the *kedaton,* or palace, its magic powers undiminished from the days of Sultan Awal, the first of the line. In 1983 Gunung Gamalama, the great volcano that dominates Ternate, began rumbling ominously. The crown was hurriedly escorted around the island in a ceremony of appeasement, and the volcano obediently quieted. Batu Angus or "Burnt Rock"—a lava flow from the 18th century, testifies to Gamalama's potential fury.

Tidore rises from the sea just one kilometer from Ternate, appearing like a mirror image of the latter. Tidore had its own sultanate, which was also a force to be reckoned with in the region. In the early days of the European presence here, Portugal, Spain and Holland often found themselves pawns in the age-old rivalry betwen the two islands.

Tidore's Gunung Kiematubu is just as stern and arbitrary as Gamalama, and in 1968 an entire village was buried in lava and ash.

The little islands south of Ternate and Tidore—Mare, Moti and Makian—are within easy reach of Ternate's Bastiong dock. These are ringed with lovely coastal villages where fish are harvested from rich reefs, and the region's utilitarian pottery is made. Motoring south, Halmahera's mountains are a constant presence to the east.

Until recently, only the most determined travelers could visit Halmahera. The island was, and still is, rugged, densely forested, and thinly populated. But within just the past few years, two airstrips have opened up this peculiarly shaped island. A quick hop from Ternate and you can reach two points on the east coast of north Halmahera: Galela and Kao.

The area around Kao is the home of the Tobelorese, seafarers who settled much of northern Halmahera. Today, families harvest coconuts for copra and grow the recently introduced and profitable cacao, which thrives here. Professional divers, staked with compressors and tanks by local entrepreneurs, comb the reefs for pearls, *trepang,* lobsters and fish. A regional delicacy is the coconut crab, a large terrestrial crab that uses its strong claws to split whole coconuts and feed on the meat inside. It is said that these tough creatures can even cut their way out of a tin can.

Morotai, off northern Halmahera, was the site of a crucial U.S. base in World War II. From Morotai, General MacArthur's huge bombers finally reached the Philippines. In 1973, Morotai was in the headlines again when Japanese Private Nakamura, who had been hiding on the island for 28 years, was coaxed out and gently told the war was over.

Morotai offers potentially exciting diving, and local fishermen know where wrecked P51 Mustangs and destroyers lurk within scuba range. The islands off Morotai have shallow, undisturbed reefs for snorkeling, and white sand beaches for sunbathing.

Overleaf: The 1,729-passenger Pelni liner Umsini calls at Ternate on its way from Jakarta to Jayapura. **Opposite:** A Tobelorese girl from North Halmahera.

TERNATE

Ancient Clove Island Under the Volcano

In 1858, British naturalist Sir Alfred Wallace, taken by the Ternate's "grand views on every side," made the little island his headquarters during his explorations of the archipelago. Charmed by the forest-clad slopes of Gunung Gamalama, the coral filled seas surrounding the island and the retired, earthquake-crumbled fortresses, he returned again and again to Ternate after collecting jaunts to distant New Guinea and the southern Moluccas. The beauty of Ternate, and its companion Tidore, has not changed since Wallace's day.

Once wracked by political turmoil and fierce competition for its clove riches, Ternate has receded from the forefront of world politics. But in the region, the island is still, after Ambon, the second-most important commercial center and transportation hub.

Ternate is the administrative capital of Maluku Utara, the *kabupaten* that encompass-

es the north Moluccas. Daily flights connect Ternate with Manado in north Sulawesi and Ambon, and on a weekly basis planes head for the towns of Galela and Kao in North Halmahera, and Morotai Island. Passenger ferries ply the route between Ternate and the West and North of nearby Halmahera.

Ternate is a tiny island, less than 10 kilometers in diameter, dominated by Gunung Gamalama. This still active volcano, whose 1,721-meter top has erupted in lava and ash at least 70 times in the last half-millenium, keeps all development in a tight circle along the coast.

The clove islands

Ternate and Tidore, and Moti, Mare and Makian to the south, were once the world's only source of cloves. The Portuguese were the first Europeans to reach the islands, establishing themselves on the twin islands in 1521. The Spanish arrived 50 years later, and intrigues between the two Iberian powers lasted until the turn of the century.

When the Dutch arrived in the early 17th century, they allied themselves with the Sultan of Tidore and forced out the Portuguese and Spanish. A half-century of bad blood between the sultan and the Iberians allowed the Dutch to negotiate a

Below: *A view of Ternate town from the sea, with Gamalama hidden in the clouds behind.*

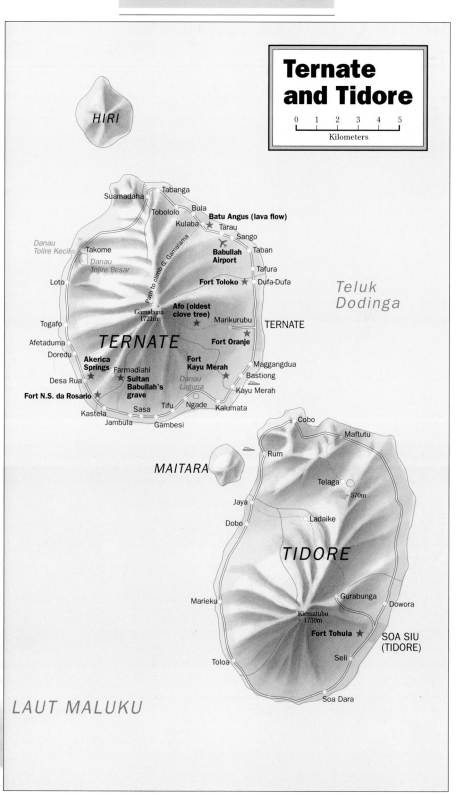

Ternate and Tidore

0 1 2 3 4 5
Kilometers

HIRI

Tabanga
Suamadaha
Tobololo
Bula
Batu Angus (lava flow)
Kulaba
Tarau
Sango
Danau Tolire Kecil
Takome
Taban
Danau Tolire Besar
Babullah Airport
Loto
Tafura
Fort Toloko
Dufa-Dufa
Path to climb G. Gamalama
Teluk Dodinga
Afo (oldest clove tree)
Togafo
Gamalama 1721m
Marikurubu
TERNATE
TERNATE
Fort Oranje
Afetaduma
Doredu
Akerica Springs
Farmadiahi
Fort Kayu Merah
Maggangdua
Bastiong
Desa Rua
Sultan Babullah's grave
Danau Laguna
Kayu Merah
Fort N.S. da Rosario
Tifu
Ngade
Kalumata
Kastela
Sasa
Jambula
Gambesi

MAITARA
Cobo
Maftutu
Rum
Telaga
+ 570m
Jaya
Dobo
Ladaike
TIDORE
Gurabunga
Marieku
Dowora
Kiematubu 1730m
Fort Tohula
SOA SIU (TIDORE)
Toloa
Seli
Soa Dara

LAUT MALUKU

monopoly on the clove trade, but their control was never absolute. In 1583, they shifted the center of clove production to Ambon, an island they held more firmly in their grasp. Subsequently, clove trees on Ternate and the nearby islands were almost wiped out. (See "The Spice Trade," page 26, and "The Dutch Monopoly," page 30.)

Today, Ternate and the other neraby islands are once again important clove producers—the North Moluccas has some 3,000 hectares under cultivation—but most of the world's supply of the spice comes from two small islands off Tanzania. Today the region's economy is more diversified.

Timber cutting and processing provide the most employment. The Barito conglomerate runs two huge mills, at Sidangole on Halmahera and at Falobisahaya on Mangole, which churn out planks and plywood. A nickel mine operates on Gebe Island—this is where the French obtained the first clove and nutmeg seedlings they smuggled out in the 18th century, thus breaking the Dutch monopoly—and manganese has been exported since 1989 from tiny Doi Island, off Halmahera's northern tip. Pearls and tuna are sent out of Bacan Island. Copra, Cacao and cloves are the district's chief cash crops.

Just a few kilometers in back of Ternate town, just short of the TV tower, a path leads from Tongole village to the largest and **oldest clove tree** on Ternate, and probably in the world. The tree is called Afo, named for the man who planted it, more than 400 years ago, and in defiance of the Dutch ban. A while back it was measured at 36.6 meters, with a trunk 4.26 meters around, but it has shrunk somewhat. At one time it produced 600 kilos of cloves a season, but it has slowed in the last decade. It may, sadly, be dying of old age.

Ternate town

The commercial center of the island is Ternate Town, which spreads out along the southeast coast facing an excellent deepwater harbor. Ternate Town has grown over the past 350 years around **Fort Oranje**, built by the Dutch in 1607 when they set about enforcing a monopoly on the sultan's cloves.

Ternate is the second-largest city in the Moluccan region, with about 50,000 inhabitants (the island is home to maybe 80,000.) Islam was introduced into the region in the 15th century, and today, the vast majority of Ternateans are Muslims. The Ternate sultanate, before the Dutch stripped the sultan of his political power, was the most powerful in eastern Indonesia.

Despite frequent earthquakes, Fort Oranje's massive walls today are in relatively good shape, and several cannon have resisted pilferage. Today the fort is occupied by an Indonesian army unit and the local police, which keeps the place relatively free of graffiti. Don't be intimidated by the uniforms. The

public is allowed to visit the fort.

Just south of town, past the main docks, a run down, graffiti-covered fort crumbles by the seaside. Begun but never completed by the Portuguese in 1510, the fort is now called **Kayu Merah** ("Red Wood"). The view here across the narrow strait to Tidore and Maitara Islands is beautiful, and at sunset becomes truly magnificent. The fort is about a kilometer south of the Pelabuhan Bastiong boat landing, just before the village of Kayu Merah begins.

The town mosque, an old, multi-tiered wooden structure, stands next to the main road to the airport in the northern part of town. If you follow Muslim etiquette (shoes off, modest clothing), you can visit this large, airy mosque. Its foundations date back to the first sultan's conversion in the 15th century, and several of Ternate's long line of sultans are buried behind the mosque.

Just north of the mosque is the sultan's residence, the *kedaton,* perched on a small hill next to the road. The original structure is said to date back to the 13th century, but today the *kedaton* looks like a country mansion—the current structure was designed by an English architect in the late 19th century. It's not the same place Sir Francis Drake visited in 1579, which he described as full of all the exotic comforts of the East, including several harems.

Today, the *kedaton* serves as an interesting, if thinly-stocked, museum of weapons, porcelain and royal knickknacks. A painting shows former Sultan Jabir Shah, wearing the royal crown, and his father, Sultan Haji Mohammed Usman.

Opposite: *Drying cloves are a common sight around Ternate.* **Above:** *The crown of the Sultan of Ternate possesses magical powers, including the ability to quiet the Gamalama volcano.* **Right:** *A portrait of Sultan Jabir Shah wearing the crown hangs in the former palace.*

A magic crown

The *kedaton*'s prize exhibit is usually kept behind locked doors—a showcase holding the jewel-studded royal crown, called the *mahkota* or *stampal.* It is a bit complicated (more below) to get permission to have the door unlocked, and you will only be allowed to look from the room's threshold. But even from this distance you can see some dark, stringy fibers under the crown—said to be locks of Sultan Awal's hair. (In fact this "human hair" looks an awful lot like plain old cassowary feathers, but don't say so in front of your hosts.)

The sultan's hair is a repository of magic powers, and even centuries after his death it still grows, requiring a ritual haircut every now and then. This crown is said to have been a gift directly from Allah when Sultan Awal submitted to Islam.

The royal crown is associated with a host of mystical powers, which permeate everyday life on Ternate, although on a level far from evident to casual visitors. Every Sunday, Wednesday and Thursday offerings of flowers, water and betel are presented to the *kedaton*'s spirits in a late afternoon ritual. The spirits like things left as they were back in their days as humans. Even the furniture in the palace cannot be moved around. Just recently the position of a bed was shifted, which infuriated the spirits of the past, who

noisily returned the bed to its original position during the night.

The last man to officially bear the title of sultan, Ishkander Mohammed Jabir Shah, died in 1975. He had been a high official in the interior ministry in Jakarta. In November 1986, a formal, week-long ceremony took place to install his son, Mudaffar Syah. The young man was unquestionably accepted as the heir, with all the accumulated mystical powers inherent in his line, but his sultanate is non-official according to Jakarta. A former legislator, Mudaffar Syah now works in the fisheries department. But he is still available for emergencies back home.

In 1983, when the Gamalama volcano began rumbling, Mudaffar Syah hurried back to Ternate. He took the ancestral crown on a sacred canoe ride around the island, accompanied by the remaining dignitaries of the ancient way of life. Upon the completion of the ceremonial circuit, the volcano quieted.

Things have changed somewhat since 1820, when the Dutch resident had to intervene to prevent a prince from being cast into the volcano's fiery maw. The sacrifice was to have been an expiation for unspecified private and public sins, and was considered the only way to stop the pending eruption.

Mysticism is pervasive on the island, perhaps because Ternatean rulers converted to Islam at an early date, when the dominant sect in Indonesia was the mystical Sufi. And Ternate's ancient religion was an animistic mix that centered on "ownership" of the volcano. One version of local history has it that the islands' first king, a headman named Guna, acquired his right to rule when he found a solid gold mortar belonging to a spirit. In Ternate, as well as other parts of the Moluccas, early Portuguese and Dutch relics even today have magical associations.

To see the crown, special arrangements must be made through the tourism office at the *bupati*'s office, as offerings must first be made before the crown can be unveiled. Contributions should be anything over $3. A day's notice is needed for the arrangements.

A loop around the island

A narrow paved road circles Ternate, and passenger-filled minibuses head out of Ternate to the more important villages. Few, however, make the entire 45-kilometer loop around the island. The best bet to take a leisurely look around the tiny island is to charter a minibus ($3 an hour).

Leaving town north of the *kedaton,* the road runs counterclockwise around the island. A few kilometers from town, just before the fork to the airport, a path leads to the beachside village of Dufa-Dufa. (See map page 105). Dufa-Dufa sits under the dominating presence of **Fort Toloko**. This well-preserved fort is perched on upraised coral, and its entrance still bears its 16th century Portuguese seal.

Continuing in the same direction on the main road, past Tarau village, the forest is replaced by a desolate moonscape of bare, jagged black rocks, running all the way to the sea. This is **Batu Angus** ("Burned Rock"), a lava flow remaining from a disastrous eruption in the 18th century. The molten rock obliterated everything in its path.

A Japanese war memorial has been erected here, but it is periodically destroyed by the local people, whose memories of the Japanese occupation are far from fond. This desecration is thought to punish the souls of the Japanese soldiers.

There were less than one hundred well-armed Japanese on Ternate during World War II, but they did whatever they pleased. Ternateans were required to bow down within 20 meters of passing a Japanese soldier on the street. Fathers were offered a choice: either give up your daughter or your head. In either case, girls as young as ten were hauled off for the soldiers' pleasure, tied up like pigs. Theft to feed one's starving family was punished with loss of a hand—or a head. One family of ten, including a baby and an infirm grandfather, was executed for the possession of a flashlight. When air-dropped leaflets announced the end of the war, the soldiers who didn't commit suicide gave up their weapons. Some Ternateans sneaked into the

Above: *The ruins of Fort Toloko, built by the Portuguese in 1512.* **Opposite:** *Batu Angus, literally "Burned Rock," the lava flow from a devastating 19th century eruption of Gamalama.*

depot and settled old scores.

Rounding north Ternate, cone-shaped Hiri Island appears less than a kilometer away offshore. A few kilometers further, near Takome village, a short side road leads inland to lovely **Danau Tolire Besar** (Big Tolire Lake). Emerald waters fill this steep-sided, vegetation encircled crater lake. There is a path around a part of the high rim. Public transportation on the main road here is rare, and Tolire can be conveniently reached only by chartered bemo. Tolire Kecil (Little Tolire), a smaller lake, lies between the main road and the nearby beach. Its smooth surface is a perfect mirror reflecting the Gamalama volcano.

The lakes are exactly halfway around the island from Ternate Town, and with your own transportation, you can continue around the island. But the west coast attractions can be reached by public minibuses only by heading south out of Ternate town.

South from Ternate, the main road climbs to Ngade village. Just past the little settlement, a high white wall blocks the view of **Danau Laguna**, a lovely lake filled with lotus plants. The main gate is usually open. Controversy still surrounds the wall, which was erected by a local businessman who planned to turn the lakefront into a private recreation park. But no one told him of the lake's mystical importance. It seems that a long time ago, a royal princess gave birth to a crocodile. The animal-child lived in this lake and produced a line of royal crocodiles, which even today must be treated with utmost respect. This belief, as interpreted today, forbids blocking any access to the lake.

Inside the gate, curious lizards scamper off on their hind legs if startled. After checking out the lake for sacred saurians—sighting a crocodile is said to bring very good luck—walk the ridge path around the lake, which winds upward on a gentle slope. About 1.5 kilometers from the gate, a short side path to the right leads to a magnificent view of spring-fed Laguna Lake and Tidore Island.

Further along the main road is the turnoff to Formadiahi, between Jambula and Kastela, the site of the ancient palace of the sultans. Today, only the barest foundations remain, along with the grave of Sultan Baabullah (also known as Prince Baab) who succeeded in driving out the Portuguese after they murdered his father. (See "The Spice Trade," page 26.) The villagers still make offerings to his grave.

The main road drops back to the coast at the village of **Kastela**, named for a nearby fort, built by the Portuguese in the beginning of the 16th century and abandoned just 50 year later. The road cuts right through the fort, and one of its ancient wells is overgrown with thick jungle vegetation. A kilometer past Kastela, a path from Desa Rua village ends at the sacred **Akerica Springs** (also called Akesibu) where the sultans used to bathe and draw their drinking water.

CLIMBING GAMALAMA

Ternate's Moody Volcano

A climb up Ternate's Gamalama volcano can reward you with incredible panoramas and a smoldering, sulfurous crater. With these rewards come some risks, however. The climb can be hazardous—you must be very careful, particularly around the crater—but more likely, just disappointing: sometimes the top is socked in by a thick cloud bank.

Only visitors in good physical condition with a full day to spare should consider climbing 1,721-meter Gamalama. A guide is essential, and bring plenty of drinking water, a hat, sunglasses and sunscreen. The earliest possible start, even 3 or 4 a.m., will improve your chances of good weather at the top. The best plan is to spend the night at the last village up the mountainside, Marikurubu. (See map page 105.) From there a guide will charge $10 to $15 for the trek. The local tourism office can help you make the arrangements.

Climbing the mountain

The easiest path to climb Gamalama, out of a possible dozen or so routes, starts at the end of Marikurubu village. It's not too bad at the beginning but it gets steeper. By the time you have reached the last hut, you're about one-fifth of the way, and will know if you can make it or not. Remember that the top is 1,721 meters, but at the end of the paved road at Marikurubu you are already 200–300 meters above sea-level. Along this first stretch, you walk through groves of clove and nutmeg trees, along with a few cinnamon trees. Unfortunately, you won't see much of this spice paradise by flashlight.

From the last hut onwards, the path narrows a bit, and an occasional spider stretches its web across the trail. These are not very pleasant to walk into, particularly since their large occupants (span of legs the size of a man's hand; bodies 10 centimeters long) tend to run down your back. They're not dangerous though. Our guide Bakri Ali, grabbed one for me to photograph. Since your guide will

be walking ahead, he will usually pull down the webs anyway.

This trail is the easiest, because it is cleared every now and then for the sultans to carry offerings to Gamalama. If you are lucky enough to climb shortly after one of the sultans pilgrimages, the vegetation will have been well-cleared on both sides and steps of sorts cut into the path, greatly facilitating the ascent. Unfortunately, the current sultan visits Gamalama only once every few years.

It is said that whenever the sultan ascends, lots of birds fly around him. You, on the other hand, will be lucky to see a single one—but will certainly hear parrots and cockatoos in the forest. The last of the birds of paradise were killed in the 19th century to sell their skins and feathers to foreigners.

Surrounded by vegetation, you pant upwards, oblivious to the large fern trees and a marked change in vegetation. Your guide will set a gentle pace. If you want to go faster, say "tolong lebih cepat," or slower, "tolong, pelan-pelan." Whenever, you want to stop, just say "berhenti."

He will usually stop at a nice flat area, the halfway mark, where camping out is possible. The trail climbs at varying grades, with a few short, God-given level stretches to give your legs a rest. Keep at it and you will eventually reach the last camping stop, with the worst of the trail behind you. Here there are lovely stands of bamboo.

From here, it's 20 minutes (watch the thorns!) to the irregular ridge which leads to the crater. As soon as the guide reaches the beginning of this ridge, from where the top of Gamalama is clearly visible (weather willing), he will pray to the spirits, explaining to them the purpose of your visit (to have a look) and ask their permission (invariably granted).

Reaching the top

Trees killed in the 1990 explosion still stand in the foreground, and the ground is covered with tall grass that has grown since. Another 15–20 minutes—down then up—and you're out of the vegetation, walking on broken bits of hardened lava.

Here is where you can really see the scenery. East is Ternate town and the landing strip, and across the water, Halmahera. Southeast is Tidore's Gunung Kiematubu,

Opposite: *The Afo clove tree, at more than 36 meters, is the largest in the world. It is also the oldest, having been planted more than four centuries ago in defiance of the Dutch ban.*

and Makian Island. This view is, of course, a matter of luck. But according to our guide, except for the month of December it is likely that at least one side of the mountain will be clear, and often all sides offer a great perspective over the coastal villages, the seas, and the surrounding islands.

Investigating Gamalama's crater is more difficult. Recent eruptions have deepened the caldera, which is almost invariably full of smoke. Dedicated volcano freaks have been known to climb the volcano three or four times with the same result each time: a crater full of smoke. But if you've made it this far, you might as well try.

From the ridge, you first pass Sumba, a small rise where the sultan lies in his simple Muslim grave, then it's a 150-meter climb up the steep cone, over chunks of broken lava. As the recent lava flows have not yet weathered, the footing is not too slippery. In 15 minutes you can reach the caldera's rim. Sulfurous smoke wafts through surface vents here. The footing here can be very dangerous, so always follow your guide.

As forewarned, the crater was full of smoke but, having come so far, we decided to wait a bit to see if the spirits would allow us a glimpse. We had scrupulously followed our guide's instruction: 1) Don't urinate on the crater! 2) Don't wear red! 3) Don't kill any flies topside! God knows what flies are doing there, but we saw a couple of big ones,

buzzing around.

Our good behavior was rewarded, and on three occasions within a half-hour the crater partially cleared of smoke and we could see partially down into the chasm. Very steep sides dropped down 100 meters to a funnel, into which we were not permitted to look. Bakri told us that during his 50-odd recent visits to the volcano, only once could he see to the very bottom, some 200 meters from where the funnel began. And only two of his other clients had been able to see as far down as we did.

A chilling warning

Looking down the hell-hole, I shuddered, thinking of a young Swiss man who disappeared here in 1991. Just about then, after I mentally thanked the spirits for the glimpses they had given us, some strange noises from the crater made me decide not to over-stay my welcome. We decided to head back.

But the volcano is still home to spirits—ancestral and otherwise—who must be shown proper respect. The Swiss tourist had climbed the volcano, and according to his guide, who seems to have been a rather shiftless fellow, he walked off on his own while the guide took a nap. (The guide, who later admitted to never having climbed the mountain before, was tired.) The guide came back down, and everyone assumed that the tourist had descended by one of the other paths.

A month later, a Swiss anesthesiologist and volcano buff arrived in Ternate to climb Gamalama. She heard rumors of her disappeared countryman, and decided to get to the bottom of the matter. She opened the bags—still at the man's hotel—and found out who he was, contacted the Swiss Embassy in Jakarta and the man's parents. Then she organized a search. No trace of the man could be found. Finally, following unanimous local advice, she contacted trance mediums. They failed to locate the body, but said that the spirits of the volcano have decided to keep the young man.

Mudaffar Syah, the current sultan of Tidore, normally lives in Jakarta, but at the time was in Ternate. His initial contacts with the spirits were inconclusive, so he decided to climb the volcano, accompany by some respectful subjects. He spent the night on the volcano meditating, and had a vision: the young tourist fell into the crater, disappearing forever, taken by a group of spirits called *manusia mamole.*

And this seems to be the final word on the unfortunate matter.

Preparations for the climb

There are a few things to do a day or two before the climb. First, go to Marikurubu village, about 3 kilometers behind Ternate town, and make your arrangements with Bakri Ali, the island's best guide. By late 1991, he had climbed Gamalama over 50 times, including more than 30 times with tourists. If Bakri is not available, locate Hanafi or Yusman, who also live in the same village. Don't climb with just anyone who volunteers to take you up. Although they claim plenty of experience, many of these free-lancers may never have climbed Gamalama. (Remember the Swiss climber.)

At the very top end of Marikurubu village, stop by the volcanology station to check on the volcano's current behavior—if the station advises against it, cancel your planned climb. It would also be good form to tell the village chief of your intention to climb, and with whom. If you would like someone to make all these arrangements for you (plus a certain early morning pickup at your hotel), you can rely on Pak Umar. (See "Ternate/Tidore Practicalities" page 193.)

You will also need to bring food for yourself and guide, plus drinking water, 2–3 liters per person. During the rainy season, there may be some rainwater in a small pool near the top, but it's best not to rely on this. Wear long pants—there are small but persistent thorns lining the path near the top. Make sure your guide takes a *parang* (machete) with him. A *tongkat* (walking stick) is very handy, and your guide will cut you one when you start. His fee for the day's climb includes carrying your camera, food and water.

You can sleep at your hotel in Ternate, but it is better to stay at Marikurubu, preferably at your guide's house (pay him $5–$8 extra). You could also overnight partway up the volcano. There are huts along the first part of the path, with the last one 1–1.5 hours' walk from the village. There is also a fairly flat area about 45 minute's climb from the top where your guide could build a *pondok* or temporary shelter. Only by sleeping there can you catch the sunrise, around 6.20 a.m., but there are no guarantees that it won't be cloudy.

To guarantee a chance of a cloud free panorama, plan on spending 2–3 days at the *pondok*. In that case you will need an extra porter to bring food, plenty of water, and a sleeping bag or good blanket.

Bakri can climb Gamalama in 2 1/2 hours, and once he did it with a young German in 3 hours. For most mortals, however, it's 6–7 hours up, and 3–4 hours down, plus topside viewing time.

Opposite, above: *Guide Bakri Ali nonchalantly displays one of the large spiders that weave their webs across the path to Gamalama.*
Above: *The volcano's smoking crater.*

TIDORE

Ternate's Twin and Former Rival

Tidore Island, slightly larger than Ternate, is just a kilometer from her better known twin's closest shore. Like Ternate, Tidore is also dominated by a volcano, 1,730-meter Gunung Kiematubu, which rears up in a perfect cone to form the southern part of the island.

The early history of Tidore was dominated by its rivalry with Ternate. In the late 16th and early 17th centuries, Tidore supported any European power against Ternate. When Ternate kicked the Portuguese out in 1574, Tidore invited them to build a fort.

This fort was captured by the Dutch, allied with Ternate at the time, in 1606. But the Dutch V.O.C. spice monopoly did not yet have enough manpower to maintain their fort, and the Tidorese welcomed the anti-Dutch forces of Spain. Soon thereafter, however, the determined forces of Holland assumed control, and this was the end of independent Tidore. After the death of Ahmadul Mansur in 1905, the sultan of Tidore's throne was left vacant and a line of 22 sultans came to an end.

Relaxed pace

The boat ride from Ternate's Bastiong dock to Rum on northwest Tidore takes no more than 15 minutes, and the boats run every half hour or so. (See map page 105.) A public minibus from Rum takes about an hour to reach Soa Siu, the island's principal town and the site of the former sultanate. On the way to Soa Siu, on the southeast side of the island, the road passes a lava flow that devastated the town of Soa Dada in 1968.

Soa Siu (sometimes called Tidore town) is the capital of the Central Halmahera District (Kabupatan Halmahera Tengah), which includes Tidore and central Halmahera. The pace of life on Tidore is relaxed, even in the capital city. In the past, administrations banned Chinese and Arab merchants, and the town remains very poorly stocked. There is, for example, no beer at all on the island.

Seaside villages ring the island, and most of the 35,000 Tidorese are concentrated on the southern coast. A paved road follows most of Tidore's 45 kilometer circumference, but gets progressively worse the further one gets from Soa Siu. Plans call for paving the remaining seven-odd kilometers. The scenery from the perimeter road is superb.

In the early morning hours on Tidore men and women set off to the gardens to cultivate vegetables and the island's staple, manioc. Copra, cloves, nutmeg, mangos and a bit of cacao and coffee are also harvested as cash crops. The island's weekly markets: Rum village on Sundays, Toloa on Wednesdays, and Soa Siu on Tuesdays and Fridays.

Visiting Tidore

There are two **crumbling fortresses** on the island, and their foundations date back to the 16th century. The low, vine-covered walls of one are just north of the Rum boat landing. The other fort—Tohula—is in just as bad shape, and lies a short, steep climb up from the main road just before Soa Siu. You will probably have to ask someone to point it out.

Just north of Soa Siu the clear seas are fine for **snorkeling**. Off Maitara Island's north and northeast coasts (get there from Rum) the coral is reported to be first-rate.

Of the **sultan's palace**, located above Soa Siu, only a few bits of masonry and a stairway remain. At one end of a field that used to be the front lawn of the palace (now used for football games) lie the graves of Nuku, Tidore's best known sultan, and Jainal Abidin Syah, the last of the line.

The local museum, **Sonyine Malige** ("Beautiful Spot" in Tidorese) is usually locked tight. To get it opened, go during regular office hours to the local education and culture office (Kantor Pendidikan dan Kebudayan, "P dan K") to find the man with the key. To see the "sacred" part of the museum, you must follow the etiquette that applies to a mosque—no shoes. This area houses the royal paraphernalia, including fine clothes, weapons, musical instruments, a beautiful old Koran, and the ancient sultan's crown.

The last sultan's immediate family lives in Jakarta, but other family members on Tidore make certain that the island stays on the crown's good side, thus averting disasters. Every Wednesday night, between 8:00 p.m. and 8:30 p.m., offerings of incense and betel nut are made to the crown. After admiring the crown, you should make an offering yourself—Rp500–Rp1,000 will be satisfactory.

Gurabunga village

If you decide on more than just a quick trip to Tidore, visit **Gurabunga village**, at the foot of Kiematubu. On Tuesdays and Fridays, market days in Soa Siu, public transportation (50¢), is available till 4 p.m. Otherwise, charter a minibus in Soa Siu, $3 one way.

Gurabunga is the center of *adat* traditions for Tidore, perhaps because of its protected, inland position. Local history says that when the sultan of Baghdad sent his four sons to rule over the clove islands—one each to Ternate, Tidore, Bacan and Jailolo—the man who founded the Tidore dynasty, his task finished, vanished into thin air.

The spot where he disappeared is Gurabunga village. A small traditional structure houses an alter at this spot, a little way into the forest above Gurabunga, under the care of Pak Sowohi (alias Aja Ibrahim), who enjoys chatting. A special room in the house is where Sowohi (literally "guardian") communicates with the sultan's spirit. This house is the venue for ritual sessions of song and drama to request the spirit's intervention in times of seasonal change or trouble.

From Gurubunga, you can climb **Kiematubu**, about four hours for the fit. Report to the village head and get a guide. The climb is steep and dangerous and wet. The views from the top can be magnificient, weather permitting. You can also skirt the mountain on a footpath from Gurabunga to Ladaike. The views of Maitara and Ternate are magnificent. From Ladaike, you can hike down to Jaya, and catch a bemo to Rum.

Opposite: *Maitara Island, and behind, Tidore.*
Above: *A woman with one of the distinctive funnel-shaped baskets made in Dowora.*

HALMAHERA

Sprawling and Wild North Moluccan Isle

The four fingers of Halmahera cut a striking figure on the map of the North Moluccas. Separated by three great bays, these long peninsulas are reminders that the island was once two separate islands that, over the eons, slowly crashed together.

The separate mountain chains now come together in a jumble of peaks in the center of the island. Only the northern finger is volcanic, and three cones still occasionally smoke and rumble. The whole of the island is mountainous, rough, and densely forested.

North to south, Halmahera measures 330 kilometers and at its widest point, 160 kilometers across, for a total land area of just under 18,000 square kilometers. Although Seram is slightly larger, Halmahera spreads over a much greater area and is a more imposing presence. The most recent estimates of Halmahera's population (1977) suggest more

than 186,000 people live here. Most of these are Muslims, with a significant Christian minority, attesting to the early presence of the Portuguese. A significant, but unknown number of Halmaherans still follow a variety of traditional religions.

Only recently has this island been well connected to the rest of the Moluccan region. Halmahera now receives daily flights from Manado and Ambon, although they are sometimes cancelled and are often overbooked. From Ternate, daily ferries and several scheduled flights each week carry passengers to various points on the North Peninsula. Once there, a partially paved 130-kilometer network of roads opens Halmahera's wonderful beaches, reefs, World War II relics and people to the traveler.

Jailolo: the former sultanate

Before the arrival of the Europeans, this small town, just a bit north of Ternate on Halmahera's west coast, was perhaps the most important political power on Halmahera. Although historical evidence is faint, Jailolo must have had a measure of power and autonomy during the early 16th century, because records show that a combined force of Ternateans and Portuguese overwhelmed the sultanate in 1551. But after this point, the Dutch and the Sultan of Ternate determined

Below: *A moody afternoon off Halmahera.*

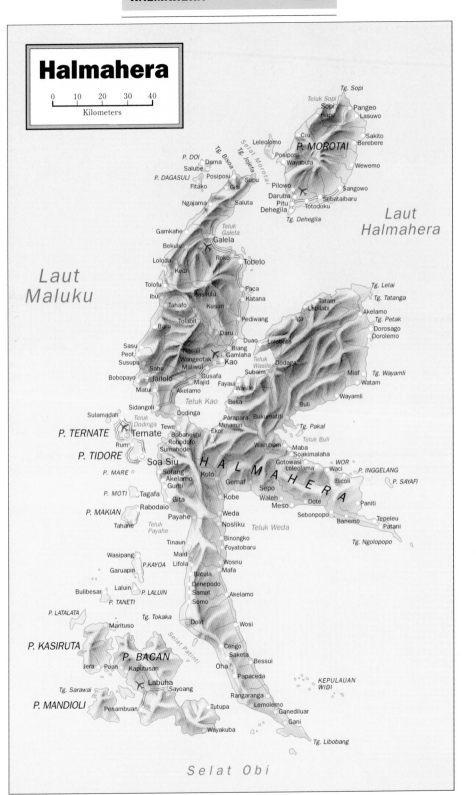

Halmahera

0 10 20 30 40
Kilometers

Laut
Halmahera

Laut
Maluku

Tg. Sopi
Teluk Sopi
Sopi
Pangeo
Hapa
Lasuwo
Ciu
Sakito
Leleolomo
P. MOROTAI
Berebere
Posiposi
Wayabula
P. DOI
Dama
Tg. Bisoa
Selat Morotai
Tg. Jolefa
Wewemo
Salube
Fitako
Posiposi
Supu
P. DAGASULI
Gisi
Pilowo
Ngajama
Saluta
Daruba
Sangowo
Pitu
Sebataibaru
Dehegila
Totodoku
Tg. Dehegila
Gamkahe
Teluk
Galela
Bekulu
Galela
Roko
Loloda
Kedi
Tobelo
Tolofu
Paca
Tg. Lelai
Ibu
Rasilulu
Katana
Tatam
Tg. Tatanga
Tahafo
Kusuri
Lepilabi
Akelamo
Baru
Tolabit
Pediwang
Iga
Tg. Petak
Daru
Dorosago
Duao
Dorolemo
Sasu
Biang
Lolobata
Peot
Ngoali
Gamlaha
Teluk
Susupu
Wangeotak
Kao
Wasile
Dodaga
Sahu
Maliwul
Subaim
Miaf
Tg. Wayamli
Bobopayo
Jailolo
Gusafa
Watam
Matui
Akelamo
Majid
Fayaui
Wasile
Wayamli
Sidangoli
Dodinga
Besa
Buli
Sulamadah
Teluk
Dodinga
Parapara
Bukumatiti
Tewe
Minamin
Tg. Pakal
P. TERNATE
Ternate
Bobanelgu
Ekor
Teluk Buli
Rum
Robodoro
Wailuhum
Maba
P. TIDORE
Sumahode
Soakimalaha
Soa Siu
HALMAHERA
Gotowasi
WOR
P. MARE
Sofang
Kulo
Loleolama
Waci
P. INGGELANG
Akelamo
Gemaf
Bicoli
P. SAYAFI
P. MOTI
Gumi
Sepo
Tagafa
Gita
Kobe
Waleh
Dote
Paniti
P. MAKIAN
Rabodaio
Meso
Tahane
Payahe
Weda
Sebonpopo
Banemo
Tepeleu
Teluk
Nosliku
Patani
Payahe
Teluk Weda
Tinaun
Binongko
Tg. Ngolopopo
Foyatobaru
Wasipang
Maid
Wosnu
P.KAYOA
Lifola
Mafa
Garuapin
Batula
Laluin
Denepodo
Bulibesar
P. LALUIN
Samat
Akelamo
P. TANETI
Semo
P. LATALATA
Tg. Tokaka
Dolit
Wosi
Marituso
P. KASIRUTA
Cengo
P. BACAN
Saketa
Jera
Poan
Kaputusan
Oha
Bessui
Labuha
Papaceda
Tg. Sarawai
Sayoang
KEPULAUAN
WIDI
P. MANDIOLI
Penambuan
Rangaranga
Tutupa
Lemolemo
Ganediluar
Gani
Wayakuba
Selat Patinti
Tg. Libobang
Teluk Kao
Selat Obi

Jailolo's fate for more than two centuries.

In 1798, the Sultan of Tidore, who had just expelled the Dutch from his island, proclaimed a noble from Makian as the Sultan of Jailolo. This re-established the sultanate, which lasted only until 1832, when the Dutch forced the aristocracy into exile. There was a last attempt to regain power through a revolt led by Baba Hassan in 1876, but steam-powered Dutch warships quickly crushed the rebels. During a tax revolt in 1914, the Jailoloans killed the colonial district officer. The final gesture of defiance took place in 1917, on the island of Waigeo off western New Guinea.

Today, the sultan's palace is said to be past even the crumbling stage. The local indigenous people, the rice-growing Sahu, still perform traditional dances to celebrate the harvest around August and September. The Sahu have recently converted to Christianity. Daily motorboats run to Jailolo from Ternate and back, the two-hour trip costing $1.50. There are three small *losmen* in Jailolo, with minimal amenities, which cost about $5 a night. Public minibuses service the vicinity of Jailolo, including Bobaneigo, the cross-over point between Halmahera's east and west coasts.

Tobelo: Halmahera's northeast coast

Halmahera's northern peninsula, the largest of the island's "fingers," remains actively volcanic. Its eastern coast, dotted with off-shore islands, is a paragon of tropical island beauty: bright, wide beaches, profusions of coconut trees, and clear, coral-filled waters.

The coast's dominant ethnic group are the Tobelorese. Originally seafarers, perhaps even more like pirates, the Tobelorese originally settled such strategic colonies as Morotai, north of Halmahera, and Bacan, west of Halmahera's southern tip. The Papuan languages spoken in northern Halmahera are related to those spoken in western New Guinea, but the people are more Malay in appearance.

The principal city on this coast is Tobelo, with a population of close to 13,000. The city stretches along the main coast road, and well-stocked Indonesian-Chinese–run stores attest to a strong local economy. Business in Tobelo is based on copra and cacao, as well as hotels and anything else that seems financially feasible. The Copra and cacao is gathered and prepared by local families, who sell their crop to the Indonesian-Chinese merchants for bulk shipment to Surabaya, Java.

While coconut trees are native to the Old World and have always been around, cacao is

Above: *A Halmaheran boy.* **Opposite:** *A coconut crab,* Birgus latro. *This unique animal is the largest terrestrial arthropod. It has very strong claws, and is thought to be able to crack coconuts. In addition to these, the crabs eat pandanus fruit, carrion and each other.*

a tropical New World tree that was introduced by the Dutch in the 19th century. Cacao farming, for cocoa and chocolate, is now encouraged by the Indonesian government and bumper crops are produced in Halmahera. Copra and cacao sales, while not making the Tobelorese millionaires, have brought a welcome increase in the area's standard of living.

The increased wealth of Tobelo has allowed its people to switch from a tuber staple to rice, imported by traders from South Sulawesi. Recent Javanese transmigrants—over 3,000 families—add to the local rice supplies from their settlements around Kao Bay. All the Tobelorese villages hug the coast, and fish and shellfish provide the greatest source of protein in the local diet.

Today's large-scale rice imports from Sulawesi are a continuation of historical contacts with that island. The traditional dress of the Tobelorese, now worn only on ceremonial occasions, such as weddings, consists of cloth from the Mandar area of south Sulawesi. Early Bugis (a South Sulawesi ethnic group) traders introduced Islam to the Tobelo region, but only 30 percent of the Tobelorese are today Muslims.

Most of the Tobelorese were converted by Dutch Protestant missionaries. The Utrecht Missionary Society first arrived in Galela in 1866, and remained at this lone location for 30 years, until another mission was established in Tobelo in 1897. In those days, the Galela district still had to provide their absentee overlord, the Sultan of Ternate, with a yearly tribute of 20 men for general service, four *kora-kora* war canoes and, for each adult, a head tax consisting of a basket of rice.

The Muslims' relative lack of success in converting the Tobelorese is perhaps partly the result of the Portuguese, who brought Christianity with them to the Moluccas before the Muslims succeeded in dominating this area. Stone walls, said to be the ruins of Portuguese forts, can be found in two locations near Tobelo: in the village of Mede, 7 kilometers north of Tobelo, and Gamhoku, the same distance south of the city. Francis Xavier, the famous Jesuit, might have paid a brief visit to this area in 1547. Records show that he traveled to an island called "Moro" from Ternate. Although Morotai Island, just north of Halmahera would seem to fit, it is more likely that Saint Francis sailed to the much closer Halmahera. "Moro" probably comes from "Mauro," the general Iberian term for a Muslim or Moor.

The Moros and Tobelo tradition

Be that as it may, there are reports of a small Tobelo clan called "Moro"—Christians all—considered to be of Portuguese descent. The Moro clan is locally considered to be the most refined. Marriages take place only within the clan. During a recent wedding of a couple who broke this regulation, the angry

ancestral spirits spoiled the feast by throwing sand on all the food that was so carefully prepared for the guests. On the island of Seram there is another Moro clan, to which all sorts of supernatural powers are attributed.

A special race of child-sized spirits are said to appear at night on a deserted mini-island called Tuputupu, near Tobelo. But they don't seem to bother strangers. Locals are still amazed by a Frenchman who spent a week alone on this island, returning no worse for his sojourn among the dwarf ghosts.

Traditional Tobelo rituals can still be witnessed. These include the small ceremony after a birth and elaborate weddings. The traditional bride price, formerly made up of heirloom treasures, is now, thanks to the

Christian influence, a more prosaic Rp 60,000 ($31). Around August and September, harvest celebrations enliven Tobelo. The Wangonira, a group of just 50 people living in the mountains about 10 kilometers from the city, are said to be the most traditional in the area, despite their having converted to Protestant Christianity some 20 years ago.

Kao: quiet, friendly little town

This district center on the southern end of the north peninsula's east coast has 2,000 inhabitants and is growing. Three contiguous villages, Kao, Jati and Kusu, make up Kao. There is no electricity here yet, although lines were strung in 1986. Local status is still

apparent at night: area officials and wealthy Indonesian-Chinese families run private generators, the less fortunate use petroleum pressure lanterns, and the rest make do with flickering oil lamps.

Kao's two parallel main streets of sand follow the coast. There are no exclusive suburbs here. In the center of town, where the market, the mosque and the church are located, nondescript concrete and tin-roofed houses shelter the town's wealthiest citizens. Further out, the middle classes make do with more modest lodgings but those who can afford it still have a hot tin roof—something of a status symbol. At the edges of town, the poorer families enjoy a much cooler life in their traditional thatched huts and houses.

The people of Kao are very friendly. On any stroll, you will be invited many times to sit, chat and have some tea, even if you can't speak a word of Indonesian. Calm reigns until Thursday and Friday nights, when the market becomes active and things liven up.

Kao's main line of communications is the 80-odd kilometer, mostly dirt road to Tobelo in the north. This road took a long time to complete (December 1986), as poorly-built bridges tended to collapse during the yearly torrential rains. The new artery has allowed Kao to receive and provide a market for some 700 transmigrant families from crowded Java who have settled in the region. Boosted by these industrious arrivals, the district population is approaching the 20,000 mark.

Four languages were spoken in the Kao area: Boeng, Kao, Pagu, and Modal. (Now add: Javanese, and the two languages of the Makian Island transmigrants.) Back in the head-hunting days each of the four traditional groups was led by the Sultan of Ternate. But Islam never made great inroads. The Dutch Protestant Church, beginning its efforts in earnest in 1906, had much better luck and the region is now mostly Christian.

Traditions are still visible in dances, including the Moluccas-wide *cakalele* war dance, and wedding ceremonies and music provided by brass gongs, drums and flutes. The last family of *orang hutan* (forest people), of the nomadic Tukuru ethnic group, came out of the woods in 1984. One hopes for their happy integration into the settled Protestant lifestyle. Previously, two Tukuru tried Kao life, found it wanting, and returned to the depths of their forest.

Aside from manioc, yams and vegetables in subsistence gardens, Kao's cash crops are the crucial copra and the recently encouraged cacao. Deer, which in the past frequently included 12-point bucks, are now getting scarce, as the Chinese pay dearly for the horns, which are ground up as a medicine. But wild pigs are still abundant. The sea supplies plenty of fish, as well as *trepang* and mother-of-pearl shell for export. The interior's timber resources, first exploited in 1972, now support a sawmill at Gamlaha on Tanjung Loleo. The enterprise, owned by the Barito conglomerate, also processes lumber shipped in from adjacent coastal areas. Rattan processing began in the region in 1987, and holds lots of promise.

World War II on Kao

The district center of Kao was the Japanese headquarters for thousands of servicemen from 1942 to 1945. After their setback in the New Guinea campaign, the Japanese forces regrouped here. Eventually, 42,000 men were stationed in Kao, and another 20,000 in the inner reaches of the bay. Kao was in those days jokingly referred to as "Little Tokyo" or "Tokyo Two."

There were about 300 Japanese bombers and Zeroes stationed here and the long runways built just outside of Kao were protected by more than 60 heavy, stationary anti-aircraft guns and many lighter, mobile units. Older locals, who remember the war well, say there were too many ships stationed off Kao to even count.

The Japanese led the good life until late in the war. Over 100 slave girls, from Hong Kong, Singapore, China, Java and Manado, were housed in special "entertainment barracks." Then General Douglas MacArthur selected Morotai for the next Allied stepping stone. The Allies first turned their superior air power against the Japanese installations at Kao, which they quickly destroyed.

An elderly resident of Kao, the former village chief, recalls the incredible spectacle of swarms of U.S. fighters dive-bombing ships, sinking four or five at a clip, occasionally losing one of their ranks to Japanese anti-aircraft guns. The surviving Japanese, neutralized without fuel or war supplies, were simply ignored by the Allies in their rush to Manila. During the last phases of the war, when the Japanese food stocks dried up, the soldiers turned to the local food supply. Hundreds of Halmaherans died of starvation.

Although most of the war relics have been stripped and removed, four heavy anti-aircraft guns still point their rust-jammed barrels at the sky, protecting the north-west corner of the overgrown Japanese-built airfield. In 1986, a small part of the multi-strip complex was reconditioned and renamed Kuabang Kao, after a local anti-Dutch hero. Merpati lands there from Ternate on Tuesdays, Thursdays and Saturdays.

Snorkeling on World War II wrecks

Although there's no scuba equipment available in Kao, a couple of drowned Japanese World War II supply ships offer excellent snorkeling possibilities. The ships were sunk by U.S. fighters about one kilometer offshore. A portion of the upper rear deck on one of the ships lies above the water and enough earth has accumulated there to support some vegetation. Flocks of gulls perch on the rusting

hulk. The labyrinths of the submerged hold shelter many fish and local fishermen occasionally report seeing big groupers hanging around. An outboard canoe covers the distance from shore in about 10 minutes, and entrepreneurs will take you there for $10 round trip, including the waiting time while you snorkel.

Across Kao Bay, where the mountains descend abruptly to the sea, two Japanese war ships lie completely underwater, the

Opposite: *World War II relics like this anti-aircraft gun can be found around Kao.* **Above:** *A bunker on Bobale Island, built by the Japanese. It is now used as a shelter by coconut farmers.*

upper decks a few meters below the surface. Fishermen report masts breaking the surface at low tide near the large transmigration site of Wasile (where over 2,300 Javanese families have transmigrated). This sounds like some potentially exciting scuba diving.

The ships are sunk close to shore, near the village of Foli and the P.T. Nasa Patma lumber camp. About $50 should cover the four to six hour round-trip by outboard from either Kao or Bobale Island. Foli and Lolobata (to the northeast) were secondary Japanese naval bases during World War II. Dozens of other Japanese ships still lie beneath Kao Bay, an occasional slick of old fuel oil betraying their presence.

Bobale Island

Bobale is one of the prettiest and most accessible of the many islands off the east coast of Halmahera's northern finger. The island is offshore from Daru Village, between Tobelo and Kao. From Kao, an hour's drive over bumps, mudholes and solid, but nerve-rattling, bridges will get you to Daru. From, Tobelo, its three hours of the same. Daru has 900 people and one well-stocked store.

From Daru, Bobale's tropical charms are just a half-hour away by outboard, $1–$2 if a boat is headed there anyway, or $13–$15 if you have to charter a boat.

When you land on the island, there is nothing but coconut trees in sight from the fine, white beach. A short walk, however, reveals a surprisingly large and neat village of 650 people. Many of the men, who have attenuated Papuan features, sport trim beards. The Tobelo language is everyone's mother tongue, although the villagers speak Indonesian as well.

A couple of wide, clean roadways with concrete drainage ditches lead to the town's central church. Procedure here (as in other villages) requires an immediate visit to the village chief (*kepala desa*) or, in his absence, one of the pastors (*guru gereja*). They will make the necessary arrangements for overnight stays and meals. (Count on paying about $6 for room and full board.)

While the men work the sea, the women tend manioc, yams, corn, vegetables and bananas in the gardens. About half of Bobale's inhabitants also own gardens on the "mainland." Beginning in April and continuing for several months, families work the extensive coconut plantations, splitting the nuts, scooping out the meat and drying it to produce copra. Oxcarts haul the coconuts to the smoke-drying racks.

A brisk half-hour walk from the village to the island's northeast coast (best done during the cooler early morning) brings visitors to an extensive Japanese bunker, mostly underground. It is kept neat and clean by a family who sleeps there when working on their nearby coconut plantation. The bunker overlooks

sharp, rugged coral formations on either side of a partially submerged cave.

Older villagers remember cordial relations with the 300-odd Japanese stationed here during World War II. They dug one of the village's four wells, down to the 7-meter-deep water table. Now, several times a day, housewives saunter to one of the wells to gossip and fill long bamboo tubes with water for their families.

Diving off Bobale

Serious divers will want to contact one of Bobale's two eight-man scuba teams. These pros go out almost daily (except Sundays), year-round, for dives up to 50 meters. Although they find the occasional pearl, the bulk of their trade is in mother-of-pearl and other shells, *trepang* and spear-fishing. An average day's haul could include 20 kilos of mother-of-pearl shell (sold at about $4 a kilo) and several 2–10 kilo fish for the men's families. And, on lucky days, a pearl or two.

Chinese businessmen in Tobelo have staked each team with a compressor, three regulators and several tanks. The contract with one of the teams calls for 30 percent of the profits while the other one makes a flat $350 payment every three months. Each group of divers owns its own boat. Work proceeds from morning until early afternoon in various locations, and the compressors are kept onboard to refill the tanks when needed.

In the old days, when Bobale (a part of the district of Kao) was under the power of the Sultan of Ternate, the area's yearly tribute consisted of "one flask half-filled with pearls," along with 12 men for general service and 4 *kora-kora* war canoes.

A visitor who has scuba experience and speaks a few words of Indonesian can join one of these regular work sessions—and get in one deep dive—for $10 to $15. Or go along for free if it's just to watch and swim. The variety of fish and seeing the men at work are a

unique experience. If you wish to charter the boat and rent the equipment for a couple of dives, count on paying $30 to $50.

Ask the *kepala desa*, Frans Kodobik, about the nearby location of a World War II fighter plane in about 30 meters of water. Snorkeling is good near the north and east shores while line and net fishing are excellent in varying locations. Sport fishermen can angle for tuna and other game fish.

With all the fishing going on, one is naturally served fine seafood. A whole lobster

appears to be a quite usual dish. A special request might yield a huge coconut crab, *ketang kenari,* on the dining table or the scallop-like pearl oyster, *daging siput.* The latter is best with a bit of lime, *jeruk nipis.*

Trekking in Halmahera

For an inland adventure, try trekking in the mountains behind Wasile. The forest is beautiful and thick, and the nomadic, animist Togutil tribe is reported to be still living in this area, which has attracted a group of very determined missionaries. The Christians have established themselves at a place called Lilei, east and around the peninsula from Wasile, where they built a strip for their light plane, usually parked in Ambon. The missionaries are learning the Togutil language and will do anything to induce the nomads out of the woods and into the evangelical fold.

A somewhat easier trek, but still only for hikers in good shape, is to Telaga Lina (Lake Lina), which can be reached in two easy days from Kao. The last village, Kai, is about five kilometers from the lake. The lake is full of huge eels and shrimp, and megapode birds make their nests on the shore.

Opposite: *Pearl divers set out from Bobale island.* **Above, left:** *A blue ring angelfish, an aquarium specimen in the west, is a diver's dinner.* **Above, right:** *Pearls are rare; mother-of-pearl provides most of the divers' income.*

MOROTAI

World War II Relics and Snorkeling

Morotai Island was at the center of world attention for a few short, but action-packed weeks during World War II when General Douglas MacArthur landed his powerful Tradewind Task Force there. A crucial step in the Pacific island-hopping strategy, the base at Morotai brought the Philippines within easy range of U.S. Superfortress bombers.

Seven long strips were laid down on Morotai, and the hundreds of planes stationed there destroyed the Japanese fortifications in the Philippines. It was striking from Morotai that MacArthur finally made good on his promise: "I shall return."

When the Allies pulled out of Morotai, the island lapsed back to its usual isolation—until 1973. For 28 years, Private Nakamura, who had been hiding in the mountainous interior, was finally coaxed out of the jungle by Japanese officials playing the wartime national anthem over a loudspeaker. He turned over his still functioning rifle and his last five cartridges while being gently told that the war was over.

Perhaps the loyal old chap should have been left on Morotai. The official reception and the honors showered on him, along with the suddenly fast pace of modern Japan, ended his life in less than three years. The local district officer, carefully investigating evidence from inland villages, is convinced that there are still three more Japanese soldiers holding out inside the island.

They have plenty of room to roam in Morotai's sparsely populated 1,800 square kilometers—80 kilometers north–south and no more than 42 kilometers wide. Just 41,000 people live in the rugged, forested island. Just north of the much larger Halmahera, almost all of Morotai's inhabitants trace their origins to the districts of Tobelo or Galela which at one time claimed sovereignty over Morotai. The population is just about evenly divided between Christians and Muslims.

Daruba town

The island's largest town, **Daruba**, is in the island's south, near the coast. Some 6,000 people live in Daruba. Electricity was scheduled for mid-1988, but as of this writing, they were still waiting. There is no movie house yet. A few Indonesian-Chinese families, each maintaining a well-stocked store on the main

street, are the kingpins of the local economy. They warehouse copra, cacao and cloves gathered by local families for export.

All but two of Morotai's villages hug the coast, and crops are planted only a short distance from the sea. Fishing supplements the diet, and some *trepang,* shells and smoked tuna are shipped to Ambon. In early 1988, sailing boats arrived with tough Madurese fishermen. There is an early morning fish market just off the Daruba dock and the vegetable market is active every day, although Mondays are the busiest.

In 1985 a lumber company started sending *Agathis* and other logs to the sawmill and plywood factory at Sidangole on Halmahera, just across from Ternate. The timber road has been extended over 40 kilometers from the north coast to the mountainous interior.

World War II relics

Until early 1988, there were plenty of war relics lying around Morotai—airplanes, tanks, trucks. These anachronistic machines, rusted to the color of clay and choked with thick jungle vegetation, were plaintive reminders of the peculiar horrors of World War II. But despite the vociferous protests of the people of Morotai, these were judged to be just steel scrap by the powers that be and disappeared into the hot jaws of the Krakatoa Steel Mill in Java. The scavengers left the many unexploded bombs and hand grenades, and the few pieces hopelessly mired in mud.

There are still a couple of armored amphibious landing craft, overgrown with vegetation but in good shape, northeast of Daruba, just out of town and about a kilometer off the paved road to Sabatai Tua village. But don't ask the residents about any relics they salvaged personally. They think the government will confiscate them. Rifles, helmets and even dog tags are hidden away, and already are beginning to assume the status of sacred heirlooms.

Hundreds of **burned out jeeps** and trucks are heaped in a pit one kilometer from Totodoku village. A paved road leads to the grave from Daruba, passing the airport, from which it is about 5 kilometers to Totodoku. The bomber strips at the airport are long and solid enough to handle anything today's commercial aviation could send there, including DC-10's and 747's. The wreck of what was probably a reconnaissance plane remains at the airport, its "Harvard" plate still legible.

The paved road continues 17 kilometers beyond Totodoku, and will eventually reach **Berebere**, the principal town on Morotai's north coast, 68 kilometers from Daruba. Until

Opposite: *Daruba village on Morotai was the scene of a successful Allied assault in World War II.* **Below:** *A heavy, U.S.-made armored carrier, a relic of the Allied base here, lies abandoned on an island off Morotai.*

then, the only regular access to Berebere is aboard a weekly outboard powered "longboat" from Daruba.

Fishermen know the location of a couple of P-51 Mustang fighters that crashed in the bay close to Daruba and Pulau Babi. It is said that when the sea is clear, the planes are visible under only a few meters of water. A downed bomber has been reported at around 30 meters within scuba range, about two hours by outboard from Daruba.

The bay in front of Daruba is dotted with offshore islands, and fishermen ply the waters in canoes and sailboats. Near town, former military docks and pontoons are slowly surrendering to the waves. The remains of the catwalks, which must have covered huge spreads of mud, are in evidence as the preferred fencing material in Daruba.

The Tradewind Task Force

It was the mud, together with undetected coral heads, that slowed down the allies' Tradewind Task Force upon its initial amphibious landing at Morotai. But the task force's engineers quickly blanketed the mud with catwalks so that the matériel could be unloaded. Out of the assault force's 61,000 personnel, fully two-thirds were engineers and service workers brought in for the speedy construction of the airstrips. Only then could the Allied attack be launched on Japanese bases in the Talaud Islands and on Mindanao in the Philippines.

Allied intelligence had detected an important Japanese concentration of ships, men and planes around Kao Bay, facing Morotai, but only 500 troops on the island itself. To ensure that the invasion would remain an unpleasant surprise, MacArthur held off his covering attack until the morning of the landings, when he unleashed a veritable hell on the unsuspecting Japanese.

Waves of 5th Air Force bombers and fighters, from their bases in the north of Irian Jaya's Bird's Head region, rained bombs on the Japanese installations. Their forces were complemented by fighters launched from six Allied carriers. War correspondents reported MacArthur's fascination as he watched from the deck of the *Nashville,* his command ship, as the Seventh Fleet and the airplanes pounded both Kao and Galela Bay, where he thought an expedition to reinforce Morotai might be staged. Facing this incredible concentration of firepower—MacArthur's specialty—all Japanese counter-attacks were squashed before they could get underway.

On Morotai itself, the perimeter of a 31 square kilometer area was quickly secured. Most of the defenders were killed as they attempted to escape by barges, blown out of the water by U.S. Navy PT boats. Only Private Nakamura and a few others who fled into the mountainous interior survived. Historians have called the Morotai operation one of the most economical and effective undertakings in the Southwest Pacific War. MacArthur, in his droll and confident way, remarked that, "The enemy, as usual, was not in the right place at the right time."

Diving off Morotai

MacArthur had his mind on other things but today's visitor to Morotai can enjoy the water without worrying about how to invade the Philippines. The offshore islands are excellent locations for snorkeling, swimming and scuba diving. White sand beaches line most of these islands. The east shores, facing Daruba, tend to shallow coral approaches with the usual variety of tropical reef fish

In contrast, the western shores drop off steeply, and here is where the bigger fish tend to congregate. Sharks, large rays and tuna and other pelagic and deep-water

Above: *Jeep axles, trucks and other World War II junk still clog the harbor at Daruba.* **Opposite:** *Sumsum Island near Morotai is said to have served as McArthur's temporary headquarters.*

species can all be sighted in a 45-minute scuba session at 20–25 meter depths.

Local store and business owners maintain a dozen sets of scuba gear, used to collect *repang,* shells and pearls. Complete gear with a full tank can be rented for about $15, but check out the equipment carefully as not much fuss is made over maintenance or safety inspections. Outboard-powered canoes, usually used by tuna fishermen, can be rented for either sport fishing, diving or just cruising for $15 to $20 for a half-day.

Sumsum Island

Pulau Sumsum, about a quarter hour from Daruba, should be included in a visitors' island-hopping strategy. Several atolls just south of Sumsum offer protected dives with a variety of coral and drops of 20–25 meters to the sandy bottom A World War II ship is said to have sunk in this area.

A couple of shacks on Sumsum's east beach serve as temporary quarters for fishermen and their families, who camp here for a few days at a time while fishing. Any longer stays are precluded by the lack of water. Yet, according to local lore, Sumsum was general MacArthur's headquarters during the Morotai phase of the Pacific campaign. Large, rusting tanks on the beach are said to have been the water containers he and his staff used. Inland, a short walk on the faintly discernable path leads past a couple of large,

caterpiller-treaded carriers with the manufacturer's plate still intact: "Forged Track Wagon by the Athey Truss Wheel Co. of Chicago, Illinois."

The path continues under squawking, rainbow-colored parrots to dumps of rusting steel drums, broken glass and finally to the spot where MacArthur was supposed to have slept. (From the looks of this place, he probably stayed onboard his command ship.) Only two rusty metal sheets in a small clearing mark the general's memory.

A half-hour or so from Sumsum is another small island, **Pulau Dodola**. Dodola is two islands at high tide, but at low tide, when it reunites with its satellite atoll, just one. Another great little island for an off-beat vacation, limited only by the lack of water.

Morotai today

Things did begin to change a bit on Morotai in the mid-1980s when Merpati began its Saturday flights from Ternate to the U.S.-built airfield ($30) and a ferry service, averaging three times a week, started operating a Ternate–Daruba–Tobelo run (See "Halmahera Practicalities," page 197). But foreign visitors are few and far between. In the 1970s, some Japanese veterans dropped by, and some Dutchmen invaded Morotai on a "nostalgia" tour. Other than these, local informants can remember only two lepidopterists who visited the island to collect butterflies.

BACAN

Butterflies, Birds and Damar Trees

The mountainous and forested Bacan Islands, south of Ternate and just west of Halmahera's southernmost arm, are rarely visited by travelers. The islands offer not really spectacular attractions, except perhaps for the unparalleled scenery on the boat trip from Ternate, their off-beat character make them an interesting stop for those looking for a place well off the tourist track.

There are a few inexpensive and attractive *losmen* in Labuha, the largest city in Bacan, and you can make one of these your base for explorations. Don't expect anyone here to speak English, however.

The largest island in the group is Bacan (in the past, its southeastern peninsula was called Seki), and Kasiruta and Mandioli are also of significant size. (See map page 117.) There are dozens of smaller ones. The Bacan *kecamatan* or sub-district includes 56,000 people, of which some 8,000 live in the capital, the town of Labuha. (See map page 199.)

History of Bacan

Since history was first recorded here, which didn't happen until the arrival of the Portuguese, Bacan was subservient to the Sultan of Ternate. In 1513, the first Portuguese trading fleet to reach the spice islands, under the command of Captain Antonio de Miranda Azevedo, established a trading post on Bacan as well as on Ternate. A few of Azevedo's men were left on Bacan to buy cloves for the following year's expedition from the Moluccas. This decision set the stage for Bacan's relations with the west.

Things got off to the worst possible start. The Portuguese behaved arrogantly and abominably, committing outrages—"especially towards the women," according to one account—until the Bacanese had had enough, and murdered all seven of them. The shipment of cloves these men had stayed behind to buy and prepare, was brought by the Sultan to Ternate to fill the hold of

Ferdinand Magellan's last ship, as stocks at the time on Ternate were insufficient. This ship was the first to make it all the way around the world. Bacan also contributed a slave and two birds of paradise as gifts to Charles V.

Bacan surfaces again shortly thereafter as a place of refuge for rebellious Ternateans, and at the receiving end of an expedition of punishment sent by the Portuguese governor. When the attack did not yield the desired results, Governor Galvão challenged Bacan's sultan to a personal duel, to determine who was to submit to whom. The challenge was accepted, but the duel never came off.

The Portuguese must eventually have done something right, however, as in 1557, just a decade later, Father Antonio Vaz converted the sultan of Bacan and many members of his court to Catholicism in what was regarded as "the great missionary coup of the century." The king went on to marry a half-sister of Sultan Hairun of Ternate. She had also become a Catholic.

The Christian victory was short-lived, however. Under pressure from Ternate, which invaded in 1578, Bacan's king apostasized. Still, a nucleus of a Christian community was created in Bacan, and it persists to this day. Local Christians were later joined by co-religionists from Tobelo, then a few more from Ambon. Eventually, the number justified a small Roman Catholic hospital, run by an elderly nun from Holland. Today, Protestants far outnumber Roman Catholics, who are called "RK" from Roman Katolik, the Indonesian spelling.

In the British naturalist Alfred Russel Wallace's times, the Christians in the Moluccas were called "Orang Sirani," and even though they were darker skinned than Malays, were thought to have descended from the Portuguese. Back then, in the mid-19th century, they dressed in white and black, dancing "quadrilles, waltzes, polkas and mazurkas with great vigour and much skill," Wallace reports. Unfortunately, none of this dancing seems to take place today.

Following the 1578 invasion, Bacan seems to have become wholly subservient to Ternate. The island provided a wife to Sultan Said of Ternate, and was the site of a small

Overleaf: *A wooden boat being built in Bacan.*
Opposite: *Cacao, introduced in the 1970s, is now a major cash crop on Bacan. The dried fruits of this small tree, a native of South America, are the main ingredient in chocolate.*

Spanish fort built in 1606. After Dutch hegemony was secured in the 17th century, Holland's power on Bacan was based in Fort Barnaveld.

In 1705, an international incident was barely averted when the sergeant in command of the fort, with help from the sultan, captured the famous English explorer, William Dampier. His ship was seized, its cargo looted and everyone aboard was threatened with execution—presumably for violating the trade monopoly. When the Dutch realized their over-zealous sergeant's momentous mistake, Dampier was released, his ship restored and the English were wined and dined in Ternate.

Gold, pearls and damar

Bacan's importance at this time can be assessed by Dutch East Indies Company's stipend to the sultan. It was a bit higher than the salary of the Dutch governor on Ternate, but only 1/9 of what was paid to the Sultan of Ternate and 1/3 of that paid to the Sultan of Tidore. These sums were paid as a kind of compensation for the extirpated clove trees.

According to at least one report, gold was washed on Bacan since at least 1774. During the mid-19th century, a party of 20 skilled Chinese gold workers were brought from western Borneo, but no gold rush materialized. The Dutch brought in Javanese convicts to extract coal, but after delivery of a few tons

to a bunkering station for official steamboats, the mining was suspended as the grade of coal was not sufficiently high.

During the last two decades of the 19th century, a prominent Amsterdam merchant invested heavily in a farming venture on Bacan. Counting on an energetic sultan and a skilled and educated community of a few hundred Christian Bacanese, Mr. Soeterwoude tried to plant vanilla, coffee, tobacco and potatoes. The land chosen was for the most part unsuitable, and his crops were plagued by floods, drought, rot, blight, insects, and rodents. He persisted, with great infusions of cash, until creditors forced him out of business in 1900. They tried to run the show themselves, but did no better.

The only economic potential on Bacan, aside from pearl and mother-of-pearl gathering operations, was the collection of damar pitch. Wallace mentions a "forest of immense trees, among which those producing the resin called dammar (*Dammara sp.*) are abundant." Several villages, he reports, were engaged in searching for damar, used principally for torches. The sticky resin accumulates in large masses, either attached to the trunk of the trees or underground, around its roots. Today, damar (also dammar) is used in varnishes. *Damar* is the word generally used by Indonesians for any resin that will burn. Copal, often confused with damar, is called *damar putih,* and comes from the *Agathis*

alba tree. Other kinds of "damar" are collected from *Shorea, Hopea* and other tree species.

During the late 19th century, Bacan and Ternate were the only places in the north Moluccas that could boast of a school with a Dutch curriculum, and the services of a Protestant minister who preached, baptized and married the faithful on regular visits. Although some Catholics kept the faith, most of Bacan's Christians seem to have become Protestant sometime during Dutch colonial times. Of the 7,700 Christians in the Bacan subdistrict, only 193 are RK's.

While the Bacan's sultanate's little remaining political power vanished after Indonesia's independence, the family still owns a fair bit of land. This included an area around

Penambuah, sold to a tuna fishing and freezing company for its operations. But the *camat,* or chief sub-district official, has preempted the (modest) sultan's residence as his home and only he holds the key to where the crown is kept. (He was away in Ambon during our visit, so we did not see the crown.) Perhaps this reflects the old Indonesian belief that whoever controls the *pusaka* (heirlooms) rules the land.

Visiting Bacan

Labuha, the islands' capital, is connected by air and sea to Ternate. The flight or boat ride down lead past some of the most beautiful scenery in Indonesia.

Begin at **Fort Barnaveld**, located at the edge of town behind a *pesantren* or Muslim school called Kairaat (also Al Chairaat). Surrounded by a two-meter-wide moat filled with stagnant water (and there are lots of mosquitoes!) the old fort remains in fairly good shape, although its thick masonry walls bristle with vegetation. The entrance is on the north side, where we startled a large monitor lizard. Stairs lead to the ramparts of the fort, where four ancient cannon still point from their emplacements, backed by a roofless blockhouse.

Some confusion exists about both the age and identity of this fort. Locals say that there is another one by the same name on Kasiruta Island, on the shore next to a village called Kasiruta Dalam. In the old days, they say, this is where the sultan lived. History mentions a Portuguese fort built in the Bacan Islands, but we have found no references more specific than this.

The Spanish also are said to have built a small fortified outpost here. The Dutch Fort Barnaveld could have been erected at the site of an older Portuguese Fort, or Spanish Fort—or both. Wallace writes of his visit to "Kasserota (formerly the chief village) situated up a small stream, on an island close to the north coast of Batchian."

Back to less shaky historial ground, fanatic history buffs or nostalgic Hollanders will want to look at the last controlleur's house. Locally, this is called **Rumah Putih**—the "White House." It is located 4–5 kilometers from Labuha, off the paved road to Penambuah and Sawadai, after the village of Makian. Although you can drive to within 400 meters of the house, you need a guide to find it as there are several paths around.

This roofless building with white walls stands behind a grove of cacao trees. Nearby, a creek locally called *air belanda* (literally Dutch water or stream) offers a small pool of sorts for swimming, called **Kolam Belanda** (Dutch Pool). An old narrow steel foot bridge, a colonial legacy, spans the creek here and leads to a nearby village.

In addition to the old fort, Labuha offers a view of two inlets lined with wooden houses built on stilts. The best vantage point is from the old, partially collapsed wooden bridge over the inlet north of town. If the bridge gets repaired, it will open the way once more, over a paved road, to nearby **Amasing Kali** village. The town's dock, at the bottom of a U-shaped bay facing southwest, also shows signs of imminent collapse, which is why passengers have to use the port of Babang, an inconvenient 16 kilometers away.

Labuha's market is active every day from 6 a.m. till noon. It is busiest from 7 a.m. to 8 a.m. The market is held in a large, lugubriously dark open-ended warehouse building. Some activity takes place just outside the warehouse, and this part of the market is colorful in the early morning sun. Fresh fish are sold behind the market building (always sold out by 9:30 a.m.) but the site always offers a good view across Labuha harbor, criss-crossed by little canoes and backed by the huge mass of almost flat-topped Mount Sibela, at 2,110 meters the highest point in North Maluku.

The port village of **Babang** holds a weekly market on Mondays. **Wayua**, on the coast south of Labuha and one of the larger villages on Bacan, with 1,000 inhabitants, has a Saturday market. Boats occasionally motor to Wayua from Labuha (3 1/2 hours), but it's easier to reach from Babang. From there, it's an hour down the east coast to **Songa** where immigrants from Makian specialize in making rotan or reed baskets called *saloi*. From Songa, land transportation is available across the narrow neck of land to Wayaua.

The **Kayoa islands** north of Bacan, quite easy to get to from Ternate, offers the area's best snorkeling. It is said that Pulau Nusadeket and Pulau Nusara islands, both close to Labuha, are as yet unspoiled and provide decent reefs and white-sand beaches.

Seaside **Penambuah** village, at the end of an awful dirt road just off the paved road between Labuha and Sawadai, was humming with activity during our visit. A large freezing plant and docking facility were being completed to freeze tuna for export to Japan and Thailand. But there was a major problem with the dock as the Balinese engineer in charge had made some serious miscalculations. We were told that when the poor man realized his mistake, he committed suicide by hanging himself in his bathroom.

The fish-processing area gives a good view onto **Mount Sibela**. Its' upper portions are often wrapped in clouds. The clearest view is available at the end of the rainy season, around late April and early May. A lake, **Danau Seki**, is said to fill the crater, with a small island protruding from the whitish water. Large butterflies called *kupu-kupu raja* ("king butterflies") supposedly live near the mountain top, which is an overnight hike from Penambuah. We were told that one of these butterflies, with a wingspan of 1 1/2

meters and resplendent with 12 colors, lives at the top, guarded by monkeys. Let us know if you meet this magnificent animal. Better yet, photograph it and we'll include the shot in our next edition.

Wildlife

If you happen to encounter this giant, you will perhaps feel the same emotions as Wallace did when he captured a new species of birdwinged butterfly on Bacan:

"The beauty and brilliancy of this insect are indescribable, and none but a naturalist can understand the intense excitement I experienced when I at length captured it," he writes in The Malay Archipelago. "On taking it out of my net and opening the glorious

wings, my heart began to beat violently, the blood rushed to my head, and I felt much more like fainting than I have done in apprehension of immediate death. I had a headache the rest of the day, so great was the excitement produced by what will appear to most people a very inadequate cause."

Although few others would faint from excitement, the butterfly he dubbed *Ornithoptera croesus* seems truly to have

Opposite: *A successful hunter returns home with his catch. Wild pigs are found on all the larger islands of Maluku.* **Above:** *A girl with a pet Bacan macaque, a tail-less monkey probably introduced long ago from Sulawesi.*

been a fine looking specimen: velvety black with fiery orange markings on the wings. Wallace did not find butterflies particularly abundant on Bacan, but he did find a number of rare species.

Bacan is also home to an endemic race of large, black tail-less monkeys. You can see troupes of them wandering dry riverbeds near the coast or, occasionally, scampering across the road between Labuha and Babang. The Bacanese call them *nonok* or *yakis*. They seem to be specimens of the Celebes crested black macaque (one of the subspecies of *Macaca nigra*), a Sulawesi endemic.

The animals were common here in Wallace's time—he called it a "baboon"—and the first biogeographer concluded that they must have been introduced by people as pets. The monkeys don't seem to be found on Halmahera, and thus the Bacan population is the easternmost point on the globe where monkeys of any kind live.

We were also told of a troupe of unusually white-haired monkeys of the same species which guard the island. They live somewhere inland from Bacan's northeast coast. The white-haired guardians must be protected, but black ones are fair game, hunted by local Christians (but not by Muslims—monkey flesh is not hallal). Cacao growers detest the beasts, who have taken a liking to the ripe pods. Some of the local Chinese in Labuha eat the brains of the still-living monkeys, which are considered a potent tonic.

Aside from the (real) monkeys, Wallace found few other mammals: a species of cuscus, a small flying opossum, the civet cat and nine species of bats. Like most of Maluku, the number of mammals here is disappointing, but Wallace struck it rich with a completely new species of bird of paradise, later named *Semioptera wallacei*, Wallace's standard wing.

While a lesser variety of birds than he had expected, Wallace still managed to bag red lories, lorikeets, the green parrot, fruit pigeons, blue kingfishers, green and purple doves, and three other species new to science: a blue roller (*Eurystomus azureus*), a racket-tailed kingfisher (*Tanysiptera isis*) and a golden-capped sunbird (*Nectarinea auriceps*). White and sulfur-crested cockatoos are also found in Bacan.

Wallace found the forest on Bacan to be particularly rich. "Batchian is an island that would perhaps repay the researches of a botanist better than any in the whole Archipelago," he writes.

Today, the Bacanese hunt wild pigs with dogs and harpoon-like spears with detachable points. We encountered a successful hunter on the side of the road, carrying his quarry strapped to his back like a knapsack.

While wild pigs and most of Bacan's game cannot be eaten by Muslim Bacanese, the plentiful fish found in the seas around Bacan are popular with everyone. The only exception is the sailfish. Stories circulate of these fish rescuing fishermen at sea, and eating them is locally taboo.

Cacao and copra

Cacao was first planted here in the 1970s, and is now common throughout the island. Groves of the small trees line many a stretch of road. The value of the cacao harvest has reached and slightly surpassed the traditional export crop, copra (dried coconut meat).

At roadside everywhere, including Labuha, mats are set in front of homes to dry the beans, which give off a slightly acrid, but not unpleasant smell. Freshly harvested beans are a light cream color, and darken to reddish brown as they dry.

Local ethnic-Chinese businessmen, who control the economy, buy up the copra and cacao crops as well as the bits of the fragrant *gaharu* or aloes wood. This material, a resin produced by a gall in the shrub *Aquilaria agallocha,* is worth up to $500 a kilo in the Arab market, making it perhaps the world's most valuable incense resin.

That the (few) local Chinese merchants have done well here is attested by a quick visit to their cemetery, the large graves reached by a privately financed paved road.

The hills hold gold, copper and coal (but not enough of any of them to warrant mining) also yield semi-precious mineral stones of various colors, believed by some to hold magical powers. These stones, made into rings, are called simply *batu bacan* or Bacan stones.

The pearl industry here, like elsewhere in eastern Indonesia, is controlled by the Japanese. The secret of inserting the irritant that will make a pearl grow is closely guarded. The first farm was established a decade ago near Jojame village on Bacan's north coast and a second one in 1990 at Belang-Belang, just northwest of Labuha.

During the '70s and up to the mid-'80s, several lumber companies were active on Bacan. They built the dock at Babang and cut many now neglected dirt roads to strip out ebony and *meranti* trees. Operations have now wound down here but lumbering is still going on at nearby Kasiruta Island.

PART V

Southeast Maluku

This chain of tiny islands, stretching from Wetar, near East Timor, to the Aru group, next to New Guinea, is probably the most remote part of all of Indonesia. This is a place where one can literally lose oneself for months on end, island-hopping from one tiny tropical outpost to the next, each more surprising and beautiful than the last.

Relatively little is known about the histories and cultures of the people living on these islands. Because they are so isolated, and their islands produce little of economic value, many have had contact with the outside world in just the last decades. Several of the islands, including the Leti Islands and the Tanimbars, are well known to collectors of art, because of their wooden ancestor figures of unusual aesthetic quality.

No beaches in the world surpass the powder-fine sands of the Kei archipelago, first stop on the air route from Ambon to the southeast. Skilled boat builders, Kei craftsmen formerly exported their fine ships to many merchants throughout eastern Indonesia. From Tual, the capital of the region, public minibuses carry passengers to all parts of Kei Kecil Island.

Daily boats from Kei Kecil run to Kei Besar, with its shore hugging villages linked only by footpaths. Although completely lacking in tourist facilities, traditional villages on Kei Besar, the largest island in the group, reward the traveler willing to explore just a bit beyond the boundaries of the convenient tourist trail. Exploring the rest of the tiny archipelago will require organizing a local boat. From the air, these tiny atolls look like true tropical paradises.

The Tanimbar Islands to the southwest had a nefarious reputation right up into the first decades of this century. Europeans always remarked upon how handsome the Tanimbarese men were, but their head-hunting for the most part kept visitors away. The Tanimbarese are also famous for their wood-en ancestral figures, and distinctive gold jewelry. Warfare ended several generations ago, and the art of goldsmithing has faded. Traditional dancing and singing, and weaving, are still practiced here, however. These low-lying islands spread out over stunning, blue-green seas. Saumlaki, the principal town, boasts air-conditioned *losmen*, delicious seafood and fantastic snorkeling.

The Aru archipelago, the largest of the island groups and the furthest to the east, is one of the most interesting places in the world for a naturalist. Birds of paradise live in Aru's thick forest, and the coastal waters are home to the increasingly rare dugong, a large sea mammal, and sea turtles. From Kei there is irregular boat service to Dobo, the largest town on the islands, and Merpati has recently posted a flight to the Benjina airstrip on Wamar Island. It is very difficult to thoroughly explore the islands, however, as there are no roads and local boats tend to have small motors. Give yourself plenty of time if you visit here.

The Southwestern Islands, between Timor and the Tanimbars, are isolated, and their contact with the outside world is occasional at best. There is no airport anywhere in this district. In Ambon, this part of Maluku is called "Tenggara Jauh," the Far Southeast. Here is a place where a caucasian visitor may meet people who have never seen a white face before. Visiting Tenggara Jauh requires patience and a sense of adventure.

Many of these islands are constantly plagued by seasonal drought, and populations are sparse. Corn is often the staple crop here. The Damar islands are a stretched out chain of tiny volcanos, but because of the threat of eruption, almost nobody is left here.

Overleaf: *Kei Islands beaches are considered to be among the finest in the world.* **Opposite:** *A woman from the Tanimbars wears a pendant and distinctive ancestral headpiece of gold.*

KEI ISLANDS

Blue Water, Beaches, and Megaliths

In clear weather, the flight from Ambon to the Kei (pronounced "Kay") archipelago is itself worth the trip. A half-hour after take-off, the small twin-propeller airplane passes over the Bandas, tiny green jewels in the middle of the Banda Sea. Then, after an hour flying over the deep blue water, the westernmost atolls and tiny fringe islands of the the Kei archipelago begin to appear.

The beauty of these coral islands rivals any you will see in the South Pacific. From the air, the transparent waters present finely blended shades of color depending on the depth and bottom. From deep blue, almost black, to rich cobalt blue, through dark emerald greens and then, in the shallow reefs near the islands, bright turquoise and foam white. The islands' thick vegetation, dominated by stately coconut palms, crowds right to the edge of the water, held back only by a ring of

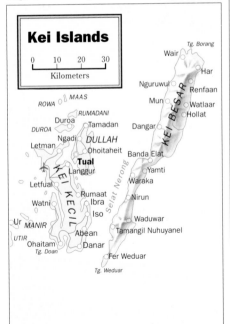

brilliant white sand.

[Note: Although you will have your camera out during the flight, put it back before landing. Dumatubun airport is part of a military base where photography is forbidden.]

Three main islands make up the Keis, and hundreds of smaller ones for a total of 1,800 square kilometers. Kei Besar ("Greater Kei") is long, thin and mountainous, while Kei Kecil ("Lesser Kei"), made up of Nuhuroa Island and the smaller Dullah Island, is mostly lowland and coastal swamps. Tual, the Keis' main city, hosts the administration of the *kabupaten* Maluku Tenggara, the Southeast Moluccas district. This includes Aru, Kei, Tanimbar, Babar and all the southwestern islands up to Wetar. An expanding network of roads connects Kei Kecil's villages.

About 100,000 people live in the Keis, some one-third of the entire population of the southeastern Moluccas. Although the records of Europeans passing through the Keis note that the islanders were Papuan, with curly hair and dark skin, because of intermarriage with immigrants from western Indonesia, the Kei islanders today look far less like their neighbors in New Guinea.

The Kei aristocrats, called Mel-Mel, are said to have originally came from Bali and have much fairer skin than most Kei islanders. The Mel-Mel, with straight hair and Malay features, comprise the nobility caste, ruling over an indigenous (Papuan Kei) middle caste.

Christianity in the Keis

Tual's urban spread began in 1882 when Ambonese colonial post-holders began to arrive. Jesuits started spreading their faith shortly afterwards, although many of the locals were already at least nominally Muslims. Even today, Arab merchants, thanks to their Muslim connections, give the Chinese some competition in Tual town.

The Roman Catholics set up an important center at Langgur (on Nuhuroa Island, just across a tiny channel from Tual) from which to carry out missionary work in both the Keis and western New Guinea. Using a potent combination of moral persuasion and the threat of Dutch force, the Jesuit missionaries were able to check warfare in the Keis by about the 1930s.

Their work suffered a setback during

Opposite: *The sea off the Kei islands takes on various shades of blue, green and turquoise.*

World War II when the Japanese arrived. The invaders murdered the bishop and 13 Dutch priests. The airfield used today was first built by the Japanese, and its presence attracted some Allied bombing but no full-scale amphibious assaults.

The Catholics now maintain a large center in Langgur, including an excellent technical school, a hospital, and a real Montessori kindergarten. They claim 34,000 adherents, about one-third of the Keis' population. To commemorate the first 100 years of Roman Catholic presence in the Keis, and to pay homage to the martyred bishop and priests, the church commissioned a Javanese artist to sculpt a memorial. The long relief traces the history of Catholicism in the Kei Islands.

Traditions on Kei

British naturalist Sir Alfred Wallace, who passed through the Keis in 1857, marvelled at the skills of the local shipwrights. He watched them assemble up to 30-ton wooden vessels with "axe, adze and auger," using nary a nail or scrap of iron on the whole boat. Planks taken from the island's magnificent hardwood trees were fastened together with wood pins and rattan. "The best European shipwright cannot produce sounder or closer fitting joints," Wallace proclaims. These boats were traded for brass guns, gunpowder, cloth, axes, Chinese ceramics, knives and rice brandy. Tobacco was the small change.

While there's still some old style boat-building on Kei Besar, Islam and Christianity have shouldered out most of the practices associated with the islands' traditional animism. Two large, exquisite Dongson-style drums were found on the Keis, the eastern-most extension of the artwork of this ancient North Vietnam culture. These drums had functioned as sacred objects in the islands' ancestral and spirit religion. Despite the current preference for church marriages, ancient gongs and brass cannon are still part of the bride price.

Touring Kei Kecil

Just a half-hour from Tual is Dullah village, a small beach-front fishing colony that is home to the **Belawang Museum**. So far the Belawang's collection contains just one object, but it is a splendid one—a huge ceremonial canoe, carved with great dragons, and with a roofed platform amidship for royal passengers. Canoes like these, with carved bows and sterns rising to two-meter peaks, were further decorated with the best shells and cassowary feathers. The raja of Banda Elat village donated the craft to the nascent museum. Banda Elat was founded by Bandanese refugees who fled their homes in 1621 during the Dutch massacre (See "History of the Bandas," page 86).

A couple kilometers further north along the coast from Dullah, there's a lonely

Japanese **World War II bunker** sinking into the sands of a good swimming beach. Returning to Tual, after Dullah, a paved side road leads to an **orchid garden**, whose several varieties bloom in April and May. From the garden, a short pathway leads to a freshwater lake. Swimming is not advisable here: informants say the quicksand-like mud will absorb any would-be swimmers as soon as they step into the shallows.

On Nuhuroa Island, south of Langgur, a pleasant paved road follows the bay. The road's slight elevation offers a nice panoramic view. The nondescript waterside village of Satehan, 11 kilometers from Langgur, looks out at an interesting mini-island, **Pulau Kapal** ("Ship Island"). The island shelters a 5-meter stone, shaped like a ship. The Kei islanders believe that their ancestors sailed from Bali on this boat, which is one of the largest and most interesting megalithic remains in the region.

If you have doubts about the stone boat's seaworthiness, the trip out to the little island in one of the tiny local canoes, without so much as an outrigger, will make you believe anything can cross the seas. Although these tiny craft will not overturn unless you panic, for peace of mind either leave your camera behind or bring a waterproof container.

Dazzling beaches

Knowledgeable travelers have remarked that the Kei's fine-grained, snow white beaches surpass any in the world.

One of the finest beaches on Kei is **Ohoideertutu beach**, 12 kilometers from Tual, which can be reached by public transportation. Ngur Bloat or **Pasir Panjang beach**, 17 kilometers from Langgur on Kei Kecil's northwest coast, sweeps around a majestic, curved bay, fringed with coconuts. The road here is terrible, however, and taxi drivers are seldom willing to risk their springs by making the trip.

Ohoideertawun beach, 15 kilometers from Langgur, is easier to reach, as only the last three kilometers are still unpaved. The sacred Luat cave at the end of this beach is inscribed with strange, still undeciphered writing. **Werabel Lake**, deep and filled with fish, is near this beach.

Kei Besar

If you have spare time, hop on one of the frequent boats to Kei Besar. There are only footpaths around this long, mountainous island and no tourist facilities. Bring your passport and some knowledge of Indonesian, because you might have to explain to local police what you are doing so far off the beaten path.

The large village of **Banda Elat** was settled by refugees from Banda after the Dutch massacre there in the early 17th century. Craftsmen make pottery nearby, building up the vessels from coils of clay. Most of Kei Kecil's timber has been cut, but the old art of boat-building is still carried on at Kei Besar. Most of the tools are also traditional.

During certain periods of calm seas, the men of Kei Besar go shark fishing. Coconut shells are strung on rattan hoops, and these underwater rattles are used to attract the sharks. When they come into view, harpoons are flung into the critters and they're hauled aboard. The best diving (few, if any, sharks) is off Kei Besar's eastern coast.

Tanimbar-Kei

Although many traditions are maintained by the 40,000 residents of Kei Besar, the Tanimbar-Kei islanders are the most traditional in the archipelago. Called Tanebar-Evav by its inhabitants, this island lies off southwestern Kei Kecil. Although the language spoken here is similar to that used on Kei, many of the old ritual words are still used in various ceremonies.

Half of each year is devoted to the cultivation of millet, essential for the rituals long abandoned elsewhere in the Keis. Tanimbar-Kei islanders consider the huge leatherback sea turtle, *Dermochelys coriacea*, to be the sacred vessel of their spirits and ancestors. There are still some 300 determined animists on the little island, and the others maintain at least a partial belief in spirits.

Evav's cash economy depends on copra sales to the Indonesian-Chinese merchants in Tual who also buy seaweed for *agar-agar*, mother-of-pearl, *trepang* and shark's fin. Manioc and sweet potatoes, cultivated by the slash-and-burn technique, are supplemented by fishing.

Weather

The rain in Kai falls chiefly in two periods: from June through July during the southeast monsoon, and more heavily, from December to March or April, during the period of northwest winds. The skies dump 2,000–3,000 millimeters of water on Kei Kecil and over 3,000 millimeters on Kei Besar in an average year.

Opposite: *A powdery sand beach at Kei, only one of many in this little-known island group.*

ARU ISLANDS

'Promised Land' for a Naturalist

The Aru Islands are thoroughly unlike any others in Southeastern Maluku. In fact, this sprawling mass of mangrove swamp and palm forest, harboring some of the most interesting wildlife in the region, is geologically part of western New Guinea. Although there are six principal islands and more than 100 smaller ones, the large islands are divided by such narrow straits that they appear as one large piece of land that has cracked in five places.

The Aru islanders are racially close to the Irianese, just 110 kilometers to the north. Because of intermarriage with Malays, however, today most of the people of Aru are mestizos. Until World War II, the Aru islanders followed their traditional religion. They were also generally peaceful, unlike the tribes along Irian's south coast, with the only conflicts arising over failure to pay the bride price or some similar misconduct. There are still mysterious nomadic tribes in the interior of Wokam, and their existence was a surprise even to the coastal Aru islanders until the late 1940s. About 25 of Aru's separate islands are known or believed to be inhabited.

The Aru archipelago spreads over 6,325 square kilometers. The main "island" is cut by five small channels into six islands: Kola, Wokam, Kobroor, Maikoor, Koba and Trangan. These seawater channels are one of the Arus' most interesting features. They are as narrow as rivers, sometimes shrinking down to the size of streams. This is a geographical feature unknown anywhere else in the world.

Perched at the end of the Sahul Shelf, the Arus are thought by geologists to have been connected to New Guinea some 10,000 years ago when sea levels were lower. The topsoil is thin, covering uplifted coral and limestone. The elevation of the islands seldom exceeds 70 meters and the interior is covered with lowland, deciduous tropical rainforest, an ecosystem found almost nowhere else in Indonesia. These forests contain huge palm trees and strange tree ferns, usually found only at higher elevations. Mangrove swamps ring the islands and clot the mouths of the channels. Some 2,180 millimeters of rain drench the islands each year, mostly from December through April.

The island group's administrative center, Dobo village on the little island of Wamar, maintains communications with Ambon and

Tual in the Keis through on occasional mixed passenger and cargo boat. Merpati has very recently scheduled a flight to the Benjina airstrip on Wamar.

Tradition in the Arus

Dobo started out as a trade entrepôt, and was inhabited only during that part of the year when traders arrived. Wamar island offered shelter to vessels, and the sea breezes kept away the mosquitoes.

During colonial times, the westernmost islands were inhabited mostly by Christians and a few Muslims, most of them engaged in the Papuan slave trade. Teachers from Ambon taught reading and writing in Malay, along with the rudiments of the Dutch Reformed Church. A divine service was held every Sunday on Wokam Island, featuring lots of psalm singing.

According to early accounts, most of the Aru islanders lived under the rule of elders in villages of 10–20 houses. They fished with iron tipped arrows, and cultivated corn, yams, sugar cane, vegetables and a little rice. They wore strips of white or blue calico as a loincloth or sarong. The Aru islanders lightened their hair with lime, and wore armbands of shells and brass wire, and a variety of gold and silver jewelry.

Those not yet converted to Christianity were animists, and created wooden posts sculpted with spirits in the form of lizards, crocodiles and snakes. When an important man died, all of his wealth was destroyed, even the gongs were broken and thrown away. The body was placed on a bier, covered with many fine cloths and Chinese porcelain set underneath to catch the drippings. These body fluids, mixed with *arak,* brandy distilled from sago or rice, were drunk by mourners as proof of affection for the deceased.

A trade emporium

Dobo was Indonesia's easternmost trade emporium, as New Guinea's aggressive cannibals kept even the most determined Chinese or Bugis merchants from her coast. Each year, the beginning of the northwest monsoon brought large trading brigs from Surabaya and Makassar, and smaller vessels from Goram and the Kei Islands.

Locally made trading vessels, up to 22 meters long and 16 tons, collected trade goods from around the Arus to bring the merchandise to Dobo.

From January through July, Dobo's population of Muslim and Chinese businessmen, sailors, and local traders rose from 300 (the village of Wamma was a short distance away) to 700. Dobo had no government, but a shared sense of purpose—trade—kept the

Opposite: *Krai village on the east coast of the Aru group.* **Below:** *A girl from Aru peers out from the palm-front walls of her house.*

ALAIN COMPOST

peace. Dobo, located on a spit of land jutting out from Wamar, was just wide enough for three rows of houses, all repaired seasonally.

The following items left Aru: pearls, including the occasional very valuable black ones, mother-of-pearl (Aru's is still considered the best), bird of paradise plumes, *trepang,* dried sharks' fins, birds' nests (then, and now, worth their weight in silver), tortoiseshell, and timber and ornamental woods. One important item from the past that is no longer traded are slaves from New Guinea.

Brought to Aru were: knives, choppers, swords, muskets, small brass cannon, gunpowder, elephant tusks, brass gongs from Java, Dutch coins of gold and silver, textiles, Chinese porcelain, bottles of rice brandy, tobacco and the ingredients of the betel chew.

Taking inventory during his visit in the mid-19th century, naturalist Alfred Russel Wallace estimated the total value of the merchandise in Dobo at £18,000.

The imports were either practical items (knives, etc.) or luxury items required in the bride price (tusks). These were most difficult to gather unless the young man was lucky enough to be the son of a wealthy father. The imported items also served as status symbols, the source of prestige and power. Nobody accumulated wealth. At a man's death, all his possessions were destroyed.

Some of the birds of paradise, as well as the beautiful Aru pearls, made their way

through many hands to Europe. Of the many varieties of shells brought to Europe, those of Aru were the most valuable, although Sula's pearls were considered the best.

Several species of sea cucumbers are collected in Aru for *trepang.* They are collected by hand in shallow water, then immediately boiled in sea water with papaya leaves. They are then buried, dug up and washed, prior to drying and storage. The drying *trepang,* Wallace remarks, looks like "sausages rolled in mud and thrown up the chimney." Eventually, the animals are cooked in a highly prized type of Chinese soup.

The pearl trade

The Aru pearl trade was quite lucrative. It must have been, as divers plunged 9 meters to bring up the oysters. The constant pressure change often brought on nosebleeds, and a 19th century traveler observed that the divers were "liable to be destroyed by the numerous sharks." As outsiders realized the potential of the pearl trade, Australian, Japanese and Filipino divers started working the Arus—to the outrage of the Aru islanders as well as the Chinese and Arab merchants who were staking them.

Late in the 19th century, Sheik Said Baadilla, the Banda Arab community's first citizen, drove out some of the foreigners by financing several well-equipped schooners. Thanks to both local and foreign divers, he became the Pearl King of the Moluccas. On a visit to Holland, Baadilla made a royal gift to Queen Emma: a flawless pearl the size of a pigeon egg.

Above: *A hunter gets ready to pull in a dugong, a large and harmless sea mammal. The animals are hunted for their teeth, which are used to make cigaret holders. Dugongs are endangered throughout Indonesia.* **Opposite:** *The saltwater channels between the larger islands of Aru are unique in the world.*

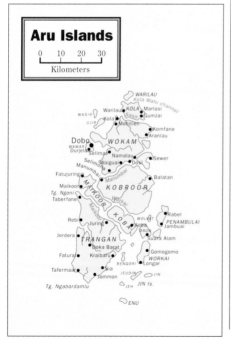

Aru Islands

0   10   20   30
Kilometers

WARILAU
Kola Watu channel
WASIR   Warilau KOLA Marlasi
Kola Basir Gumzai
UJIR   Mohitien
Komfane
Aranlau
Dobo   WOKAM
WAMAR Durjela Selimap Namalau
Selim Waiguai Dosi   Sewer
Manumbai
Fatujuring   Manumbai Balatan
Maikoor   KOBROOR
Tg. Ngoni
Taberfane
Workai
Rabel
Rebi   Jurin WOLGAT PENAMBULAI
Kobra Jambuai
GAUN
Jerdera   Suara Alam
TRANGAN
Boka Barat
Fatural Kraibaru Gomogomo
BENGORI WORKAI
Longar
Tafermaar Sia
Jommon JEUDIN JIN
Tg. Ngabordamlu   JEH JIN Is.

ENU

After Baadilla's death in 1930, foreign companies reappeared. Before World War II, American, Australian, Dutch and Japanese pearling companies operated in the Arus. The Japanese companies were able to furnish very valuable information to their invading countrymen in 1942.

During the war, Allied planes bombed the Arus, especially Dobo and Taberfane, where the Japanese maintained a seaplane base. The Japanese bases were put back into use when Indonesia mounted her military campaign to reintegrate western New Guinea back into the fold. In the "Battle of Aru," an Indonesian torpedo boat was sunk by a Dutch warship. Paratroopers took off from Aru to land in the south coast jungle, and from there contested West Irian.

Sir Alfred Russel Wallace

During his famous sojourn in the archipelago in the mid-19th century British naturalist Sir Alfred Russel Wallace spent several months exploring the Arus. In Dobo from March to June 1857, he added over 9,000 specimens to his collection.

Wallace's stay coincided with an attack by four large pirate canoes manned by Sulu pirates from the southern Philippines, their first strike after an 11-year lull. When pursued by a Dutch warship, the clever pirates simply headed straight into the wind and rowed for their lives. Steam-powered warships slowed down, but did not eliminate, the pirates, who still operate today—not, however, in the Arus.

As soon as Wallace set up camp at Dobo, he began collecting animal life. On his very first day of searching, he "trembled with excitement," he recalls in *The Malay Archipelago,* as his net swooped down on the great bird-winged butterfly, *Ornithoptera poseidon.* Lost in admiration, he gazed at "the velvet black and brilliant green of its wings, seven inches across, its golden body and crimson breast." After capturing 30 species of butterflies in one day, mostly rare or new to science, Wallace decided that the Arus were for him "the promised land."

The only trouble in paradise was its immense variety of spiders, particularly one species that strings its strong and glutinous nets across footpaths. While freeing himself with "much trouble," the naturalist remarks that the nets' inhabitants, "great yellow-spotted monsters with bodies two inches long, and legs in proportion, are not pleasant things to run one's nose against while pursuing some gorgeous butterfly, or gazing aloft in search of some strange-voiced bird."

But it would have taken an army of spiders to deter our determined naturalist from pursuing his birds, particularly the birds of paradise, and he was probably the first European to see them in their native forests. Wallace became attuned to the sounds of the forest birds: "lories and parakeets cry shrilly;

cockatoos scream; king-hunters croak and bark; and the various smaller birds chirp and whistle their morning song." But his siren's song was the loud "wawk-wawk-wawk-wok-wok-wok" of the birds of paradise.

Birds of Paradise

The strange ornamental breast fans and spiral tail wires of the birds of paradise are unknown on any other of the 8,000-odd species of birds on the earth. The silky yellow nuptial plumes of the greater bird of paradise does not begin appearing until June, and reaches what Wallace called "full perfection" only in September and October. In As the plumage starts appearing, the birds begin their characteristic dancing parties in food trees—mahogany and wild nutmeg—that are clear enough to show the nervous males off to their potential mates.

To catch any but the most fleeting glimpse of these birds, birders and photographers should copy the technique of the hunters and erect a blind of leaves high up in the trees where the birds are known to gather and climb there before dawn.

Local hunters shoot birds of paradise during the height of their plumage, using smooth-tipped arrows so as not to damage the feathers. By the late 19th century, the Italian naturalist, Dr. Oduardo Beccari, wrote that some 3,000 bird of paradise skins were exported yearly from Dobo to Makassar. The skins were worth 16 to 18 shillings, or 15 large bottles of *arak*. Despite the fact that the birds are now protected by law, the clandestine trade continues today. One of the stuffed birds now costs the resident Indonesian-Chinese businessmen about $20, and by the time the skins reache Ambon, the price has doubled.

The number of birds of paradise has dropped so low that wildlife specialists fear the birds will soon be too scarce to maintain viable groups. A nature preserve has been proposed for Kobroor island, in order to put at least a partial brake on the trade in illegal birds and wildlife. Kobroor was selected because it has only 22 villages, with a total population of 6,500. The preserve will also halt the planned exploitation of the timber and other natural resources of the area. There are still 165 species of birds in the Arus, of which an observant watcher can easily see 45 in an afternoon's stroll.

Colonial neglect

The archipelago had been claimed for Holland back in 1623 by Captain Jan Carstenz. Some of the native Aru leaders were taken to Banda, wined, dined and given the royal treatment, and returned home after signing a treaty in 1640. A couple of Portuguese encampments had been built in the Arus, but by the time Carstenz arrived, the Iberians had abandoned their positions.

The Dutch built their own fort on Wokam island in 1659 to protect the spice trade, but this was soon deemed useless and was abandoned. The Dutch were busy in Ambon and Banda, and paid no attention to the Arus.

In 1825, Lieutenant Kolff called at the Arus as part of a Dutch "prise de conscience" triggered by the visit to the Moluccas by the Governor-general of Netherlands India. Kolff described the Papuans of Kabroor as having clear skin, fine hair, neat dress and pleasing head ornaments. They were more oriented to agricultural than maritime pursuits, he writes, but they had "great taste" in weapons and the decoration of their *prahus*. The men and women both wore strings of beads, resulting in "by no means an unpleasant appearance."

Holland left the Arus alone, and they were commercially and politically autonomous until 1874, when the indigenous trading was finally recognized as being too important to continue without a semblance of control. A post-holder was stationed to Dobo. He joined the three Ambonese schoolmasters who were there in Wallace's time.

The Dutch Protestant Church had been given permission to proselytize in 1870, and under the influence of Ambonese pastors, the chiefs and nobles of the northwestern Arus converted to Christianity. Roman Catholic missionaries were denied access until the 1930s. The people of Wadia, at the northern end of the archipelago, opted for Islam.

In 1882, Anna Forbes visited the Arus and could write that Dobo was a permanent, fair-sized village, "wonderfully civilized for this out-of-the-world corner." Mrs. Forbes' Dutch steamer was met by wide, flat-bottomed boats in which some locals lived with their families, sleeping and cooking in *atap*-covered huts "between elaborate carvings crowned with bunches of cassowary feathers on both prow and stern."

The Arus today

Some 45,000 people live in the Arus today, double the figure at the end of World War II. Almost three-fourths are Protestants, the rest are Catholic or Muslim. There are also some very strong traces of animism and traditional religion. The Aru islanders are dispersed in 122 villages, an administrator's headache.

Opposite: *The beautiful and harmless green tree python,* Chondropython viridis, *is found in Aru and New Guinea.* **Right:** *A boy in the Kei islands holds the flipper of a leatherback sea turtle. These huge animals are hunted for food.*

The largest city is Dobo, which has about 3,500 people, mostly non-Papuan: Chinese, Makassarese and Bugis.

The Papuan inhabitants of the Arus live by subsistence farming, supplemented by fishing and hunting of wild pigs and introduced deer. Sago is the most important staple. Some obtain cash income by collecting live butterfly larvae. Although five languages are traditionally spoken, the islanders share a common mythology.

Some 4,000 Indonesian-Chinese live in Aru. Just about every village has one or more Chinese storekeeper-merchants who control the economy, buying the pearls, mother-of-pearl, timber, trepang, agar-agar and copra that is collected. The Chinese work mainly with Kei and Tanimbar Islanders.

In 1969 a Japanese company started pearling operations, investing a cool $1 million at Fatujuring, some 35 kilometers south of Dobo. A dozen Japanese foremen operate in the Arus today, mostly off the north and east coasts, keeping divers under contract. The locals still sell their pearls to the resident Chinese shopkeepers.

A government managed trading corporation tried to control Aru's economy but inefficiency led to its early demise. Foreign trawlers take advantage of Aru's relative isolation, and Japanese and Taiwanese boats are periodically caught fishing illegally off the Aru group.

THE TANIMBARS

Islands of Dances and Gold Treasure

The Tanimbar group lies due south of the tip of Irian Jaya's Bird's Head Peninsula, and forms part of the arc that includes the Kei Islands to the northeast, and Babar and Leti to the southwest. The Tanimbars are a racial mixture of Malay and Papuan blood, with dark skins and frizzy hair, but non-Irianese facial features.

The Tanimbar group contains 66 islands, one of which, 500-square-kilometer Yamdena, dominates the group. Yamdena and six of the smaller islands are populated. All of the islands are low-lying, with few hills exceeding 200 meters, and coastal swamps abound. In south central Yamdena, a quirk of geology has left a four-hectare salt deposit. The salt is 30 centimeters deep in places, and the deposit served as the area's chief supply until it became easier to buy the staple condiment from Chinese merchants.

Christianity has succeeded here, but ancestral beliefs are still strong. Before 1907, when the Dutch police began to clamp down, head-hunting, cannibalism and inter-village warfare were common. Some areas, out of the reach of Dutch law and order, continued these deadly cultural practices up to World War II.

Saumlaki Town

The Tanimbars are split into two *kecamatan*s or districts, with the north controlled out of Larat, on Larat Island off Yamdena's northern tip, and the south out of Saumlaki. The population of the Tanimbars pushes 70,000, having more than doubled since World War II. Saumlaki was a regular port of call for steamships and the center of the Dutch colonial presence in the islands. Today, Saumlaki's 3,400 people make it the largest urban area in the Tanimbars.

The pleasant little town of Saumlaki, on the south coast of Yamdena island, hugs the sea on the protected shore of a long peninsula. The local population professes the Roman Catholic faith. The Protestants started later than the Catholics, and the Protestant faith has spread to parts of the west coast of Yamdena and the islands to the north. Some 200 Muslims from overcrowded western Indonesia have drifted into town, working mainly as day laborers. Many are up by dawn to take advantage of the cool morning hours

to shop for fish, fruit and vegetables at the bustling open market which is finished by about 10:30 a.m.

Saumlaki faces a wide bay whose entrance is protected by several small islands featuring excellent skin diving. Beautiful local orchids bloom from March to June in the natural preserve of Anggarmasa Island.

History of the Tanimbars

Until the early 20th century, very little was known about the Tanimbars. Commercial possibilities were limited and, like some of the other islands on the southern fringe of the Moluccas, warfare and head-hunting gave the region a particularly fierce reputation, keeping casual tourists at bay and even deterring well-equipped expeditions. Passing boats testified only to Yamdena's large size and low, forest-covered elevations. It wasn't until the first decade of the 20th century that it became known that the interior was completely uninhabited.

Before the Dutch became well-established in the area, allied villages participated in constant and fierce battles. Head-hunting took up a significant percentage of the man's energy. Villages were located on cliffs for defense, at times enclosed by a high, double palisade and protected by sharpened bamboo spikes. Anna Forbes, who chronicled the trip she and her husband naturalist Henry Forbes took through the region in the 19th century, tells of a human arm casually hanging from a branch and "recently gibbeted heads and limbs" hung in the trees as trophies after public dismemberment.

Still, Forbes was fond of the Tanimbarese, and seems to have found the men particularly handsome. The Taminbarese, she writes,

*Opposite: Traditional dances are still performed in the Tanimbars, as part of seasonal agricultural celebrations. **Above:** The drummer is the backbone of the group.*

were "mostly fine athletic men, with an intelligent expression of countenance…. [They were] powerful, athletic fellows, having rich chocolate colored skins and flowing manes of gold-hued hair, which gave them a most prepossessing air."

The yellow locks required constant care. Every few days they were bleached with a mixture of coconut and lime. The youths' heads were carefully bound with colored kerchiefs. Although many of the young men are still quite handsome today, the tradition of the golden manes belongs to the past.

Following in the wake of Chinese merchants, in 1907 the Dutch picked Saumlaki as their administrative headquarters. Three years later, the first Catholic missionaries arrived. It took another couple of decades before the dialects of the Tanimbars were grouped into four mutually unintelligible Austronesian languages: Yamdena, Fordata, Selaruan and Seluwasan, the latter named for the medium-sized island clustered of the southern tip of Yamdena.

World War II woke up a sleepy Saumlaki. A Japanese naval task force landed at dawn, after an all-night shelling. But the landing party was greeted by a deadly surprise. Strong defensive positions had been prepared by Ambonese sergeant Julius Taija with a couple of machine guns and some vintage rifles. Eighty of the first 100 Japanese assault troops were killed. But other Japanese quick-

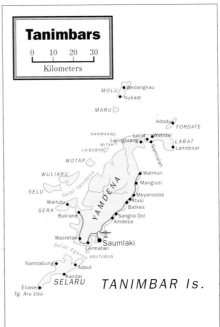

ly landed and began to outflank the handful of defenders. The natives of the colonial army cast off their military clothing and blended into the population. According to one local story, a Dutch soldier from among the defenders hid in a village for the remainder of the war. Another says the Ambonese sergeant hopped a boat to Australia and became a lieutenant in the Dutch military intelligence.

Saumlaki was turned into a secondary Japanese base with an airfield and up to 1,000 soldiers. Relations were not particularly amicable. The local girls were rounded up for the soldiers' recreation, drunk soldiers beat up some of the natives, and the Japanese forced the Tanimbar islanders to build their roads and to grow food for them. A school to teach the Japanese language functioned for about two years with about 50 young students. The children, and some adults, participated in drills carrying wooden rifles. Everyone had to make their own clothing. Local cotton was hand-spun and woven into cloth.

As the fortunes of war turned, the island felt bombing raids from Australia and three Allied fighters were brought down here. MacArthur's island-hopping strategy skipped the Tanimbars, so the Japanese, cut off from supplies, sat tight until the peace treaty was signed, and were evacuated. Since the airfield opened on Saumlaki in 1980, two groups of Japanese veterans who had served there returned for "nostalgia" tours. The friendly reception committee included local men who could still speak passable Japanese.

Gold and the social order

Even today Tanimbarese dancers wear locally woven sarongs, and some still have old ivory bracelets, ancient beads, and headdresses of a stuffed bird of paradise or heirloom gold jewelry. The gold pieces in particular—necklaces or forehead ornaments—are of a distinctly Tanimbarese design.

Gold objects served as exchange items in marriage alliances between the clan of the wife-taker and that of the wife-giver. The complicated exchanges included "female" gifts from the wife-givers's clan: finely woven sarongs, gold filigree earrings, necklaces of Venetian and chalcedony beads, armbands cut from shell and a variety of garden produce. The wife-taker's presents were "male" gifts of greater prestige value: ivory tusks, metal earrings, swords, palm brandy, pigs, and fish, but the most important were gold pendants with thick chains and clasps. These pendants were almost always adorned with a human face, sometimes complemented by horns, boats, half-moon motifs or, occasionally, an animal such as a turtle.

The binding of noble families with commoner households through complicated exchange pathways was based on wife-giving and wife-taking, with what one commentator has called the "life blood" flowing in the wife-

takers' direction. The lion's share of the best gold pieces was controlled by the richest nobles. The precious metal objects were the tangible highlights of lavish state visits which took place every decade or so to renew mutual defense pacts between allied villages.

The Tanimbar aristocrats, like their counterparts in the megalithic cultures of Nias, Sumba and Flores, competed with each other in lavish displays of wealth. But on Tanimbar, writes Forbes, they "went about the business of regal one-upmanship with particular verve." Dressed in gray coats with all the important gold pieces of their respective villages underneath, they strutted and "flashed their gold at each other in the ultimate test of rank and power." Surely this ranks among the most magnificent of the many ostentatious displays devised by the rulers of eastern Indonesia.

Metal and metalworking was associated with the supernatural, and high social status, on Tanimbar as well as in the Indies' other megalithic cultures. As there was no indigenous gold on Tanimbar, the metal had to be imported. Supplies came from three sources: Tanimbar merchant-sailors who acquired the metal in their trade with other islands in the Moluccas; Makassarese and Buginese who traded gold for shells and *trepang;* and later, Dutch and English ships seeking spices.

Gold was imported either in the form of finished jewelry or coins. These coins, and at times the jewelry, were melted down by local smiths, recast and worked into the local, raised motif style. The Tanimbarese were stung once with fake gold from Singapore, traded by a Dutch ship. Decades later, they refused real gold sovereigns naturalist H.O. Forbes tried to exchange here for supplies.

Treasure baskets

Some of the ancient gold pieces form part of the set of core heirlooms which, because of their association with power and ancestors, cannot be alienated from a clan. Stored in baskets and accompanied by stirring histories, these treasures can be viewed by visitors— for a fee. Before the basket is opened, prayers and palm wine (recently, beer) are offered to the ancestors.

Each piece is carefully unwrapped and revealed, one at a time. If one's knowledge of Indonesian is up to it, the story of each item and its pedigree will be recounted: who originally owned and deposited the items, and that person's accomplishments in life, including feats of war. In addition to the gold jewelry, the baskets contain antique porcelain, ivory bracelets, ancient beads, and carved tortoise-

Opposite: *A small village on the coast of Yamdena Island.* **Below:** *Teenagers pose under a cliffside statue of the Virgin Mary near Saumlaki. Most Tanimbarese are Christians, although ancestral beliefs remain strong.*

shell combs—some crumbling with age. Everything can be photographed, but can be worn only by someone in the clan's blood lines. Should an outsider be so presumptuous to put on the treasures, he would fall sick, a victim of the anger of the ancestral spirits.

After the visitor has seen the objects, they—as well as the basket and everyone's head—are rubbed with coconut oil to calm the spirits who had been keeping an eye on their possessions. A prayer is offered to the Christian God, just in case.

Antique jewelry or old wood carvings are difficult to purchase here, even for thousands of dollars. These and other ancient objects possess supernatural powers and, treated properly, the power of ancestors works

through the heirlooms to keep the living in good health and bless them with abundant harvests. Back in Forbes' time ancestral skulls were kept in homes to ward off evil. The graves of powerful aristocrats, replete with human figures shooting guns or gesticulating wildly, also served to keep nefarious forces safely at bay.

Although museum pieces are difficult to obtain, there are well-made local souvenirs available to anyone. Colorful cloths, woven on backstrap looms, go for $10–$30, less than half the price in Ambon. Small woodcarvings of human figures, usually with very thin, graceful limbs, can be had for $3–$10, depending on size. These carvings come

from the village of Tumbur and are brought to Saumlaki for sale. The Catholic Church, to its credit, started this cottage industry a few years ago and markets some of the better figures in Holland.

Young artisans are picking up the carving tradition of their forefathers, which had been dormant for generations. In the old days, Tanimbar artists carved beautiful figureheads on their outrigger *prahus,* intricate patterns on the central pillars of their houses and powerful ancestral figures.

Dance and ritual

The Tanimbar islanders have kept many of their old rituals and dances alive. Dancing is still an integral part of planting and harvest celebrations, weddings and funerals. Some of the old inter-village alliances are still strong, and these are celebrated occasionally with ritual dances and gift exchanges.

At the end of October in every odd-numbered year, a series of stunning dances conclude the Catholic retreat and conference at Saumlaki. At the local high school, the Church has organized a dance team, in an effort to ensure that the youth will not neglect their cultural heritage. Indonesian independence day, August 17, is celebrated each year with songs and dances from the past, and the appointment of a new village chief triggers a celebration.

If the traveler does not have the good luck of having his visit coincide with a ritual, splendid dances with up to 60 participants can easily be organized with one or two days' notice for a very reasonable fee ($30–$100). Visitors who leave their portable tape recorders at home do so at the risk of extreme frustration—the songs accompanying the dances are masterpieces of lively and distinct harmonies and rhythms.

Megalithic remains

Tanimbar's ancient beliefs, partially followed today, link the southern Moluccas with other megalithic cultures in the archipelago. This interrupted chain starts in Nias, off Sumatra, skips to central Sulawesi and down to Flores and Sumba, and ends in the easternmost Moluccas.

The village of Sanglia Dol, on Yamdena's east coast, holds some of the area's best megalithic remains. A monumental stone staircase, 50 meters long, reaches up some 30 meters from the beach to the village overlooking the sea. Unfortunately, the head of a human figure, carved of stone and guarding the foot of the staircase, has recently been "lost." But the best surprise awaits at the top of the stairs: a large, raised stone platform with the flowing lines of a boat. This stone ship measures 18 meters bow to stern, and 8 meters in beam.

The megalith sits in the village square and its stone prow, intricately carved and with a graceful upward sweep, face the sea. In former days, ritual offerings were made here to Ubila'a, the supreme deity, prior to war raids and when alliances were renewed. The boat-shaped stone altars or platforms, called *natar,* had once been a feature of every Tanimbar village, but most have been allowed to decay. Sanglia Dol's Catholic citizens have lovingly maintained their *natar* and still hold occasional rituals there. There may be a fee ($3–$6) to photograph the platform. Great dances are held here, with a day or two's notice and about $55 for the dancers.

Although Sanglia Dol is one of the most traditional villages in Tanimbar, even her dead are no longer placed in the traditional boat-shaped coffins. These coffins, as well as the boat-shaped platforms, were used in the past to commemorate the arrival of the clans' founders. Sanglia Dol's houses are of "modern" design: cracked bamboo walls and thatch roofing—or tin sheets if the owner can afford them. The high huts on stilts, with a trapdoor entry at the bottom, went out of fashion when the head-hunting stopped. Most of the villages have also left their elevated, defensive positions for the more convenient seaside, just below their former homes.

Local industry in Tanimbar

The pearling operations and the general economy of south Tanimbar is run by some 30 Indonesian-Chinese families. The earliest of these merchants arrived just ahead of the Dutch administration during the first decade of this century. The Chinese settled and quickly took over commerce from the Buginese and Arab sailors who, according to Mrs. Forbes, exchanged ivory and gold for *trepang* and tortoiseshell. Although tending to marry among themselves, the Chinese seem well integrated into the community. All of the well-stocked stores on Saumlaki's main street are owned and operated by them. They also buy the copra crop, which is the mainstay of the economy and the sole source of cash income for most local families: some $400 to $600 a year.

The crucial *lontar* palm—here called *koli*—provides palm wine, locally called

sagero. This toddy is also distilled into a fierce brandy called *sopi.* These local drinks are not often seen in Saumlaki, but in the surrounding villages they provide happiness and many headaches.

Well-kept gardens provide the Tanimbars' staple sweet potatoes and manioc, as well as beans, corn, onions and leaf vegetables. The forests are beginning to yield a lumber crop, prepared at the local sawmill for shipping to Surabaya. Ironwood and a yellowish wood used for dye-making in Java are exported.

The local harvest from the sea includes many delicious varieties of fish. Little two-meter sailing canoes return after a couple of hours' work with a veritable cornucopia: several kinds of fish, all neatly tied together by

species, and a large canvas bag filled with shrimp, crabs and a lobster or two. A bit is kept for the family and the rest is sold in the market, yielding perhaps $12.

Trepang heads the list of commercial crops from the sea. Several varieties of shells, including the important *Trochus* are sent to Ujung Pandang, some destined for abroad, the rest processed there into buttons and other mother-of-pearl items.

Opposite and **Above:** *Antique gold headpiece and necklace. The Tanimbars were famous for their goldsmiths, and the two pieces above, recast from coins and other gold pieces bought from traders, are of very high artistic quality.*

SOUTHWESTERN ISLANDS

The Most Isolated Part of Indonesia

Although lately a number of Moluccan islands have become increasingly attractive to European tourists and scientists, many inhabitants of the islands between Timor and Tanimbar have never seen an orang barat (Westerner) before. Partly this is because of the isolated position of these islands, and partly by the many years of struggle for independence in East Timor, which made the area inaccessible to strangers.

It is true that after the Dutch left in 1949, legends and calendars with white-faced biblical scenes kept the memory of Caucasians alive, but still the innocent westerner will clearly remember a visit to the islands, if only because of the reaction to his appearance.

The enthusiastic curiosity with which he is received in the dusty villages, almost all situated along the coast, makes him soon forget the inconveniences of the past several days spent aboard a rusty coaster from Ambon. Particularly if the landing, which requires riding through the breakers on a dugout canoe, goes smoothly. There are no airstrips on the islands, nor ports with quays. The coasters from anchor everywhere there are roads.

Unlike the Aru, Kai and Tanimbar Islands, which participated in archipelago-wide trade since before the arrival of the Dutch East India Company, the Southwestern Islands have never been economically important. Damar was the only spice producing island in the region, but since it was too small to exploit, and too far from their base to control to their satisfaction, the Dutch simply chopped down Babar's nutmeg trees.

Only Luang, surrounded by a girdle of magnificent coral islands, had some economic significance. Once a year the island was visited by Makassarese and Buginese, who were seeking profitable reef products such as *trepang*, and mother-of-pearl. Today, the situation remains basically the same. The Southwestern Islands do not have much to offer the world market.

Barren, dry islands

This unattractive economic situation cannot be divorced from the unfortunate geography and climate of these islands. Most are raised coral limestone, barren, infertile and barely forested. The limited annual rainfall threatens to transform already eroded islands like Leti and Luang into empty moonscape. During the dry season—from October to December—some of the islands take on the appearance of a scorched savanna, most unusual for this part of the world.

Because of the lack of water, the islanders seasonally rely on drinking the sap of the drought-resistant *lontar* palm (*Borassus sundaicus*). Worrying every year whether the drought will spoil the corn crop is not the kind of thing that makes one very cheerful.

Considering this, it is hardly surprising that the islanders have so many rituals designed to bring about rain. The methods vary from simply sprinkling water onto their children to lavish dances. Ancestor worship plays a key part in these ceremonies.

This continues despite the presence of ministers belonging to the Gereja Protestan Maluku, the Protestant Moluccan Church, from which all the islanders are at least nominally members. But prudence perhaps justifies this departure from Christian dogma. If the rain waits too long to come, after the corn has been planted at the end of the dry season, famine is unavoidable.

These rain-making rituals are pale reminders of the grand fertility feasts that were held in these islands up until the beginning of the 20th century. Although the performance differed somewhat on each island, all the people of the region shared a core world view. The mythology that shaped the feasts was this: Heaven was considered to be male, with rain the analog of sperm. This would fertilize the earth, which like in most other cultures, was taken to be female.

The correct performance of such a feast, which would go on for months, often required a human head, or even more than one. Although the inhabitants of the Southwestern islands usually organized head-hunting raids to Wetar for this purpose, they sometimes made do with a head obtained by mere chance. Knowledge of this practice, made the few traders who plied the region change course when they approached these islands,

Opposite: *A journey to the southwestern islands is an unforgettable adventure.*

and up until the beginning of the 20th century the region was considered very dangerous for travelers.

'The Far Southeast'

The isolation of what the Ambonese call Tenggara Jauh, the "Far Southeast," continues today. On average, once a month, a freighter leaves Ambon for the Southwest Islands. Stalls on board the boat offer the people of the anchorage the opportunity to buy modern goods: usually a garment, a plastic bucket or some batteries for the radio, an important status symbol in many villages.

Money is scarce in the region due to the tradition of barter trade, which flourishes locally during the change of the monsoons. During the west monsoon, from December to March, and the east monsoon, from April to October, the seas are very difficult to navigate in the small village *prahus*.

After first filling up the water supply in Saumlaki on Tanimbar, the coaster sets course for the Southwestern islands. The Babar archipelago is called at first; from here the boat navigates for about a week in a big loop along Luang–Sermata, the Leti group, Kisar, Wetar, Roma and Damar.

The Babar archipelago

This little archipelago is made up of six islands, five of them no bigger than pinheads. The name has nothing to do will the small French elephant so well-known in Europe, although elephant tusks do belong to the sacred objects of some families.

Economically, the archipelago is self-supporting. Babar, the largest and central island, is relatively fertile and, if it rains, even disposes of a surplus of corn, the staple food. This is exchanged for articles coming from the surrounding rocky islands, every single one known for a specific product.

Approximately 17,000 people live on the Babar islands, in 46 villages, the largest of which is Tepa. Many of these villages are arranged according to a spatial structure that goes back to Dongson culture. The village is laid out as a ship sailing west. The families living within the villages have symbolic roles, reflected in the position of their houses: the helmsman, living on the east side, the bailer, in the middle, and the pilot, whose family lives in the front (i.e., on the western side). Some of the villages on other Southwestern islands have, or have had, similar symbolism.

In the past, the people of Babar were warlike enough to almost match prevailing colonial standards. One English trading vessel was boarded here, and its entire crew dispatched. Right through the nineteenth century, the Dutch had little control over what one report called Babar's "unruly natives."

Around New Year in every village a great feast is held, which is quite reminiscent of the early fertility feasts. Traditional dances are performed, and in the beginning the ancestral spirits are welcomed to the celebration. The aim has remained the same throughout the years: a big yield of fish and palm wine, but especially, lots of children.

Should you want to visit Babar, there is a 12 room *losmen,* the Sumber Jaya, in the sub-district capital of Tepa. All facilities enclosed, $6. From Tepa there are occasional local ships to Yamdena on Tanimbar, where there are three weekly flights to Ambon.

Luang and Sermata

To the west of the Babar archipelago, and part of the same subdistrict—Kecamatan Pulau-Pulau Babar—are Luang and Sermata. Some 3,500 people live here, divided by the flat Pulau Kelapa, "Coconut Island." On these islands, a traditional caste system still dominates social relations.

Members of the Luang island nobility emphasize the importance of their island as the "cultural center" of the region. Proof offered for this is the distribution of the island's language, the Lteri Lgona, which is spoken from West Babar to Kisar. Undoubtedly this distribution is closely connected with the character of Luang's economy.

The people of Luang are, compared to the inhabitants of the other Southwestern islands, a relatively rich seafaring people. The barren soil makes agriculture pointless, and the men therefore concentrate on trade. Like the other islanders, they are supported by their wives, in the case of Luang however, the women weave *ikat* fabric for export instead of planting corn. Trade earnings are considerble, and already the first video cassette recorder in the area has arrived in Luang.

The Leti group

The islands of Leti, Moa and Lakor form a separate subdistrict, with the *kecamatan* capital in Serwaru on Leti. The villages on the three islands have a total of about 15,000 inhabitants. Like Luang, but hardly noticeable to the outsider, the caste system still functions here. All outer appearances have disappeared. Because of the arrival of western clothing, class can no longer be displayed, as it was in the past, in the length of the sarong or loin cloth. However, marriage between a member of the nobility and lower class is still virtually impossible.

Unlike the rest of the Southwestern islands, there is no bride price in these islands, and descent is matrilineal. After the wedding, the husband would traditionally move into his new wife's parental home. Now, however, the single-family dwelling is becoming popular, and couples live on their own. Still, children are born into their mother's family, not their father's.

The Leti group is well-known to western art-dealers. The ancestor sculptures of Lakor are renowned. With the arrival of missionaries, these masterpieces have become very scarce. Today, a sculpture—it it hasn't been burned or cast into the sea by the minister—will bring thousands of dollars.

Kisar

Kisar is the only major southwestern island that is primarily Islamic, instead of Christian. Wonreli, on Kisar, is the principal town of the Terselatan Islands, which include Wetar, Roma and Damar. The *kecamatan* has some 20,000 people. Kisar is well-known for its islanders with reddish-blond hair and western looks, the so-called "mestizos," descendants of 19th century European soldiers.

The village of Oirata on Kisar is quite special, as it is a Timorese settlement where a non-Austronesian language is spoken, a holdover from the region's aboriginal people. Kisar is also known for very old and unique textile designs. The *ikat* woven here features animal, human, and bird-with-rider themes, with bright colors and stripes. A special cloth, *kain sinun,* features a tree of life and a man with upraised arms, in dark blue or black.

Opposite: *Fishing by torchlight in the shallows off Babar.* **Right:** *Traditional weaving still brings income in parts of the Southwest Islands.*

Wetar

From time immemorial Wetar has been called at especially for beeswax. (In addition to heads, of course, which were needed for the great fertility feasts). The wax was used to build molds for casting jewelry, using the lost-wax technique. The number of goldsmiths on the Southwestern islands has diminished and so has the number of gold objects. These ornaments, like the ancestor sculptures, are extremely popular with western collectors, and to protect these items of cultural value, there is even an official ban on exports.

Wetar is now undergoing dramatic changes, thanks to a gold mine that recently started operations there.

Roma and Damar

Unlike the other Southwestern islands, which consist of raised coral, Roma and Damar are volcanic. Soil conditions are identical to those of Banda, and on Damar nutmeg was once the most important export products as well. To monopolize the spice trade, the V.O.C. cut down 3,000 nutmeg trees on the island in 1648. Naturally, this infuriated the the Damarese, but unlike the people of Banda, they were at least allowed to live.

Nowadays Damar, and to a lesser degree Roma, are famous for their hot springs, which are said to have a salutary effect on the skin.

—*Nico de Jonge*

NICO DE JONGE

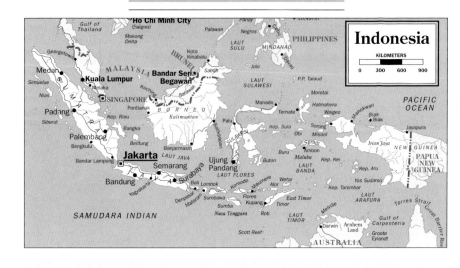

Indonesia At A Glance

The Republic of Indonesia is the world's fourth largest country, with 200 million people. The vast majority (88%) are Muslims, making this the world's largest Islamic country. More than 400 languages are spoken, but Bahasa Indonesia, a variant of Malay, is the national language.

The nation is a republic, headed by a strong President, with a 500-member legislature and a 1,000-member People's Consultative Assembly. There are 27 provinces and special territories. The capital is Jakarta, with 9 million people. The archipelago comprises just over 2 million sq km of land. Of 18,508 islands, about 6,000 are named, and 1,000 permanently inhabited.

Indonesia's $175 billion gross national product comes from oil, textiles, lumber, mining, agriculture, and manufacturing. The country's largest trading partner is Japan. Annual per capita income is $940. Much of the population still makes a living through agriculture, chiefly rice. The unit of currency is the rupiah, which trades at approximately 2,400 to US$1 (1997).

Historical overview. The Buddhist Sriwijaya empire, based in southeastern Sumatra, controlled parts of western Indonesia from the 7th to the 13th centuries. The Hindu Majapahit kingdom, based in eastern Java, controlled even more between the 13th to the 16th centuries. Beginning in the mid-13th century, local rulers began converting to Islam.

In the early 17th century the Dutch East India Company (VOC) founded trading settlements and quickly wrested control of the Indies spice trade. The VOC was declared bankrupt in 1799, and a Dutch colonial government was established.

Anti-colonial uprisings began in the the early 20th century, when nationalism movements were founded by various Muslim, communist and student groups. Sukarno, a Dutch-educated nationalist, was jailed by the Dutch in 1930.

Early in 1942, the Dutch Indies were overrun by the Japanese army. Treatment by the occupiers was harsh. When Japan saw her fortunes waning toward the end of the war, Indonesian nationalists were encouraged to organize. On August 17, 1945, Sukarno proclaimed Indonesia's independence.

The Dutch sought a return to colonial rule after the war. Four years of fighting ensued between nationalists and the Dutch, and full independence was achieved in 1949.

During the 1950s and early 1960s, President Sukarno's government moved steadily to the left, alienating western governments. In 1963, Indonesia took control of Irian Jaya and began a period of confrontation with Malaysia.

On September 30, 1965 the army put down an attempted coup attributed to the communist party. Several hundred thousand people were killed as suspected communists.

In the following years, the powers of the presidency gradually shifted away from Sukarno and General Suharto became president in 1968. His administration has been friendly to Western and Japanese investment and the nation has enjoyed three decades of solid economic growth.

MISS YOUR LOVED ONES BACK HOME?
PUT YOURSELF IN THE PICTURE WITH 001

When you're far away from home, nothing brings you closer to loved ones than a phone call. And it's so easy with 001. Indosat offers International Direct Dial to over 240 countries. Plus, you save 25% during discount hours on weekends*, and around the clock on national holidays and weekends. Call today, and share the good times!

IDD = **001** | COUNTRY CODE ▸ AREA CODE ▸ TELEPHONE NUMBER

From Hotel = HOTEL ACCESS CODE ▸ **001** | COUNTRY CODE ▸ AREA CODE ▸ TELEPHONE NUMBER

001 I D D   **NUMBER ONE** 〰 **INDOSAT**

* For information, call 102.

PERIPLUS TRAVEL MAPS
Detailed maps of the Asia Pacific region

This five-year program was launched in 1993 with the goal of producing accurate and up-to-date maps of every major city and country in the Asia Pacific region. About 12 new titles are published each year, along with numerous revised editions. Titles in **BOLDFACE** are already available (32 titles in mid-1996). Titles in *ITALICS* are scheduled for publication in 1997.

INDIVIDUAL COUNTRY TITLES
Australia	ISBN 962-593-150-3
Burma	ISBN 962-593-070-1
Cambodia	ISBN 0-945971-87-7
China	ISBN 962-593-107-4
Hong Kong	ISBN 0-945971-74-5
Indonesia	ISBN 962-593-042-6
Japan	ISBN 962-593-108-2
Malaysia	ISBN 962-593-043-4
Nepal	ISBN 962-593-062-0
New Zealand	ISBN 962-593-092-2
Singapore	ISBN 0-945971-41-9
Thailand	ISBN 962-593-044-2
Vietnam	ISBN 0-945971-72-9

AUSTRALIA REGIONAL MAPS
Brisbane	ISBN 962-593-049-3
Cairns	ISBN 962-593-048-5
Darwin	ISBN 962-593-089-2
Melbourne	ISBN 962-593-050-7
Perth	ISBN 962-593-088-4
Sydney	ISBN 962-593-087-6

CHINA REGIONAL MAPS
Beijing	ISBN 962-593-031-0
Shanghai	ISBN 962-593-032-9

INDONESIA REGIONAL MAPS
Bali	ISBN 0-945971-49-4
Bandung	ISBN 0-945971-43-5
Batam	ISBN 962-593-144-9
Bintan	ISBN 962-593-139-2
Jakarta	ISBN 0-945971-62-1
Java	ISBN 962-593-040-x
Lake Toba	ISBN 0-945971-71-0
Lombok	ISBN 0-945971-46-x
Medan	ISBN 0-945971-70-2
Sulawesi	ISBN 962-593-162-7
Sumatra	ISBN 0-945971-47-8
Surabaya	ISBN 0-945971-48-6

Tana Toraja	ISBN 0-945971-44-3
Ujung Pandang	ISBN 962-593-138-4
Yogyakarta	ISBN 0-945971-42-7

JAPAN REGIONAL MAPS
Kyoto	ISBN 962-593-143-0
Osaka	ISBN 962-593-110-4
Tokyo	ISBN 962-593-109-0

MALAYSIA REGIONAL MAPS
Kuala Lumpur	ISBN 0-945971-75-3
Malacca	ISBN 0-945971-77-x
Johor Bahru	ISBN 0-945971-98-2
Penang	ISBN 0-945971-76-1
West Malaysia	ISBN 962-593-129-5
Sabah	ISBN 0-945971-78-8
Sarawak	ISBN 0-945971-79-6

NEPAL REGIONAL MAP
Kathmandu	ISBN 962-593-063-9

THAILAND REGIONAL MAPS
Bangkok	ISBN 0-945971-81-8
Chiang Mai	ISBN 0-945971-88-5
Phuket	ISBN 0-945971-82-6
Ko Samui	ISBN 962-593-036-1

Distributed by:

Berkeley Books Pte. Ltd.
(Singapore & Malaysia)
5 Little Road, #08-01, Singapore 536983
Tel: (65) 280 3320 Fax: (65) 280 6290

C.v. Java Books (Indonesia)
Jl. Kelapa Gading Kirana
Blok A-14 No. 17, Jakarta 14240
Tel: (62-21) 451 5351 Fax: (62-21) 453 4987

Practicalities

TRAVEL ADVISORY, TRANSPORTATION, AREA PRACTICALITIES

The following On The Road sections contain all the practical knowledge you need for your journey. **Travel Advisory** provides all the non-transport information: facts about Indonesia, from the economy and health precautions to bathroom etiquette. It is followed by a handy language primer. **Transportation** section deals exclusively with transportation: getting to Indonesia and traveling in Maluku.

The **Practicalities** sections focus on each destination and have all the local details on transport, accommodation, dining, the arts, trekking, shopping and services, plus maps. These sections are organized by area and correspond to Parts II to VII in the first half of the guide. The margin tabs make cross-referencing simple and fast.

Ambon 1
Lease 2

Seram 3
Banda 4
Ternate 5
Halmahera 6
Southeast 7

Travel Advisory

TOURIST INFORMATION

Overseas, you can contact the Indonesian embassy or consulate, or one of the following **Indonesia Tourist Promotion Board** offices:
ASEAN & Southeast Asia, 10 Collyer Quay #15–07, Ocean Building, Singapore 0104. ☎ (65) 534-2837, 534-1795. Fax: (65) 533-4287.
Australia & New Zealand, Level 10, 5 Elizabeth Street, Sydney NSW 2000, Australia. ☎ (61 2) 233-3630. Fax: (61 2) 233-3629, 357-3478.
Europe, Wiesenhuttenstrasse 17, D-6000 Frankfurt/Main 1, Germany. ☎ (49 169) 233-677. Fax: (49 169) 230-840.
Japan & Korea, Sankaido Building, 2nd Floor, 1-9-13 Ahasaka, Minatoku, Tokyo 107. ☎ (81 3) 3585-3588. Fax: (81 3) 3582-1397.
North America , 3457 Wilshire Boulevard, Los Angeles, CA 90010-2203. ☎ (213) 387-2078. Fax: (213) 380-4876.
Taiwan & Hong Kong, 66 Sung Chiang Road, 5th Floor, Taipei, Taiwan. ☎ (886 2) 537-7620. Fax: (886 2) 537-7621.
United Kingdom, Ireland, Benelux & Scandinavia, 3–4 Hanover Street, London W1R 9HH. ☎ (44 171) 493-0334. Fax: (44 171) 493-1747.

The **Directorate General of Tourism** in Jakarta has brochures and maps on all Indonesian provinces: Jl. Kramat Raya 81, PO Box 409, Jakarta 10450. ☎ (021) 310-3117/9. Fax: (021) 310-1146.

Local government tourism offices, *Dinas Pariwisata*, are generally only good for basic information. More useful assistance is often available from privately run (but government approved) **Tourist Information Services**. Be aware that many offices calling themselves "Tourist Information" are simply travel agents.

In Maluku, the main office is: **Maluku Regional Tourist Office**. PO Box 1112, Ambon. ☎ (0911) 52471. Faces the Governor's office building; use the entrance on Jl. Sultan Hairun, in front of Restaurant Halim. The tourist office is behind the first door on the right of the ground floor.

VISAS

Nationals of the following 46 countries do not need visas, and are granted visa-free entry for 60 days upon arrival at major gateways.

Argentina	Iceland	Philippines
Australia	Ireland	Saudi Arabia
Austria	Italy	Singapore
Belguim	Japan	South Korea
Brazil	Kuwait	Spain
Brunei	Liechtenstein	Sweden
Canada	Luxembourg	Switzerland
Chile	Malaysia	Taiwan
Denmark	Maldives	Thailand
Egypt	Malta	Turkey
Finland	Mexico	United Arab
France	Monaco	Emirates
Germany	Morocco	United Kingdom
Greece	Netherlands	United States
Hungary	New Zealand	Venezuela
	Norway	Yugoslavia

Be sure to check your passport before leaving for Indonesia. You must have at least one empty page to be stamped upon arrival and the passport must be valid for at least six months after the date of arrival. For visa-free entry, you must also have proof of onward journey, either a return or through ticket. Employment is strictly forbidden on tourist visas or visa-free entry.

Visa-free entry to Indonesia cannot be extended beyond two months (60 days) and cannot be converted to any other kind of visa.

A visa is required in advance for all other nationals or arrivals at minor gateways.

Upon arrival you will be given a white embarkation/disembarkation card to fill out. Keep this card with your passport as you must present it when leaving the country.

Other Visas

The 2-month, non-extendable tourist pass is the only entry permit that comes without a great deal of paperwork.

A social visa, usually valid for 4–5 weeks, can be extended for up to 6 months, but is difficult to get. You must have a good reason for being in Indonesia (relatives, language study), and a sponsor who will assume financial responsibility for you. The process can take days or even weeks, and extensions are at the discretion of the immigration office where you apply.

A business visa requires a letter from a company stating that you are performing a needed service for a company in Indonesia. It is valid for up to one year, but you must leave the country every 4 months. This is not intended as an employment visa, but is for investors, consultants, or other business purposes. You are not to earn money in Indonesia on a business visa.

Two other types of visas are available: the temporary residence card (KITAS) for research, formal study or employment, and the permanent residence card (KITAP). Both are difficult to get. When dealing with the authorities, be on your best behavior and dress appropriately. The Immigration Office in Ambon is on Jl. Dr. Kayadoe, ☎ 53066.

Customs

Narcotics, firearms and ammunition are strictly prohibited. The standard duty-free allowance is: 2 liters of alcoholic beverages, 200 cigarettes, 50 cigars or 100 grams of tobacco.

There is no restriction on import and export of foreign currencies in cash or travelers checks, but there is an export limit of 50,000 Indonesian rupiah.

All narcotics are illegal in Indonesia. The use, sale or purchase of narcotics results in long prison terms, huge fines and death, in some cases. Once caught, you are immediately placed in detention until trial, and the sentences are stiff, as demonstrated by Westerners currently serving sentences as long as 30 years for possession of marijuana.

FOREIGN EMBASSIES & CONSULATES

All foriegn embassies are in Jakarta:
Australia Jl. H.R. Rasuna Said, Kav. C/15–16, ☎ 522-7111.
Austria Jl. P. Diponegoro No. 44, ☎ 338-090.
Belgium Jl. Jend. Sudirman, Kav. 22–23, ☎ 571-0510.
Brunei Darussalam Jl. Jend. Sudirman, Kav. 22–23, ☎ 571-2180.
Canada Wisma Metropolitan I, 15th Floor, Jl. Jend. Sudirman, Kav. 29, ☎ 525-0709.
China Jl. Jend. Sudirman, Kav. 69, ☎ 714-596.
Denmark Bina Mulia Bldg., 4th Floor, Jl. H.R. Rasuna Said, Kav. 10, ☎ 520-4350.
Finland Bina Mulia Bldg., 10th Floor, Jl. H.R. Rasuna Said, Kav. 10, ☎ 516-980.
France Jl. M.H. Thamrin No. 20, ☎ 314-2807.
Germany Jl. Raden Saleh 54-56, ☎ 384-9547.
Greece Jl. Kebon Sirih No. 16, ☎ 360-623.
India Jl. H.R. Rasuna Said No. S-1, ☎ 520-4150.
Italy Jl. Diponegoro 45, ☎ 337-445.
Japan Jl. M.H. Thamrin No. 24, ☎ 324-308.
Malaysia Jl. H.R. Rasuna Said Kav. X/6/1–3, ☎ 522-4947.
Myanmar Jl. H. Agus Salim No. 109, ☎ 314-0440.
Mexico Wisma Nusantara, 4th Floor, Jl. M.H. Thamrin No. 59, ☎ 337-479.
Netherlands Jl. H.R. Rasuna Said, Kav. S-3, ☎ 511-515.
New Zealand Jl. Diponegoro No. 41, ☎ 330-680.
Norway Bina Mulia Bldg. I, 4th Floor, Jl. H.R. Rasuna Said, Kav. 10, ☎ 525-1990.
Pakistan Jl.Teuku Umar No. 50, ☎ 314-4009.
Papua New Guinea Panin Bank Centre 6th Floor,

Jl. Jend. Sudirman No. 1, ☎ 725-1218.
Philippines Jl. Imam Bonjol No. 6–8, ☎ 314-9329.
Singapore Jl. H.R. Rasuna Said, Block X Kav. 2, No. 4, ☎ 520-1489.
South Korea Jl. Gatot Subroto, Kav. 57-58, ☎ 520-1915.
Spain Jl. Agus Salim No. 61, ☎ 331-414.
Sweden Bina Mulia Bldg. I, Jl. H.R. Rasuna Said, Kav. 10, ☎ 520-1551.
Switzerland Jl. H.R.Rasuna Said B-1, Kav. 10/32, ☎ 516-061.
Thailand Jl. Imam Bonjol No.74, ☎ 390-4055.
United Kingdom Jl. M.H. Thamrin No.75, ☎ 330904.
United States of America Jl. Medan Merdeka Selatan No. 5, ☎ 360-360.
Vietnam Jl. Teuku Umar No. 25, ☎ 310-0357.

Passport Loss

If you lose your passport, it will be difficult to get new documents to leave the country unless you have the proper official forms from the police. Always keep a photocopy of your passport, visa, driver's license and travelers check numbers (plus receipts) separate from the originals. You can then prove your identity in case of theft or loss.

Should theft occur, report to your consulate. Verification of your identity and citizenship takes two or three weeks and involves going to the immigration office in Ambon.

WHAT TO BRING ALONG

Pack light. The smaller flights only allow 10 kgs (22 lbs) of checked luggage. You can leave some of your stuff in Ambon, as you may pick up souvenirs and clothing in your travels. Keep in mind that you will be in the tropics, but that it can get cold in the mountains. Bring wash-and-wear, **light cotton clothes**. (Synthetic fabrics are really uncomfortable in the tropics.) A light rain jacket with a hood and a good sweater (it can get very cold at night at higher elevations, for example if you are climbing Gamalama) are also essential. Tennis shoes are fine for basic footwear, but if you plan to do any hiking you will need sturdy shoes or boots (depending on the difficulty of the trek). Bring a pair that is already broken in. Also, bring a cap to keep the sun off during long boat rides or walks.

Trekkers should pack a light sleeping bag and a lightweight tent, a sweater, compass, Swiss Army knife, portable kerosene stove, canteen, soap, toilet paper, and a mosquito net. Definitely, bring a good **medical kit** and scissors (to keep your beard trimmed).

Don't bring too much, as you will be tempted by the great variety of inexpensive clothes available here. For those wanting to travel light, a *sarong* ($5–10) is one of the most versatile items you could hope for. It serves as a wrap to get to the bath, a beach towel, pajamas, bed sheet, fast drying towel, etc.

If you visit a government office, men should wear long trousers, shoes and a shirt with collar. Women should wear a neat dress, covering knees and shoulders, and shoes.

Indonesians are renowned for their ability to sleep anytime, anywhere; so they are not likely to understand your desire for peace and quiet at night. Many consider sponge rubber **earplugs** the most important 4 grams they carry.

Pack spare **eyeglasses** or **contact lenses** and **medical prescriptions**, legible and with generic (not brand) names. There are no Western-style department stores in many parts of Maluku, so for things like **contact lens solutions, dental floss, tampons, sunscreen,** and **insect repellent**, if you think you might need them, pack them. Other useful items include a watch with **alarm**, a **money belt**, an English/Indonesian dictionary (easy to buy in Java and Bali), and snorkel equipment.

Tiny **padlocks** for use on luggage zippers are a handy deterrent to pilfering hands. Some come with combination locks. **Flashlights** and a small **umbrella** may come in handy, although these can easily be purchased locally.

Bring along some **pre-packaged alcohol towelettes** (swabs). These are handy for disinfecting your hands before eating, or after a trip to the *kamar kecil* (lavatory).

Passport photos may come in handy for applications/permits (for parks) or even as gifts.

On your travels you will meet people who are kind and helpful, yet you may feel too embarrassed to give money. In this kind of situation a small gift is appropriate. Chocolates, biscuits, pens, stationery from your hotel, even T-shirts with colorful logos, are appreciated.

CLIMATE

The seasonal weather in Central Maluku is completely different from western Indonesia. The northwest monsoon brings on the dry, hotter season from November to March. Temperatures can rise to an uncomfortable 38°C in the dry season (31.5°C average) and winds can reach 10–15 knots. The southeast monsoon, from May through August, brings rain, slightly cooler temperatures, and 5–10 knot winds.

During the rainy season, it often seems like the rain will never stop—some 3,360 mm of rain falls on Ambon in an average year. Temperatures drop as low as 18–20°C with a mean of 22.3°C.

The seas are calmest for boat travel and clearest for diving during October–November. Winds up to 30 knots can blow in February, causing plenty of discomfort in any kind of craft except the largest boats.

The general rule in Maluku is:

North of the equator: The northeast winds bring good weather from December to March, and the rains set in with the southeast winds from May to September.

South of the equator: From November to March, northern coastal areas suffer from unsettled weather when winds shift from west to northwest. But from May to September, east and southeast winds bring fine weather; September usually the most beautiful. The southern islands experience strong southeast winds and rain from April to September.

See individual practicality sections for area specific information.

PLANNING A TRIP TO MALUKU

Besides the weather, the most crucial factor in planning your trip is the amount of time available. Three or four days is enough time to look around Ambon, Saparua Island and southwestern Seram, and you could perhaps spend another two days in the Bandas or Ternate. But Maluku is a long way to travel to for just a few days.

If you want to visit places like the Keis or Tanimbars (which have landing fields), you should give yourself at least a week, probably more, from the time you get to Ambon. Flights are frequently cancelled and if you are counting on three flights a week, you might find that only one of them materializes. Where there are no landing fields, add a couple of extra weeks.

Unless you have a month or more, after touring Ambon and vicinity, you really should head either north or south, not both. The southern loop (linked by air) starts in the Bandas, goes on to Tual and ends in Saumlaki. A northern loop could include Bacan and/or the Sula Archipelago, Ternate, Tidore and the northern Halmahera.

However, if you are coming to Maluku only once, you should not miss the twin highlights: the Banda islands and Ternate. Both are easy to reach, have superb scenery and fine snorkeling and diving.

TIME ZONES

Maluku is on Eastern Indonesian Standard Time, the most easterly of Indonesia's three time zones, which is Greenwich mean time + 9 hours. It is one hour ahead of Ujung Pandang and Bali, and two hours ahead of Jakarta.

MONEY

Prices quoted in this book are intended as a general indication. They are quoted in US dollars because the rupiah is being allowed to devalue slowly, so prices stated in US dollars are more likely to remain accurate.

Standard **currency** is the Indonesian *rupiah*: Notes come in 50,000, 20,000, 10,000, 5,000,

1,000, 500 and 100 denominations. Coins come in denominations of 1,000, 500, 100, 50, 25, 10 and 5 rupiah. Unfortunately, the new coins are very similar in size, so look carefully. Coins below Rp50 are rarely available. In stores small change is often replaced by candies.

Banking

It is best to carry travelers' checks of two leading companies as sometimes, for mysterious reasons, a bank won't cash the checks of a company as well known as, say, American Express. U.S. dollars—checks and cash—are accepted in all banks which deal in foreign exchange, as are Australian dollars and (usually) Japanese yen, Deutsche marks, French and Swiss francs.

Although carrying cash can be a handy safety precaution as cash is still exchangeable should you lose your passport, carrying too much is not a good idea. Aside from the possible loss, banks won't take the bills unless they are crisp and clean.

State banks are open from 8am–3pm, Monday to Friday. Some private banks open also on Saturday until 11 am. The bank counters at major airports offer competitive rates. Bank lines in town can be long and slow; the best way to avoid a long wait is to arrive promptly at opening time, and don't go on Mondays.

Get a supply of Rp1,000 and Rp500 notes when you change money, as taxi drivers and vendors often do not have change for big bills. When traveling in the countryside, Rp100 notes are also useful.

Major **credit cards** may be accepted in some shops and hotels. Visa and MasterCard are the most frequently accepted.

There are no exchange controls and excess *rupiah* (bills only) can be freely reconverted at the airport.

Banking in Maluku

The only places in Maluku to change money in banks are Ambon and Ternate. Bank Central Asia (BCA) at Jl. Sultan Hairun 24 in Ambon is most frequently used by foreignors. It is best to change all the money you will need before leaving Ambon, even if this means carrying an unwieldy wad of cash.

In Ternate, a couple of banks also accept travelers' checks and foreign currency, but elsewhere, the only recourse is Chinese store owners who might change U.S. or Australian dollars for cash. The rates you will get under these circumstances, however, are not good.

Tax, service and tipping

Most larger hotels and restaurants charge 21% tax and service on top of your bill. Tipping is not a custom here, but it is appreciated for special services. Rp500 per bag is considered a good tip for roomboys and porters. Taxi drivers will want to round up to the nearest Rp500 or Rp1,000.

When tipping the driver of your rental car or a *pembantu* (housekeeper) of the house in which you've been a guest, fold the money and give it with the right hand only.

OFFICE HOURS

Government offices (except those in Jakarta which run on a five-day work week) are officially open Monday to Thursday, 8 am–2 pm, on Friday until 11 am, and Saturday until 1 pm. In large cities most private businesses are open 9 am –5 pm. Large stores from 9 am–9 pm; smaller shops close for a siesta at 1 pm and re-open at 6 pm.

COMMUNICATIONS

Mail

Indonesia's postal service is reliable, if not terribly fast. *Kilat* express service is only slightly more expensive and much faster. *Kilat khusus* (domestic special delivery) reaches its destination overnight. International express mail gets postcards and letters to North America or Europe in about 7 days from most cities.

Kantor pos (post office) branch outlets are in every little village and are open during regular government office hours. The main office in the larger towns and cities is open 8am–8pm, daily.

Post offices are often busy and sometimes it can be a tedious process to line up at one window for weighing and then another window for stamps. Hotels will normally sell stamps and post letters for guests or you can use private postal agents to avoid hassles. Look for the orange *Agen Kantor Pos* (postal agency) signs.

Poste Restaunte service is usually reliable, but it is advisable to choose the office in Ambon Town (Jl. Raya Pattimura, ☎ 52965), rather than one in a remote village.

Telephone and Fax

Long distance phone calls, both within Indonesia and international, are handled by satellite. Domestic long distance calls can be dialed from most phones. To dial your own international calls, find an IDD (International Direct Dial) phone and dial "001" or "008," otherwise you must call via the operator, which is far more expensive.

A magnetic debit (*kartu telpon*) phone card can be purchased at hotels, post offices and many other outlets. Card phones, which are increasingly popular, eliminate the need for small change.

If your hotel has no IDD link then go to the main telephone office (*kantor telepon*) or use a private postal and telephone service: *Wartel* (*warung telekommunikasi)/warpostel/warparpostel.* These small "telecom shops" are all over Indonesia and fast becoming the most convenient way to call international (you avoid hotel price hikes). They are often run by well-trained, efficient staff and offer fast IDD services at near standard rates. Open daily from 8 am to 10 pm or 11 pm; some in larger cities open 24 hours. Prices per minute are about $2.30 to the Americas and $3.10 to most European countries. Night rates are slightly lower.

International calls via MCI, Sprint, ATT, and the like can be made from IDD phones using the access code for your calling card company. Recently, special telephones have been installed in Indonesia's airports with pre-programmed buttons to connect you via these companies to various countries.

Faxes can be sent and received at *wartel* offices and most main post offices.

Courier Services

Some of the big international courier outfits operate in Indonesia, along with some domestic ones. DHL Worldwide Express and Elteha International are probably the most reliable here. **DHL**. Jl. Sultan Babullah SK 42/15. ☎ 56634, 51159.
Senawangi Sempati. ☎ 45150.
Elteha International. ☎ 55568.

ELECTRICITY

Most of Indonesia has converted to 220 volts and 50 cycles, though a few places are still on the old 110 lines. Ask before you plug in if you are uncertain. Power failures are common. Voltage can fluctuate considerably so use a stabilizer for computers and similar equipment. Plugs are of the European two-pronged variety.

HEALTH

Before You Go

Check with your physician for the latest news on the kind of malaria prophylaxis and recommended **vaccinations** before leaving home. Frequently considered vaccines are: Diphtheria, Pertussis and Tetanus (DPT); Measles, Mumps and Rubella (MMR); and oral Polio vaccine. Gamma Globulin every four months for Hepatitis A is recommended. For longer stays many doctors recommend vaccination to protect against Hepatitis B requiring a series of shots over the course of 7 months. Vaccinations for smallpox and cholera are no longer required, except for visitors coming from infected areas. A cholera vaccination is recommended for travel in outlying areas, but it is only 50% effective.

Find out the generic names for whatever pre-

Telephone Codes

From outside Indonesia, the following cities may be reached by dialing 62 (the country code for Indonesia) then the city code, then the number. Within Indonesia, the city code must be preceded by a 0 (zero).

City	Code	City	Code
Ambon	911	Mataram	364
Balikpapan	542	Medan	61
Banda Aceh	651	Merauke	971
Bandar		Metro	725
Lampung	721	Mojokerto	321
Bandung	22	Nusa Dua	361
Banjarmasin	511	Padang	751
Banyuwangi	333	Palangkaraya	514
Batam	778	Palembang	711
Belawan	619	Palu	451
Bengkulu	736	Pare-Pare	421
Biak	961	Pasuruan	343
Binjai	619	Pati	295
Blitar	342	Pekalongan	285
Bogor	251	Pekanbaru	761
Bojonegoro	353	Pematang-	
Bondowoso	332	siantar	622
Bukittinggi	752	Ponorogo	352
Cianjur	263	Pontianak	561
Cilacap	282	Parapat	625
Cipanas	255	Probolinggo	335
Cirebon	231	Purwakarta	264
Cisarua	251	Purwokerto	281
Denpasar	361	Sabang	652
Gadog	251	Salatiga	298
Garut	262	Samarinda	541
Gresik	31	Sekupang	778
Jakarta	21	Semarang	24
Jambi	741	Serang	254
Jember	331	Sibolga	731
Jombang	321	Sidoarjo	319
Kabanjahe	628	Sigli	653
Karawang	267	Situbondo	338
Kebumen	287	Solo	271
Kediri	354	Sorong	951
Kendal	294	Sukabumi	266
Kendari	401	Sumbawa	
Klaten	272	Besar	371
Kota Pinang	624	Sumedang	261
Kotabaru	518	Surabaya	31
Kutacane	629	Tangerang	21
Kuala Simpang	641	Tapak Tuan	656
Kudus	291	Tarakan	551
Kupang	380	Tasikmalaya	265
Lahat	731	Tebing Tinggi	
Lhok Seumawe	645	Deli	621
Lumajang	334	Ternate	921
Madiun	351	Tulung Agung	355
Magelang	293	Ujung Pandang	411
Malang	341	Wates	274
Manado	431	Wonosobo	286
Manokwari	962	Yogyakarta	274

scription medications you are likely to need as most are available in Indonesia but not under the same brand names as they are known at home. Get copies of doctors' prescriptions for the medications you bring into Indonesia to avoid questions at the customs desk. Those who wear spectacles should bring along prescriptions.

First Aid Kit

A basic first aid kit should consist of aspirin and multivitamins, a decongestant, an antihistamine, disinfectant (such as Betadine), antibiotic powder, fungicide, an antibiotic eyewash, Kaopectate or Lomotil, and sunscreen. Also good strong soap, perhaps Betadine or other antiseptic soap. Avoid oral antibiotics unless you know how to use them. For injuries, make up a little kit containing Band-Aids and ectoplast strips, a roll of sterile gauze and treated gauze for burns, surgical tape, and an elastic bandage for sprains. Also very important are Q-tips, tweezers, scissors, needles, and safety pins. Keep your pills and liquid medicines in small unbreakable plastic bottles, clearly labeled with indelible pen.

Hygiene

Hygeiene cannot be taken for granted in Indonesia. Few places away from the tourist areas have running water or sewerage. Most water comes from wells and raw sewerage goes into the ground or the rivers. Tap water is not potable and must be boiled.

Most cases of stomach complaints are attributable to your system not being used to the strange foods and stray bacteria. To make sure you do not get something more serious, take the following precautions:

☛ Never drink unboiled water from a well, tap or *bak mandi* (bath tub). Brush your teeth only with boiled or bottled water, never with water from the tap or *bak mandi*. Bottled water is available everywhere and usually called "Aqua", which is the most popular and reliable brand name.

☛ Ice is made in government regulated factories and is deemed safe for local immunities. Confirm that the ice is made from boiled water before relaxing with an ice drink.

☛ Plates, glasses and silverware are washed in unboiled water and need to be completely dry before use.

☛ Fruits and vegetables without skins pose a higher risk of contamination. To avoid contamination by food handlers, buy fruits in the market and peel them yourself.

☛ To *mandi* (bathe) two or three times a day is a great way to stay cool and fresh. But be sure to dry yourself off well and you may wish to apply a medicated body powder such as Purol to avoid the unpleasantness of skin fungus, especially during the rainy season.

Exposure

Many visitors insist on instant suntans, so over-exposure to the heat and sun are frequent health problems. Be especially careful on long boat rides where the roof gives a good view. The cooling wind created by the boat's motion disguises the fact that you are frying like an egg. Wear a hat, loose-fitting, light-colored, long-sleeved cotton clothes, pants, and use a good-quality sunscreen (bring a supply with you). Do not wear synthetic fibers that do not allow air to circulate. Tan slowly—don't spoil your trip. Drink plenty of fluids and take salt.

Cuts and Scrapes

Your skin will come into contact with more dirt and bacteria than it does at home, so wash your face and hands more often. Cuts should be taken seriously and cleaned with an antiseptic like Betadine or Dettol, available from any pharmacy (*apotik*). Once clean, antibiotic powder (*Sulfanilamide*) or ointment, both available locally, should be applied. Cover the cut during the day to keep it clean, but leave it uncovered at night and whenever you are resting so that it can dry. Constant covering will retain moisture in the wound and only encourage an infection. Repeat this ritual after every bath. Areas of redness around the cut indicate infection and a doctor should be consulted. At the first sign of swelling it is advisable to take broad spectrum antibiotics to prevent a really nasty infection.

Not every mosquito bite leads to malaria, but in the tropics a scratched bite or small abrasion can quickly turn into a festering ulcer. You must pay special attention to these. Apply calamine solution or Tiger Balm—a widely available camphorated salve—or some imitation thereof to relieve the itching. For light burns, use Aristamide or Bioplacenteron.

Diarrhea

A likely traveling companion. In addition to the strange food and unfamiliar micro-fauna, diarrhea is often the result of attempting to accomplish too much in one day. Taking it easy can be effective prevention. Before leaving home, ask around about what the latest and greatest of the many remedies are and bring some along. Imodium is locally available, as are activated carbon tablets (*Norit*) that will absorb the toxins giving you grief.

When it hits, it is usually self-limiting to two or three days. Relax, take it easy and drink lots of fluids, perhaps accompanied by rehydration salts such as Servidrat (local brands are *Oralit* and *Pharolit*). Especially helpful is water from the young coconut (*air kelapa muda*) or strong, unsweetened tea. The former is an especially pure anti-toxin. Get it straight from the coconut without sugar, ice or food color added. When you are ready, bananas, papayas, plain rice, crackers or dry biscuits, and *bubur* (rice porridge) are a good way to start. Avoid fried, spicy or heavy foods and dairy products for a while. If you continue to suffer for three days without relief, see a doctor.

Not all bouts of diarrhea mean dysentery. If you contract the latter, which is much more serious, you must seek medical help. Do this if your stools are mixed with blood and pus, are black, or you are experiencing severe stomach cramps and fever. If no medical help is available, try tetracycline and Diatab, effective for bacillary dysentery. If you feel no relief in a day or two, you may have the more serious amoebic dysentery which requires additional medication.

To prevent stomach problems, try to eat only thoroughly cooked foods, don't buy already peeled fruit, and stay away from unpasteurized dairy products. For constipation, eat a lot of fruit.

Intestinal Parasites

It is estimated that 80 to 90 percent of all people in Indonesia have intestinal parasites and these are easily passed on by food handlers. Short of fasting, prevention is difficult when away from luxury hotel restaurants, and even these are no guarantee. It's best to take care of parasites sooner rather than later by routinely taking a dose of anti-parasite medicine such as *Kombatrin* (available at all *apotik*) once a month during your stay and again when you get on the plane home.

If you still have problems when you get back, even if only sporadic, have stool and blood tests taken. If left untreated, parasites can cause serious damage.

Mosquito-Borne Diseases

Malaria is endemic in Maluku. It is worse along the coasts of some of the larger islands, particularly where it is swampy. It is less of a problem in the higher regions (although, the oft-heard rule of thumb that malarial mosquitos do not live at altitudes higher than 500 meters is simply not correct. People have gotten malaria at altitudes of 1,500 meters).

Malaria is caused by a protozoan, *Plasmodium*, which affects the blood and liver. The vector for this parasite is the *Anopheles* mosquito. After contracting malaria, it takes a minimum of six days—or up to several years—before symptoms appear.

If you are visiting Maluku, you *must* take malaria pills. Do not think that pills offer complete protection, however, as they don't. If you are pregnant, have had a splenectomy, have a weak immune system, or suffer from chronic disease, you should weigh carefully whether the trip is worth the risk.

Chloroquine phosphate is the traditional malaria prophylactic, but in the past 10–15 years, the effectiveness of the drug has deteriorated. Deciding on an appropriate anti-malarial is now more complicated. There are actually four forms of malaria: *Plasmodium vivax*, which is unpleasant and can lie dormant for 50 years or more, but is rarely fatal to healthy adults; *P. melariae*, which is the least serious variant; *P. ovale*, which is rare in Indonesia; and *P. falciparum*, which can be quickly fatal. *P. falciparum* is dominant in parts of Indonesia.

Malaria pills. As a prophylactic for travel, take two tablets of Chloroquine (both on the same day) once a week, and one tablet of Maloprim (pyrimethamine) once a week. Maloprim is a strong drug and not everybody can tolerate it. If you are planning on taking Maloprim for more than two months, it is recommended that you take a folic acid supplement, 6 mg a day, to guard against anemia. [**Note**: The anti-malarial drugs only work once the protozoan has emerged from the liver, which can be weeks after your return. You should continue on the above regimen for one month after returning.]

There is now widespread resistance to Chloroquine. Mefloquin (such as Larium) seems to be the most commonly used prophylaxis now. It has been shown effective, although unpleasant side effects have been demonstrated for it as well. Mefloquine is also very expensive, about $3 a tablet. However, it can be a lifesaver in cases of resistant *falciparum* infection.

These drugs are not available over-the-counter in most western countries (or, indeed, even behind the counter at most pharmacies), and if you visit a doctor, you may have trouble convincing him of what you need. Doctors in the temperate zones are not usually familiar with tropical diseases, and may even downplay the need to guard against them. Do not be persuaded. Try to find a doctor who has had experience in these matters.

You can also buy Chloroquine and Maloprim over-the-counter in Indonesia, for very little (a few dollars for a month's supply). Larium, however, may still be difficult to find. [**Note**: there is a non–chloroquine based drug sold in Indonesia called Fansidar. This drug is not effective against the resistant strains of *P. falciparum* and not for use as a prophylaxis.]

The antibiotic Doxycycline can also be used as a prophylaxis for short-term stays (2–6 weeks): 100 mg. once a day with food, starting 2 days before arrival and continued through 4 days after departure of the malarious area.

Treatment. Malaria in the early stages is very hard to distinguish from a common cold or flu. A person infected may just suffer from headache and nausea, perhaps accompanied by a slight fever and achiness, for as long as a week until the disease takes hold. When it does, the classic symptoms begin:

1) Feeling of intense cold, sometimes accompanied by shaking. This stage lasts from 30 minutes to two hours.

2) High fever begins and the victim feels hot and dry, and may vomit or even become delirious. This lasts 4–5 hours.

3) Sweating stage begins, during which the victim perspires very heavily and his body temperature begins to drop.

The classic fever/chill pattern is more likely to occur with people who are not taking prophylaxis. Those on a prophylaxis will have stronger "flu" symptoms (aches, nausea, headache).

If you think you have malaria, you should call on professional medical help immediately. A good medical professional is your best first aid. Only if you cannot get help, initiate the following treatment:

1) Take 4 Chloroquine tablets immediately.

2) 6 hours later, take 2 more Chloroquine tablets.

3) The next day, take 2 more.

4) The following day, take 2 more.

Note: If the Chloroquine treatment does not cause the fever to break within 24 hours, assume the infection is the very dangerous *P. falciparum* and begin the following treatment immediately:

1) Take 3 tablets (750 mg) of Mefloquine (Larium)

2) Six hours later, take 2 more tablets (500 mg) of Mefloquine.

3) After 12 hours—and only if you weigh 60 kg (130 lbs) or more—take one more tablet (250 mg) of Mefloquine.

The other mosquito concern is **dengue fever**, spread by the morning-biting *Aedes aegypti*, especially during the rainy season. The most effective prevention is not getting bitten; there is no prophylaxis for dengue. Dengue fever symptoms are headache, pain behind the eyes, high fever, muscle and joint pains, and a rash appearing between the third and fifth days of illness. Within days, the fever subsides and recovery is seldom hampered with complications. The more serious variant, dengue haemorrhagic fever (DHF), which can be fatal, may be the reaction of a secondary infection with remaining immunities following a primary attack.

Cases of **Japanese encephalitis**, a viral infection affecting the brain, have occured recently and are added cause to take protective measures against mosquito bites.

Prevention. Malaria, dengue fever, and Japanese encephalitis are carried by mosquitos. If you aren't bitten, you won't get the diseases.

1) While walking around, use a good quality mosquito repellent—be very generous with it—particularly around your ankles. Wear light-colored, long-sleeved shirts or blouses and long pants. (Effective insect repellent may be hard to find in Maluku, so bring some from home.)

Any chemical repellent containing deet (diethyl toluamide) should be applied with caution and never to the face. Application to clothing can be more effective. A local non-chemical solution is citronella mixed with eucalyptus oil (*minyak gosok, cap tawon*).

2) While eating or relaxing in one spot, burn mosquito coils. These are those green, slightly brittle coils of incense doped with pyrethrin that were banned in the United States some years ago. They last 6–8 hours and are quite effective. You will get used to the smell. (If you are worried about inhaling some of the poison they contain, re-read the classic symptoms of malaria above.) In Indonesia, the ubiquitous coils are called *obat nyamuk bakar*. Double Rabbit is one of the more reliable brands. (There are brands which do not contain pyrethum, so are ineffective.) In places where there is electricity, there is a smokeless repellent with a similar ingredient that is inserted into an electrical unit.

3) While sleeping, burn *obat nyamuk* and use a mosquito net. Some hotels have nets, but not many, so you should bring your own. If you set a couple of *obat nyamuk* coils going in strategic places when you go to sleep you will be protected. Remember that mosquitos like damp bathrooms—where few people bother to light a mosquito coil.

AIDS & Hepatitis B

Surprise! **Safe sex** is a good idea. HIV/AIDS documentation, awareness and education is just beginning and understanding of prevention and spread is still quite poor. Another area of concern is the Hepatitis B virus which affects liver function, is sometimes incurable and can lead to chronic liver inflammation. The prevalence of Hepatitis B in Indonesia is the basis for international concern over the ominous possibilities for the spread of the HIV virus, which is passed on in the same ways.

Medical Treatment

Pharmacies—*apotik*—in Ambon carry just about everything you might need. You can get malaria pills and an excellent anti-bacterial ointment called Bacitran. Tiger Balm is available everywhere in Asia and it is excellent for treating itching bites and muscle pains resulting from hiking or carrying a back pack. Mycolog is a brand of fungicide sold in Indonesia. Oral rehydration salts are usually sold in packets to be mixed with 200 ml of drinkable water. It's nearly impossible to purchase medicines or first aid supplies outside of larger towns.

In the larger towns, especially Ambon, there are decent government hospitals (*rumah sakit*) and medicines are widely available. Smaller villages only have government clinics (*puskesmas*), which are not equipped to deal with anything serious. Your hotel or losmen may be able to find you a doctor who speaks English.

Doctors and health care are quite inexpensive by western standards, but the quality leaves much to be desired. At least they're familiar with the symptoms and treatment of tropical diseases, which your family doctor at home might have tough time recognizing.

Consultations with doctors are very cheap in Indonesia, usually about $5–$8 for general practitioners, $8–$15 for specialists. If you check into a hospital in Ambon, get a VIP room ($20–$30 for everything—including doctors' fees—but not medicines) or a somewhat cheaper "Klas I" room. If you stay in a cheaper hospital room or a ward, your doctor will be some young, inexperienced kid, fresh out of medical school. Government hospitals, at provincial capital and district levels, have improved considerably since the late 1980s.

Misuse of antibiotics is still a concern in Indonesia. They should only be used for bacterial diseases and then for at least 10 to 14 days to prevent developing antibiotic resistant strains of your affliction. If an injection or antibiotics are prescribed, be sure it's necessary. Ensure syringes have never been used before or better yet, buy your own disposable one from an *apotik* (pharmacy) and take it to the clinic.

Emergency Medical Assistance

Even in the big cities outside of Jakarta, emergency care leaves much to be desired. Your best bet in the event of a life-threatening emergency or accident is to get on the first plane to Jakarta or Singapore. Contact your embassy or consulate by phone for assistance (see below). Medivac airlifts are very expensive ($26,000) and most embassies will recommend that you buy insurance to cover the cost of this when traveling extensively in Indonesia.

Insurance

Check your health insurance before coming to make sure you are covered. Travel insurance should include coverage of a medical evacuation to Singapore and a 24-hour worldwide phone number as well as some extras like luggage loss and trip cancellation.

AEA International Asia Emergency Assistance offers insurance packages for travelers and expatriates living in Asia. This well-respected outfit is considered to have the best response time and operation in Indonesia. AEA maintains 24-hour alarm centers in Jakarta, Bali, Singapore, Sydney, Bangkok, Hong Kong, Seoul, Beijing, and Ho Chi Minh City. Premium for one-year (approx. $125) is available for travelers and covers the cost of medical evacuation to Singapore and repatriation if recommended by the AEA doctor. Contact: **AEA International Pte. Ltd.**,331 North Bridge Road,

17th Floor, Odeon Towers, Singapore 0718. ☎ (65) 338 2311. Fax: (65) 338 7611.

International SOS Assistance Asia Pacific Regional Head Office: 10 Anson Road, #21–08/A International Plaza, Singapore 0207. ☎ (65) 221 3981. Fax: (65) 226 3937, telex: 24422 SOSAFE. Offers a range of emergency services worldwide. Numerous large corporate clients. Contact them for rates and types of coverage.

FOOD AND DRINK

Dehydration can be a serious problem, so drink lots of fluids. Symptoms are infrequent urination, deep yellow/orange urine, and headaches.

Tap water in Indonesia is not potable and should be brought to a full boil for ten minutes before being considered safe. Indonesians are themselves fussy about drinking water, so if you're offered a drink it is almost certainly safe.

Most Indonesians do not feel they have eaten until they have eaten rice. This is accompanied by side dishes, often just a little piece of meat and some vegetables with a spicy sauce. Other common items include *tahu* (tofu), *tempe* (soybean cake), and salted fish. Crispy fried tapioca crackers flavored with prawns and spices (*krupuk*) usually accompany a meal.

No meal is complete without *sambal*—a fiery paste of ground chili peppers with garlic, shallots, sugar, and sometimes soy sauce or fish paste. Fruit, especially pineapple and papaya, provide quick relief for a chili-burned mouth.

Cooking styles vary greatly from one region to another. The Sundanese of West Java are fond of raw vegetables, eaten with chili and fermented prawn paste (*lalab/sambal trasi*). Minihasan food in North Sulawesi is very spicy, and includes some interesting specialties: bat wings in coconut milk, *sambal* rat, and dog. In the more isolated parts of the archipelago, the food can be quite plain.

In most Indonesian restaurants there is a standard menu of *satay* (skewered barbequed meat)—most common are *ayam* (chicken) and *kambing* (goat)—*gado-gado* or *pecel* (steamed vegetables with spicy peanut sauce) and *soto* (vegetable soup with or without meat). Also common are Chinese dishes like *bakmie goreng* (fried noodles), *bakmie kuah* (noodle soup) and *cap cay* (stir-fried vegetables).

In most larger towns you can also find a number of Chinese restaurants on the main street. Some have menus with Chinese writing, but usually the cuisine is very much assimilated to local tastes. Standard dishes, in addition to the *bakmie* and *cap cay* mentioned above, are sweet and sour freshwater fish (*gurame asem manis*), beef with Chinese greens (*kailan/caisim ca sapi*), and prawns sauteed in butter (*udang goreng mentega*).

Indonesian fried chicken (*ayam goreng*) is common and usually very tasty—although the locally grown chicken can be a bit stringy. Then there is the ubiquitous *nasi goreng* (fried rice); the "special" (*istimewa*) comes with an egg on top and is often served for breakfast.

There are restaurants everywhere in Indonesia that specialize in food from **Padang**, West Sumatra. This spicy, very tasty cuisine has a distinctive way of being served. As many as 15–20 different dishes are displayed in the glass case in front of the restaurant. You tell the waiter what you want and he sets a whole stack of the little dishes in front of you. At the end of the meal, you are charged for what you have eaten and any untouched plates are put back in the case.

As tempting as fresh vegetables may be, avoid eating garnishes or raw salads unless the veggies are air-flown/imported.

The beers available in Indonesia are Bintang, Carlsberg, and Anker, all appropriately light for the tropics. However, as electricity is such a precious commodity, in many places the only way to quaff it cold is to pour it over ice.

Eating in Maluku

The most common meals in Maluku are *nasi ikan* (rice with fish and veggies) and *nasi ikan telur* (the same with an egg added). Ordering these meals is a good way to avoid stomach problems, as the demand is high and the ingredients therefore always fresh. As chicken is more expensive than fish, it is not sold as fast, so be more cautious about the freshness of the meal and even moreso for menu selections that are fancier and more expensive.

Unfortunately, Maluku specialties are rarely found on the restaurant menus. *RW* is finely chopped dog meat prepared with a lot of chili and served with boiled *kaspi* (manioc/cassava). *Papeda* is made from the sago palm: it looks like a plate of transparent glue which seems to have a will of its own, trying to glide off your spoon long before it's reached your mouth. It is nearly tasteless, and its consistency can make it difficult to swallow. Trying *kaspi goreng* (fried manioc) or *rujak* (fruit salad with spicy peanut sauce) is more likely to be a success.

The original staples in Maluku, sago and manioc are ground and baked as dry sugarless cakes. The red cakes are made from the trunk of the sago palm and the white ones are from manioc. Ground manioc is also sold in a not so dry form called *suami*, which is usually eaten with smoked fish and is available around the Ambon bus terminal at night.

The only Maluku specialties that are readily available in restaurants are *ikan bakar* (grilled fish), *colocolo*, and *kohukohu*. Colocolo is baked fish with a sauce of lemon, tomato, onions, and chili. Kohukohu are beans, sprouts, lemon and grated coconut.

Fruits & Vegetables

Two of Indonesia's tastiest fruits are mangosteens (*manggis*) and *rambutan*. Many other delicious fruits to feast upon are: bananas, oranges, papaya, pineapples, pomelos (*jeruk Bali*), starfruit (*blimbing*), guava (*buah biji*), and watermelon. Vegetables are fresh and grown by expert gardeners. Along with the Indonesian vegetables (cassava, sweet potatoes), there are many familiar Western vegetables cultivated, such as carrots, green beans, cauliflower, tomatoes, corn, and potatoes.

Warung (Street Stalls)

Restaurant kitchens do not necessarily have healthier food preparation procedures than roadside *warung*. The important thing at a *warung* is to watch and judge whether or not the cooks inspire confidence. *Warung* rarely have a supply of running water, so beware.

The first portion may not fill you up, so a second portion can be ordered by saying *"Tambah separuh"* (add half portion). But only the price is halved. The amount of food is more like three-quarters. Finish off with a banana and say *"Sudah"* (I've had plenty, thank you). The seller will total up the prices of what was served you and ask you how many *krupuk*, *tempe*, etc. you added; so keep track. The total will come to between Rp500 and Rp2,500 (30¢–$1.40).

Vegetarianism

Say *"saya tidak makan daging"* (I don't eat meat), *"tidak pakai ayam"* (without chicken) or *"tidak pakai daging"* (without meat). Dietary restrictions are very acceptable and common due to the various religious and spiritual practices involving food. However, finding food that truly has no animal products is a problem. Often meals which appear to be made exclusively of vegetables will have a chunk of beef or chicken in them to add that certain oomph. *Tempe* (fermented soy bean cakes) and *tahu* (tofu, soybean curd) are excellent sources of protein.

SECURITY

Indonesia is a relatively safe place to travel and violent crime is almost unheard of. However, petty crime is on the upswing. Pay close attention to your belongings, especially in big cities. Use a small backpack, fannypack or moneybelt for valuables. Shoulderbags can be snatched by thieves racing by on motorbikes, so be vigilant. Be especially wary on crowded *bemos*, buses and trains; this is where **pick-pockets** lurk. They work in groups and are very clever at slitting bags and extracting valuables unnoticed.

Be sure that the door and windows of your hotel room are locked at night, including those in the bathroom, as thieves are adept at sneaking in while you are asleep. Big hotels have **safety boxes** for valuables (passport, tickets, travelers' checks, etc.). If your hotel does not have such a facility, it is better to carry all the documents along with you during the day. Make sure you have a photocopy of your passport, return plane ticket and travelers' check numbers and keep them separate from the originals.

Surat Jalan

Technically, you need a letter from the police for traveling in remote areas, but it doesn't seem to be a problem without it. It is advisable to spend a few extra minutes at the police office in Ambon if you plan to travel anywhere outside of the Lease Islands and Banda. Bring copies of your passport and photographs.

ADDRESSES

The Indonesian spelling of geographical features and villages varies considerably as there is no form of standardization that meets with both popular and official approval. We have seen village names spelled five different ways, all on signboards in front of various government offices. In this guide, we have tried to use the most common spellings.

There are three overlapping and concurrent address systems for any given location: old street name and number, new street name with new number, and *kampung* (neighborhood) name with block numbers. To add to the confusion, the government periodically changes street names and upgrades alleyways (gang) to street which are then given new names. In essence, addresses are constantly in flux.

Every town now has its streets named after the same national heroes, so you will find General Sudirman Street in every city throughout the archipelago.

The names with the new house numbers are the preferred designations for postal purposes. However, when tracking down a hotel address you may find that old street names, *kampung* names, or local landmarks more helpful. You will also find number 38 next to number 119 and the streets referred to by different names, such as Jalan Diponegoro (an Indonesian hero), Jalan Abdi Dongo (from local history) or Gajahan Gang II (the *kampung* name and alley number).

Finding Your Way

Westerners are used to finding things using telephone directories, addresses, and maps. But in Indonesia, phone books are out of date, addresses can be confusing and maps little understood. The way to find something is to ask.

To ask for directions, it's better to have the name of a person and the name of the *kampung*.

Thus "Bu Murni, Jetis" is a better address for asking directions even though "Jalan Kaliwedas 14" is the mailing address. Knowing the language helps here, but is not essential. Immediately clear answers are not common and you should be patient. You are likely to get a simple indication of direction without distance or specific instructions. The assumption is that you will be asking lots of people along the way. Begin by asking three people. Usually, two point toward the same general vicinity. Proceed, then ask again.

Maps are useful tools for you, but introducing them into discussions with Indonesians may cause more confusion than clarity. More than likely the north arrow on the map will be turned to real north before a reading. Periplus-Travel Maps provide detailed and accurate maps of all major tourist destinations.

CALENDAR

The Indonesian government sets national holidays every year, both fixed and moveable dates. The fixed national holidays on the Gregorian calendar are the international New Year, Jan. 1; Independence Day, Aug. 17; and Christmas, Dec. 25. The Christian Good Friday, Easter Day, and Ascension Day, the Balinese new year, Nyepi, and the Buddhist Waisak are also legal holidays. These holy days and all the Muslim holy days are based on the moon, so confusion results when attempting to extrapolate several years ahead.

Muslim holidays in Indonesia in 1998:

Idul Fitri January 30-31. The end of the Muslim fasting month, Ramadan, also called Lebaran.
Idul Adha April 8. The day of Abraham's sacrifice and the day that the haji pilgrims circle the Kaaba in Mecca.
Hijryah April 28. The Islamic New Year, when Muhammad traveled from Mecca to Medina.
Maulud Nabi Muhammad SAW July 7. Muhammad's birthday.
Isra Mi'raj Nabi Muhammad SAW. November 18. When Muhammad ascended on his steed Bouraq.

The 12 lunar months of the Muslim calendar are, in order: Muharram, Safar, Rabiul Awal, Rabiul Ahir, Jumadil Awal, Jumadil Ahir, Rajab, Sa'ban, Ramadan, Sawal, Kaidah, Zulhijja.

Note: The Muslim calendar begins with the Hijriah, Muhammad's flight to Median, in A.D. 622 according to the Gregorian calendar. May 1997 A.D. corresponds to A.H. 1418. The Muslim calendar is a lunar calendar (354 or 355 days) and gains 10 or 11 days on the Gregorian calendar (365 days) each year.

Local Events

January 2 Martha Tiahahu celebration at Karang Panjang in Ambon City.

January 31 Hila/Kaitetu villages — thanksgiving festival.

March 18 *Panas Gondong* ("Hot Siblings") celebration at either Rumahkai (West Seram) or Rutong (east coast of Ambon). This event, held every five years (next in 1998), consists of a number of dances and cultural performances celebrating the reunion of the descendents of the same mother.

April 25 Anzac Day, the Australian cemetery in Tantui near Ambon Town. Hundreds of Australians land in Ambon around April 23–27 for memorial service to the Australians slain here in World War II.

May 14–15 The Pattimura celebration, in honor of Maluku's most famous patriot, begins on the 14th on Saparua Island and concludes on the 15th in Ambon Town.

July (late) Darwin–Ambon yacht race. Over 40 racing yachts cover the 600 or so nautical miles in three to five days. So far, the record stands at an even 72 hours. The entry fee runs some $400, the best way to get a permit to sail Indonesian waters.

August 17 National Independence Day celebrations, lasting throughout the week.

September 7 Founding of Ambon town; parade through the town.

October 28 Youth Festival of Tual, Kei Islands. Some traditional island events, including canoe racing.

October to January (varies) *Sasi Lompa* on Haruku Island; fishing season ritual.

November Traditional ceremony in Pelauw, Haruku Island. This three-day event takes place only once every three years at the Muslim village of Pelauw, and includes religiously induced trances and dancing at night.

December (2nd Friday) *Cuci Negeri*, "village cleansing" ritual at Soya (Ambon Island).

ETIQUETTE

In the areas of Indonesia most frequented by Europeans, many are familiar with the strange ways of Westerners. But it is best to be aware of how certain aspects of your behavior will be viewed. You will not be able to count on an Indonesian to set you straight when you commit a *faux pas*. They are much too polite. They will stay silent or even reply *tidak apa apa* (no problem) if you ask if you did something wrong. So here are some points to keep in mind:

☛ The left hand is considered unclean as it is used for cleaning oneself in the bathroom. It is inappropriate to use the left hand to eat or to give or receive anything with it. When you do accidentally use your left hand then say *"ma'af, tangan kiri"* (please excuse my left hand).

☛ The head is considered the most sacred part of the body and, hence, the feet the least sacred. Avoid touching people on the head. Go for the elbow instead. Never step over food or expose the sole of your foot toward anyone.

☛ As it is impolite to keep one's head higher than others, it is appropriate to acknowledge the presence of others by stooping (extending the right arm, drooping the right shoulder, and leaning forward) while passing closely by someone who is sitting.

☛ Pointing with the index finger is impolite. Indonesians use their thumbs (palm turned upward, fingers curled in) or open palms instead.

☛ Summoning people by crooking the forefinger is impolite. Rather, wave downward with a flat palm face down.

☛ Alcohol is frowned upon in Islam, so take a look around you and consider taking it easy.

☛ Hands on hips is a sign of superiority or anger.

☛ Indonesians don't blow their noses. Keep a handkerchief handy.

☛ Take off your shoes when you enter someone's house. Often the host will stop you, but you should go through the motions until he does.

☛ Wait for a verbal offer before devouring food and drinks that have been placed in front of you. Sip your drink and don't finish it in one gulp. Never take the last morsels from a common plate.

☛ You will often be invited to eat with the words *makan, makan* ("eat, eat") if you pass by somebody who is eating. This is not really an invitation, but simply means "Excuse me as I eat."

☛ If someone prepares a meal or drink for you it is most impolite to refuse.

Some things from the west filter through to Indonesia more effectively than others and stories of "*free sek*" (free sex) made a deep and lasting impression in Indonesia. Expect this topic to appear in lists of questions you will be asked in your cultural exchanges. It is best to explain how things have changed since the 1960s and how we now are stuck with "*saf sek.*"

Keeping Your Cool

At government offices, like immigration and the police, talking loudly and forcefully doesn't make things easier. Patience and politeness are virtues that open many doors in Indonesia. Good manners and respectable dress are also to your advantage.

TRAVELING WITH CHILDREN

Luckily for those with children, Indonesians are very gentle and love to have kids around. But you should bring essentials: sunhats, creams, medicines, special foods, disposable diapers, and a separate water container for babies to be sure of always having sterile water. Nights can sometimes be cool, so remember to bring some warm clothing for your tot. Milk, eggs, fruit which you can peel, and porridges are available in the markets here.

ACCOMMODATIONS

A hierarchy of lodgings and official terminology has been set by the government. A "hotel" is an up-market establishment catering to businessmen, middle- to upper-class travelers and tourists. A star-rating (one to five stars) is applied according to the range of facilities. Smaller places with no stars and basic facilities are not referred to as hotels but as *losmen* (from the French *logement*), *wisma* (guesthouse) or *penginapan* (accommodation) and cater to the masses and budget tourists.

It's common to ask to see the room before checking in. Shop around before deciding, particularly if the hotel offers different rooms at different rates. Avoid carpeted rooms, especially without air-conditioning, as usually they are damp and this makes the room smell.

Many of the cheaper digs have only squat toilets (no toilet paper) and ladle-type, *mandi* baths. This is usually adequate, but try to get a room with an attached bath, if possible.

Bring your own towel and soap (although many places provide these for their guests) and a packet of mosquito coils. Mosquito nets are the best protection, but they're a hassle to put up in most hotel rooms. If you request it, your room will be sprayed for insects. If you want to avoid the smell, be sure that this is done long before you are ready to sleep.

In many hotels, discounts of up to 50% from published rates are to be had for the asking, particularly if you have a business card. Booking in advance through travel agencies can also result in a much lower rate. Larger hotels always add 21% tax and service to the bill.

Bathroom Etiquette

The Indonesian-style bathroom features a tub of water (*bak mandi*) built into a corner of the bathroom. This tub is for storing clean water. Don't climb in or drop your soap into the tub. Scoop and pour the water over yourself with the ladle/dipper provided. In the rural areas, some people keep fish in the *bak mandi*—leave them alone, as the fish eat mosquito larvae.

If you wish to use the native paper-free cleaning method, after using the toilet, scoop water with your right hand and clean with the left.

This is the reason one only eats with the right hand—the left is regarded as unclean. Use soap and a fingernail brush (locals use a rock) for cleaning hands. Pre-packaged alcohol towelettes may make you feel happier about opting for this method. But don't throw the towelletes down the toilet—it will clog.

Staying in Villages

Officially, the Indonesian government requires that foreign visitors spending the night report to the local police. This is routinely handled by *losmen* and hotels, who send in a copy of the registration form you fill out when you check in. Where there are no commercial lodgings, you can often rely on local hospitality. But when staying in a private home, keep in mind the need to inform the local authorities. One popular solution is to stay in the home of the local authority, the village head (*kepala desa*).

Carry photocopies of your passport, visa stamp and embarkation card to give to officials when venturing beyond conventional tourist areas. This saves time, and potential hassles, for you and your host.

Keep in mind that people in many parts of Maluku have had limited experience with foreigners to date and are still learning how to share their homes with you. Villagers in rural Indonesia do not routinely maintain guest rooms. Things like soft beds, cold drinks and electricity are luxury items, and it is not guaranteed you will find someone who speaks anything other than Indonesian or the local language. They will, however, offer you the best they have and you should graciously return that respectful treatment. Paying a modest fee ($6) for a meal and a bed is appropriate and polite.

If a cash arrangement has not been pre-arranged, you should leave a gift appropriate to local needs—sugar, salt, biscuits, mirrors, small clasp-knives, clothing, cigarettes, or D-cell batteries for radios in remote villages. These gifts will be deeply appreciated. For children of poorer families, bring notebooks, colored pencils and inexpensive ballpoint pens. Send them prints of any photos you take of them.

BARGAINING

Other than airfares, package tours, most hotels/losmen rates, prices for prepared foods, and merchandise labeled *harga pas* (fixed price) or *harga mati* (dead price), a price in Indonesia is a flexible thing. At the market, "How much?" is not a question needing a short answer, but the beginning of a conversation.

Bargaining is not played out in extremes in Maluku as it is in other places in Indonesia. Ask for the vendor's offer, and counteroffer an amount below it, and keep smiling. Don't seem too eager to buy; feign indifference to the charms of an item if you really want to get a good price. Don't be shy about denigrating the item you want to buy: "Is this a scratch?" "But, look, it's faded here." Keep a sense of humor about the whole thing. There's no such thing as a "right price." You usually pay more than the locals, but that's the way it is.

Once a price is settled, you are obliged to buy, so don't play the game if you're not really interested in the merchandise. Always agree on a price before accepting a service.

SHIPPING & FREIGHT

Shipping goods home is relatively safe and painless. Items under one meter long and 10 kg in weight can be sent via most postal agents. All the packing will be done for you at minimal charge, although it's always advisable to keep an eye on how it's done. Buy insurance.

Larger purchases are best sent by air or sea cargo. Fowarders will handle the whole process for a price, from packing to customs. Some retailers may also be prepared to send goods if purchased in quantity.

Air cargo is charged by the kilogram (10 kg min) and can be costly. Sea cargo (min. one or two cubic meters) is around $275/cubic meter to the US or Europe and takes about 60 days. Insure your shipment: sea insurance is usually 2.75% of the claimed value.

When shipping cargo, you are responsible for clearing customs back home and for the transportation from the port of entry to your street address. This can cost up to $500 so cargo is only economical for large purchases.

PHOTOGRAPHY

Indonesians generally enjoy being photographed. However, if you are in doubt or the situation seems awkward, it is polite to ask. Some religious activities, eating, and bathing are inappropriate subjects.

Beware of the strong shadows from the equatorial sun. Late afternoon and, especially, early morning, provide the most pleasing light and the richest colors. The only way to deal with the heavy shadows in midday is to use a fill flash.

The heat and humidity of the tropics are hard on camera equipment. Be particularly careful when moving equipment from an air-conditioned room to the muggy outdoors. Moisture will condense on the inside and outside of the camera, Wait until it evaporates; don't be tempted to wipe it off. Also, watch the location of your camera bag and film. Temperatures in hot cars or on boats can be searing.

In general, stick with reliable equipment you are familiar with and bring extra batteries.

Photographic Supplies

35 mm Fuji and Kodak film is widely available in Indonesia, including color print film from ASA 100 to 400 and Ektachrome and Fujichrome 100 ASA daylight transparency film. In larger towns you can buy Fuji Neopan 100 ASA black-and-white negative film and Fuji Velvia. Slide film (100 ASA and video tapes are also readily available at reasonable prices. In Ambon, try the large photo shops on Jl. A.Y. Patty.

PROTECTED SPECIES

Indonesia is home to more than 500 animal species—more than anywhere else in the world. It also has the greatest number of endangered species in the world. Establishing an effective environmental conservation program is a formidable project. The government, with the help of private conservation agencies, such as the World Wide Fund for Nature and the Nature Conservancy, is working to create a viable network of national parks and nature reserves where fragile ecosystems and threatened species can be protected. Two of these national parks, Ujung Kulon in West Java (home to the world's most endangered large mammal, the Javan rhino) and Komodo in the Lesser Sundas (home to the Komodo dragon) have been declared World Heritage Sites by the World Conservation Union.

There are strict laws and severe penalties for trade in endangered species. The appendices of the Convention on International Trade in Endangered Species (CITES) lists more than 200 protected species of Indonesian mammals, birds, reptiles, insects, fish, and mollusks—including orangutan, parrots, cockatoo, crocodiles, tortoises and turtles, birdwing butterflies, and black coral. Visitors should be aware of the fragility of Indonesia's natural environment and not contribute to any further degradation of it.

Species Unique to Maluku

It is illegal to export any products made from marine turtle shells (e.g. jewelry, combs, fans, boxes). Also protected by international convention are the magnificent birds of paradise, cockatoos, parrots and pigeons, birdwing butterflies, cassowary birds and their eggs, giant clams, Triton's trumpet shells, the pearly or chambered nautilus shells, black coral, and ivory from the dugong.

WILDLIFE RESERVES

Forget about large mammals here, as there aren't many. Concentrate on exotic birds and marine life. With a modicum of luck, you could see some of the following: 22 species of parrots, lories and cockatoos, many varieties of colorful pigeons, large, flightless cassowaries, and the birds of paradise. And, of course, Alfred Russel Wallace's favorites, the birdwing butterflies. Sea life includes the dugong and more fish and invertebrate species than you could ever hope to identify. (See also the relevant local sections for more information.)

Pulau Pombo and Pulau Kasa Marine Reserves. Both can be reached from Ambon by paved road to either Tulehu or Waai, and then by motor launch to Pombo (half hour) or to Kasa (three hours). Scenery, snorkeling and megapode birds are the main attractions here. The megapodes build their nests of large mounds of vegetation which, when rotting, provide sufficient heat to incubate the eggs. Unfortunately, scuba diving is ruined as dynamite fishing has destroyed the reefs. Make certain you are self-sufficient on these islands, especially in drinking water. No one lives there.

Manusela Reserve. Large, thinly populated Seram is home to one of the most inaccessible reserves in Indonesia. It is a minimum of three days' walk from anywhere. But the tough terrain of steep hills, ridges and deep valleys have safeguarded a wealth of wildlife both from commercial hunters as well as lumbermen. The attraction here is the birds: bright-colored lories, parrots, cockatoos, kingfishers and pigeons, along with the more drab cassowaries, megapodes, friar birds, honey eaters and the spectacular hornbills. Add to this 90 species of butterflies, many of them found only here.

Manusela, the name of the reserve, refers to the largest village in the park as well as to the island's highest mountain. The reserve was created to protect the watershed of the Toluarang, Muai and Isal rivers.

Banda Islands Marine Reserve. The reserve covers the entire Banda archipelago. Snorkeling and scuba diving are excellent, with lots of fish to be seen—all within sight of the Gunung Api volcano. Another attraction is the big nutmeg-eating pigeon found only here.

Some experts suggest Suanggi (Ghost or Witch) Island as one of many fine places to see wildlife. It has the best beaches, reefs and nesting sites for boobies and other sea birds. Sharks patrol this uninhabited island.

Aru Tenggara Marine Reserve and Pulau Baun Reserve. Away from frequent lines of communications, but not impossible to reach if you have about a month to spare. An ideal location to see the birds of paradise and more. Before you start planning, remember two essential factors: the birds of paradise are in full, magnificent plumage only in the courting season from May to September, and you have to travel by boat, with the best time for this being between September and December—not the ideal time to see the birds.

Aside from the birds of paradise, you can also see kangaroos, wallabies, large crocodiles, monitor lizards, lots of butterflies and insects, and a plethora of birds, including cassowaries and black cockatoos which live mostly on the kanari nuts, which few other birds can crack.

You get here from Ambon by a coastal steamer that calls about once every two to three weeks. Or take one of the daily flights from Ambon to Tual and then it's some 24 hours by small passenger boat (no accommodations). Once in Dobo, make arrangements to travel by locally chartered boats. To see the birds of paradise, you will have to locate the appropriate tree, and build a blind. And then be patient.

CLIMBING VOLCANOS

Maluku province's S-shaped volcanic zone, split neatly down the middle by non-volcanic Seram, offers nine active volcanoes (that we know of).

Two are easy to reach. Banda's 656-meter Gunung Api can be climbed in an hour. (See "Climbing Gunung Api" page 99.) Ternate's 1,721 meter Gamalama is more difficult, but still only a one day round trip. (See "Climbing Gamalama" page 118.)

The rest of the volcanoes are harder to reach, and require some organization. South of Gunung Api, there are four small volcanoes in the Damar Islands chain: **Wurlali** (869 meters) on Damar, **Serawerna** (655 meters) on Teun, **Laworkawra** (781 meters) on Nila, and **Legatala** (641 meters) on tiny Serua Island.

Climbing these small peaks is not difficult, but getting to the Damar Islands is. From Ambon, try to find a mixed passenger freighter that will stop at Damar. Failing this, find one that will go to Romang or Babar, and hire a small boat from there. It might eat up most of your two-month visa time to do this jaunt.

It is a lot easier to reach the active volcanoes in North Maluku. **Keibesi** (1327 meters) on Makian Island, exploded in 1988, leaving an impressive crater and nearly split the island in two. Makian is a short (and beautiful) boat ride from Ternate.

Gamkonora (1,655 meters) is just north of Jailolo on Halmahera's northern peninsula. The best access is from one of the nearby coastal towns such as Tongutisungi. Boats make the trip frequently. Count on two days for this climb.

Dokono (1,335 meters) requires a two-day round trip from Tobelo in North Halmahera. It's at least a 12-hour slog, most of it over a very bad path. The best views of Dokono are from nearby **Mount Mamoja** (1,233 meters) whose peak is a 5–6 hour hike from Tobelo. Tobelo is easy to reach from Ternate by plane.

You need to speak a bit of Indonesian or bring an interpreter, as none are available locally. A good local guide is crucial to the success of any climb. Contact local government officials or village heads to find one.

Transportation

GETTING TO INDONESIA

You can fly direct to Indonesia from just about anywhere. Most people traveling from Europe and the US arrive on direct flights to Jakarta, while those coming from Australia usually go first to Bali. The main international entry points are Soekarno-Hatta airport in Jakarta, Ngurah Rai airport in Bali, and Polonia airport in Medan. There are also non-stop flights from several Asian cities, including Singapore, Hong Kong, Taipei, Seoul, Nagoya, Fukuoka and Osaka.

Jakarta's Soekarno-Hatta airport is served by many international airlines, with over a dozen flights a day from Singapore alone. A cut-price alternative from Europe or the US may be to get a cheap flight to Singapore and buy an onward discount ticket to Jakarta from there: the cost of these can be as low as $75 single, $150 return. An excursion fare return ticket from Singapore to Bali with stops in Jakarta and Yogyakarta, good for a month, is available in Singapore for around $300. Buy through travel agents—check the classified section of the Straits Times for details. [**Note**: you need a return or onward ticket to get a visa-free entry upon arrival in Indonesia.]

Air fares vary depending on the carrier, the season and the type of ticket purchased. A discount RT fare from the US costs from $1,000–1,200 and from Europe costs $800–1,200; about half that from Australia or East Asian capitals. Garuda Airlines now has a direct flight from Los Angeles that flies non-stop via Honolulu to Denpasar. The return flight goes through Jakarta.

Air tickets from Batam and Bintan are also inexpensive. These Indonesian islands just off the coast of Singapore can be reached via short ferry hops from Singapore's World Trade Center. Ferries to Batam cost $12 single, $17 return, and to Bintan $32 single, $45 return. Inquire at travel agents in Singapore for latest fares, then compare with direct Singapore to Bali discount rates.

Garuda offers a visit pass to foreigners purchasing outside of Indonesia. A minimum of three coupons can be purchased for $300. Additional coupons are $100 each, up to 10 coupons. One coupon is valid for one flight and you can not return to a destination already covered. If the flight is not directly to your intended destination, you are charged one coupon per stop. This program is good value for long-haul travel within Indonesia, Medan to Jakarta for instance or Bali to Biak, which otherwise is quite costly.

TRAVELING IN INDONESIA

Having arrived in Indonesia, your choices for onward travel depend, as always, on time and money. In many ways, Indonesia is an easy place to get around. Indonesians are, as a rule, hospitable, good-humored, and willing to help a lost or confused traveler. The weather is warm, the pace of life relaxed, and the air is rich with the smells of clove cigarettes, the blessed durian fruit and countless other wonders.

However, the nation's transportation infrastructure does not move with the kind of speed and efficiency that Western travelers expect, which often leads to frustration. Bookings are often difficult to make; flights and reservations are sometimes mysteriously canceled.

It is best to adjust your pace to local conditions. What seems like nerve-wracking inefficiency is really so only if one is in a hurry. If you have to be somewhere at a particular time, allow plenty of time to get there. Check and double-check your bookings. Otherwise just go with the flow. You will get there eventually. You can't just turn off the archipelago's famous *jam karet*—"rubber time"—when it's time to take an airplane and turn it on again when you want to relax.

Peak periods around the Christmas/New Year holidays and during the June to August tourist season are the most difficult. It is imperative to book well in advance and reconfirm your bookings at every step along the way. Travel anywhere in Indonesia during the week prior to the Islamic Lebaran holiday is practically impossible. Find a nice spot and sit it out.

The golden rule is: things will sort themselves out eventually. Be persistent, of course, but relax and keep your sense of humor. Before you explode, have a cup of sweet coffee or a cool glass of *kelapa muda* (young coconut water). Things might take on a different look.

Planning an Itinerary

The first thing to do is to be easy on yourself and not to plan an impossibly tight schedule.

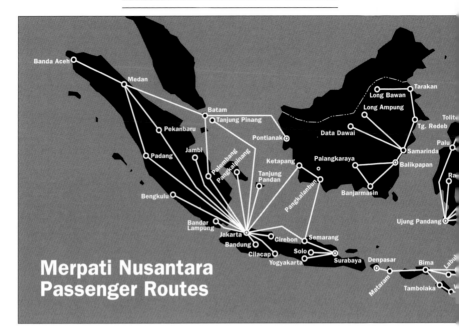

Merpati Nusantara Passenger Routes

Things happen slowly here, so adjust yourself to the pace. Better to spend more time in a few places and see them in a leisurely way, than to end up hot, hassled, and hurried. You'll see *more* this way, not less.

Better yet, do not plan an itinerary. You can do all your homework and plan your whole trip, but it may never work. Be flexible when traveling within Maluku. The Tanimbar, Kei and even Banda islands can be difficult places to get away from for any number of reasons.

Wherever you are, keep in mind that the tropical heat takes its toll and you should avoid the midday sun. Get an early start, before the rays become punishing (the tropical light is beautiful at dawn). Retreat to a cool place after lunch and go out again in the afternoon and early evening, when it's much more pleasant.

TRAVELING IN MALUKU

Maluku lies scattered in a huge expanse of open sea between Sulawesi and Irian Jaya. Few travelers get this far east in Indonesia, although there's now an improved travel infrastructure to many islands where you can soak up weeks of sun, diving, and island life.

The capital of the province of Maluku is Ambon, which is both the largest and best-connected city in the province. The province is subdivided into three districts or *kabupaten*:

1) Maluku Utara (North Maluku). Capital at Ternate. Includes Ternate, Tidore and the small islands south of them, Halmahera and Morotai, Bacan and Obi, and the Sula archipelago.

2) Maluku Tengah (Central Maluku). Capital at

Masohi, Seram. Includes Ambon and the other Lease Islands, Seram, Buru and the tiny Banda archipelago.

3) Maluku Tenggara (Southeast Maluku). Capital at Tual, Dullah Island, Kei group. Includes the Keis, the Aru Islands, the Tanimbars, and the tiny Southwestern Islands from Wetar to the Babar group.

Communications between Ambon and the district capitals is quite good and these towns all have decent accommodations and restaurants, and good local transportation. Drop in at the local tourism office (*Kantor Pariwisata*) or try to find the local high school English teacher.

With the exception of the Banda Islands, which are well set up for tourists, travel outside the district capitals requires plenty of time. In general, you will find simple accommodations and meals at any Merpati destination.

Access to the more remote parts of Maluku, which means most of the archipelago, still requires water-borne transport. It is impossible to work out a precise time schedule beforehand when traveling around in Maluku. Planes get cancelled, boat schedules change, and landslides often close roads. However, local people need to get around too and only the most remote villages will not have some kind of passenger boat arriving and leaving during the week.

Local passengers bring their own sleeping mats and food, but foreign travelers can usually obtain a crew bunk along with simple meals for a few dollars a day. These ships stop for only a few hours at each port, however, which is just enough for a quick look around. If you like the place, get off and stay, but be aware that the

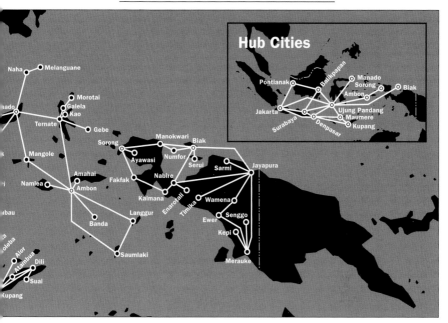

next ship to pass that way might not come along for a week or two.

Remember to allow for cancelled or overbooked flights, delayed boats and many other unforeseen hitches. The further you wander off the usual routes, the more time you should allow to get back, especially during the rainy season, usually May–August.

AIR TRAVEL

The cardinal rule is book early, confirm and reconfirm often. If you are told a flight is fully booked, go to the airport anyway and stand in line. While Garuda's booking system is computerized, the other local airlines' are not, and bookings evaporate at the last minute all the time. It is rare that flights are completely full. Always keep the following points in mind:

✈ It's practically impossible to get a confirmed booking out of a city other than the one you're in. You can buy a ticket and it may say you have a booking, but don't believe it until you reconfirm with the airline in the city of departure.

✈ Reconfirm bookings directly with the airline office in the city of departure between 24 and 72 hours before your flight, particularly during peak tourist seasons and Indonesian holidays. Your seat may be given away if you reconfirm either too early or too late (or not at all).

✈ Make bookings in person, not by phone.

✈ Get written proof or computer printout of bookings. Note the name of the person who gives it to you so you can hold them responsible if you're told you don't have a booking later.

✈ Note the computer booking code or PRN (passenger record number). Names have a tendency to go astray or be misspelled. Concrete proof of your booking is essential.

✈ If your name isn't on the computer try looking under your first or middle names as these are frequently mistaken for surnames.

✈ If you are told a flight is full, ask to be put on the waiting list, then go to the airport about two hours before departure and check the waiting list. Hang around the desk and be friendly to the staff and you will probably get on the flight. A tip will sometimes, but not always, help.

✈ There are usually alternate ways of getting from point A to B. Search them out.

✈ Generally, students (12–26 years old) receive a discount of 10–25% (show an international student ID card) and children between the ages of 2–10 pay 50% of the regular fare. Infants not occupying a seat pay 10% of the regular fare. Ask the airlines or travel agent.

Garuda Indonesia's flagship airline has been in business since 1946. It serves all major cities in Indonesia and at least 38 international destinations. They fly only jets, mainly wide-bodied, and the service is reasonably good.

Merpati A domestic network serving more than 160 airports throughout Indonesia. Merpati (literally "pigeon") flies smaller jets and turboprops (McDonnell Douglas DC-9s, Fokker VFW F-28s) as well as turbo-props (Fokker F-27s, Canadian De-Havilland DHC-6 "Twin-Otters," the Indonesian built Casa Nusantara CN-235s and CN-212s, and Boeing B-737 jets).

Merpati is not known for its punctuality, but the airline does at least connect towns and villages across the archipelago, in some cases land-

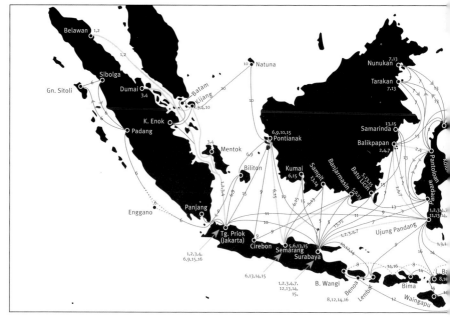

ing on a grass airstrip in a highland village of only 100 people that would take days to reach by any other means.

Merpati's standard baggage allowance is 20 kg for economy class, but some of the smaller aircraft permit only 10 kg (after which excess baggage charges of $1/kg apply).

Sempati A privately-owned competitor, with quality service and a growing network inside and outside of Indonesia. Sempati flies new Fokker F-28s and F-100s to several cities in Asia, such as Singapore, Kuala Lumpur, Taipei, and Perth. Domestically it flies between major cities such as Jakarta, Yogyakarta, Surabaya, Ujung Pandang, Jayapura, and Denpasar. Sempati has also added destinations previously difficult to reach, such as Balikpapan, Banjarmasin, Tarakan, Palangkaraya, Palu, Padang, and Manado.

Bouraq A small, private company, flying mainly older planes and a few newer B-737s linking secondary cities in Java, Bali, Kalimantan, Nusa Tenggara, Sulawesi, and other remote destinations.

Mandala Operates a few prop planes and B-737s to out-of-the-way airstrips in Sulawesi, Kalimantan and Sumatra.

NOTE: Travel agents often give cheaper fares than airline offices.

To and from Maluku

Travel to Maluku usually involves at least one transit through Ujung Pandang; usually to transfer from larger jets coming from Jarkarta and elsewhere onto smaller ones heading to Ambon. The Ujung Pandang airport is normally chaotic enough, but the place becomes a virtual madhouse during Indonesian holidays.

Pattimura airport is the largest in Maluku and is connected to many small strips on the outlying islands, as well as to other provincial centers, such as Manado and Biak.

As always with Merpati, remember to book early, confirm and reconfirm. An automatic cancellation policy means your seat is automatically wiped out of the computer if you don't reconfirm your intentions within 72 hours before your flight. The flights below are scheduled as of press time, but you should check, of course, as they could change at any time.

Regional

Bandung	MTuThFSa	$249
Biak	Daily	$103
Denpasar	Daily	$148
Jakarta	Daily,	
	via Ujung Pandang	$211
Jayapura	Daily	$155
Manado	ThSu	$107
Sorong	Daily	$58
Surabaya	MTuThFSa	$184
Timika	TuWFSu	$149
Ujung Pandang		
	2–3 Daily	$103

Provincial

Amahai	Sa	$25
Banda	MWSa	$42
Dobo	TuSu	$105
Labuha	M	$67
Langgur	TuWThFSaSu	$79
Mangole	WF	$67
Namlea	Su	$29
Namrole	WF	$25
Sanana	M	$56
Saumlaki	ThSa	$83

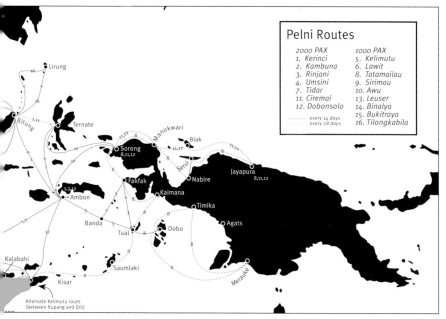

Pelni Routes

2000 PAX	1000 PAX
1. Kerinci	5. Kelimutu
2. Kambuna	6. Lawit
3. Rinjani	8. Tatamailau
4. Umsini	9. Sirimau
7. Tidar	10. Awu
11. Ciremai	13. Leuser
12. Dobonsolo	14. Binalya
	15. Bukitraya
——— every 14 days	16. Tilongkabila
········ every 28 days	

Ternate	MTuThSaSu	$71
Galela		$93
Taliabu		$75

Other airlines also have daily flights connecting Ambon with cities throughout the archipelago. Check with them if you are having trouble getting on a Merpati flight. Some of the Mandala and Bouraq aircraft have seen a good bit of use, so these are not for the squeamish.

Airline Offices

Offices in Ambon (area code 0911):
Bouraq Jl. Sultan Babullah 19. ☎ : 43143.
Indoavia Jl. A. Rhebok, ☎ 53866. Charter only.
Mandala Jl. A. Y. Patty, ☎ 42551.
Merpati/Garuda Jl. A. Yani, ☎ 52481, 52572, 52739. Fax: 52572.
Sempati Jl. A.M. Sangaji 46C. ☎ 61612.

Departure Tax

Airport tax for departing passengers is Rp9,200 for domestic flights and Rp15,000 for international flights.

SEA TRAVEL

There is four times as much sea in Indonesia as land and for many centuries transportation among the islands has been principally by boat. Tiny ports are scattered all over the archipelago and the only way to reach many areas is by sea.

To travel by boat you need plenty of time. Most ships are small and are at the mercy of the sea and the seasons. Think of it as a romantic journey and don't be in a hurry.

Pelni *(Pelayaran Nasional Indonesia)*, the national passenger line, has 17 large ships criss-crossing the archipelago—stopping at 79 ports—carrying up to 1,500 passengers each. These boats travel on fixed schedules. The first and second class cabins are comfortable. Check the route map above for destinations served and contact Pelni's main office for a current schedule.

The new German-built passenger ships are modern and comfortable. Fares are fixed, and there are up to 5 classes, determining how many people share a cabin and kinds of services. The ships which include Maluku on their runs are:
Kerinci. This ship's two-week run stops at: Ambon, Bitung, Ternate, Ambon, Bau-Bau, Ujung Pandang, Surabaya, Jakarta, Padang, Nias, Sibolga, Jakarta, Surabaya, Ujung Pandang, Bau-Bau, Ambon.
Capacity: 1,596 people. Cabins: 50 1st class, 50 2nd class, 50 3rd class, 62 4th class, deck 500 beds.
Rinjani. This ship's two-week run includes: Jakarta, Surabaya, Ujung Pandang, Bau-Bau, Ambon, Banda, Tual, Fakfak, Banda, Ambon, Bau-Bau, Ujung Pandang, Surabaya, Jakarta, Muntok, Kijang, Dumai, Jakarta.
Capacity: 1,729 people. Cabins: 20 1st class, 22 2d class, 28 3d class, 82 4th class, deck (777).
Tatamilau. Alternates two two-week routes:
A: Tual, Timika, Merauke, Timika, Doba, Tual, Saumlaki, Kisar, Dili, Larantuka, Labuanbajo, Badas, Banyuwangi, Denpasar, Bima, Labuahbajo, Larantuka, Dili, Kisar, Saumlaki.
B: Tual, Dobo, Timika, Agats, Merauke, Timika, Tual, Kaimana, Fakfak, Sorong, Manokwari,

Nabire, Serui, Jayapura, Serui, Nabire, Manokwari, Sorong, Fakfak, Kaimana.

Capacity: 969 people. Cabins: 10 1st class, 10 2d class, deck (915).

Ceremai. This ship's two-week run includes: Jakarta, Ujung Pandang, Bau-Bau, Banggai, Bitung, Ternate, Sorong, Manokwari, Biak, Jayapura, Biak, Manokwari, Sorong, Ternate, Bitung, Banggai, Bau-Bau.

Capacity: 1,974 people. Cabins: 22 1st class, 22 2d class, 48 3d class, deck (1,554).

Dobonsolo. This ship's two-week run includes: Jakarta, Surabaya, Denpasar, Kupang, Dili, Ambon, Sorong, Manokwari, Biak, Jayapura, Biak, Manokwari, Sorong, Ambon, Dili, Kupang, Denpasar, Surabaya, and back to Jakarta.

Capacity: 1,974 people. Cabins: 22 1st class, 22 2d class, 48 3d class, 48 4th class, deck (1,554).

First class on these ships is quite luxurious, two to a cabin; each cabin has its own shower and video. Second class sleeps 4 to a cabin, third class 6 to a cabin, fourth class 8 to a cabin, and the rest sleep in a large dormitory on the lowest deck. Food, included in the fares, is quite adequate and plentiful.

Of course, timing is of the essence with one of these ships—will its schedule coincide with yours? If it does, it's a great alternative to flying: a relaxed, 19th century style of travel. Tickets are difficult to come by during Indonesian holidays and school vacations, so if you can, book in advance.

Small ships. A variety of smaller Pelni ships based in Ambon make the rounds around Maluku. Here's a typical trip. Starting from Ambon, the entire route takes 17 days.

Destination	Distance	Fare
Banda	132km	$3
Tual	329km	$5
Saumlaki	536km	$8
Masela	624km	$9
Kroing	644km	$9
Tepa	669km	$10
Lelang	714km	$10
Lakor	786km	$11
Moa	796km	$11
Leti	806km	$12
Kisar	843km	$12
Ilwaki	893km	$13
Romang	961km	$14
Damar	1,047km	$15
Tepa	1,117km	$16
Larat	1,354km	$19

Other ships follow different routes. Here are the main ones:

Daya Nusantara. R7 (14 days): Ambon, Geser, Gorong, Tual, Elat, Dobo, Larat, Saumlaki, Adaut, Tual, Geron, Geser , Ambon

Daya Nusantara. R8 (14 days): Ambon, Banda, Tual, Banda, Ambon, Laksula, Namlea, Ambon.

Baruna Dwipa. R9 (14 days): Ternate, Labuha, Laiwuri, Falabesahaya, Dofa, Bogong, Sanana, Ambon, Namlea, Air Buaya, Sanana, Bobong, Dofa, Laiwuri, Labuha, Ternate.

Baruna Dwipa. R10 (14 days): Ternate, Saketa, Gebe, Wayanli, Busui, Patani, Wed, Mafa, Besui, Saketa, Ternate.

On these inter-island ships, passage is deck class only. Bring a sleeping mat, food and get on board early to pick out a decent spot as it gets very crowded. Or, try bargaining with one of the crew members for his bunk. At about $15 per day, it's worth every rupiah if you can afford it. Some ships even offer meals of rice and fish for about $1 per plate. Alternatively, the Pan Marine 2 offers better places to sleep along with bargain fares on the Ambon–Ternate–Banda run once a week.

Head office: 5th floor, Jl. Gajah Mada 14, Jakarta 10130. ☎ (021) 384-4342. Fax: (021) 385-4130. Main ticket office: Jl Angkasa 18, Kemayoran ☎ 421-1921. Open in the mornings.

Ambon: Jl. Pelabuhan 1, ☎ (0911) 53161, 52049. Fax: 53369. The office is open 8 am to 4 pm (closed 12 noon–1 pm) on weekdays, and 8 am–1 pm on Saturdays.

Coasters and local ferries

There are a myriad of options. Rusty old coasters ply routes through the eastern islands, stopping at tiny ports to pick up dried coconut meat, seaweed and other small loads of cash crops. They drop off basics like tinware, fuel and the occasional outboard motor. You could find deck passage on one of these ships at just about any harbor for very little money.

Stock up on food—you may quickly get tired of white rice and salted fish—and bring raingear and plastic to thoroughly waterproof your baggage. Try to negotiate with a crewmember to rent his bunk, which could make sleeping much more comfortable.

Overnight ferries, with throbbing motors and crowds beyond belief, offer passage to many smaller islands. On these—and on deck passage on any vessel in Indonesia—it is important to use your luggage to stake out territory early, and to set down some straw mats to have a clean place to lie. It is almost always best to stay on deck, where the fresh sea air will keep your spirits up. Below deck tends to be noisy, verminous and smelly.

Motorboats and *prahu*

The Lease Islands as well as the southwest coast of Seram maintain daily communications with Ambon via small motorboats. These can become quite crowded, but the price is right since chartering boats tends to be quite expensive.

In many places small boats are the primary means of travel. Almost anywhere there is a boat, it can be chartered, but particularly in the more remote regions, the price can be high. For example, in the Aru Islands, the most common outboard motors are just 15 HP, because of the cost of gas or kerosene and the investment for larger motors. This makes for long travel times and what might seem like an expensive rental. Fuel in the outer islands is very expensive, so don't be too shocked at the prices.

In many areas, day trips on smaller boats—*prahu*—are the best way to explore. These can be hired by the hour, with a boatman, to take you snorkeling or sightseeing along the coast, or birdwatching upriver. When renting a boat, always check its seaworthiness and assess the confidence and skill of the skipper. The larger the boat, the more seaworthy it usually is and an outrigger seems a minimum precaution for small sea-going *prahu*. Try to find a boat with a canopy or have your pilot rig one up.

When traveling by very small boat, it is good insurance to keep your camera and valuables in a plastic, waterproof box (e.g. a Pelican box).

LAND TRAVEL

The average road in Indonesia is a paved, but rough and potholed thoroughfare, traversed by a veritable zoo of vehicles: fully loaded trucks with marginal brakes and crazed drivers; full-size buses one and three-quarters lanes wide; small public minivans stopping for passengers anywhere without warning; the occasional private car; scores of motorcycles often at the hands of a young hotshot screaming along at full throttle; horse-drawn carts; bicycle pedicabs; bicycles some with children fore and aft and often piled with produce or perhaps two fighting cocks in their cages; and, of course, pedestrians.

Local Buses

The major advantages of these rattling buses is that they are extremely cheap, run every few minutes between major towns, and can be picked up at the terminals or any point along their routes. This is also their biggest disadvantage: they stop constantly to pick up passengers.

If you depart from a terminal, find a seat near a window that opens. Try not to share this breeze with passengers behind you; they are likely to have a strong aversion to wind for fear of *masuk angin* (the wind which enters the body and causes a cold).

The seats are very small, both in terms of leg room and width. You and your bag may take up (and be charged for) two seats. This is fair, but be sure you're not being overcharged. Before getting on, ask someone what the proper fare is to your destination. A few words of Indonesian are indispensable for asking directions.

Public Minivans/Minibuses

In the places in Maluku with developed road systems, the standard Indonesian form of mass transport, the "Colt" or minivan, plies the road. Along the regular route, these vehicles are quite cheap, but since their drivers always wait for a full load before departing and often swing through populated areas to round up passengers, they are a test for one's patience.

Driving On Your Own

Driving in Indonesia is not for the faint-hearted. Vehicles and creatures of every size, shape and description charge onto the road out of nowhere. The traffic is horrendous on the main highways. Drive on the left, slowly and carefully. Road construction sites are not marked and few cyclists have reflectors for use at night.

The condition of road networks has improved in recent years, however, and driving off the beaten track is one of the best ways to explore the area. Check your fuel gauge regularly as there are few gas stations away from the main roads. Small roadside fuel shops, indicated by a "Premium" sign, sell gasoline for the bit more than the Pertamina stations.

A valid international license is required for driving cars and motorbikes. Insurance is not compulsory, but strongly recommended. You can get a policy from most of the rental companies and travel agents. Check the condition of the car before signing the contract. Beware: vehicles are usually rented with an empty tank. Test-drive the car before renting.

Becak

Bicycle pedicabs (*becak*) are an important means of local transport in many towns. Used primarily for short distances, a trip costs anywhere between Rp350–2000, depending on the distance, route, and your bargaining ability.

Ojek

Increasingly popular are motorcycle taxis, where passengers ride pillion on the back of motorcycles. Usually parked at bus stations and major crossroads, these bikes can get you to obscure destinations. Bargain before you get on.

TOURS AND TRAVEL AGENTS

Hiring your own vehicle for a private tour naturally allows you much more flexibility. An AC vehicle with a driver/guide costs anywhere from $30 up to $60 per day, all inclusive. The guides on both types of tours do expect tips, however be aware that they also get a 20%–40% commission on any of your purchases in the large souvenir shops along the way.

Indonesian Language Primer

Personal pronouns
I *saya*
we *kita* (inclusive), *kami* (exclusive)
you *anda* (formal), *saudara* (brother, sister),
  kamu (for friends and children only)
he/she *dia*   they *mereka*

Forms of address
Father/Mr *Bapak ("Pak")*
Mother/Mrs *Ibu ("Bu")*
Elder brother *Abang ("Bang" or "Bung")*
      Mas (in Java only)
Elder sister *Mbak* (in Java only)
Elder brother/sister *Kakak ("Kak")*
Younger brother/sister *Adik ("Dik")*
Note: These terms are used not just within the family, but generally in polite speech.

Basic questions
How? *Bagaimana?*
How much/many? *Berapa?*
What? *Apa?*   What's this? *Apa ini?*
Who? *Siapa?*   Who's that? *Siapa itu?*
What is your name? *Siapa namanya ?*
(Literally: Who is your name?)
When? *Kapan?*
Where? *Di mana?*
Why? *Kenapa? Mengapa?*
Which? *Yang mana?*

Civilities
Welcome *Selamat datang*
Good morning (7–11am) *Selamat pagi*
Good midday (11am–3pm) *Selamat siang*
Good afternoon (3–7pm) *Selamat sore*

Goodnight (after dark) *Selamat malam*
Goodbye (to one leaving) *Selamat jalan*
Goodbye (to one staying) *Selamat tinggal*
Note: Selamat is a word from Arabic meaning "May your time (or action) be blessed."
How are you? *Apa kabar?*
I am fine. *Kabar baik.*
Thank you. *Terima kasih.*
You're welcome. *Kembali.*
Same to you. *Sama sama.*
Pardon me *Ma'af*
Excuse me *Permisi*
(when leaving a conversation, etc).

Numbers
1	*satu*	6	*enam*
2	*dua*	7	*tujuh*
3	*tiga*	8	*delapan*
4	*empat*	9	*sembilan*
5	*lima*	10	*sepuluh*
11	*sebelas*	100	*seratus*
12	*dua belas*	600	*enam ratus*
13	*tiga belas*	1,000	*seribu*
20	*dua puluh*	3,000	*tiga ribu*
50	*lima puluh*	10,000	*sepuluh ribu*
73	*tujuh puluh tiga*		
1,000,000	*satu juta*		
2,000,000	*dua juta*		

half *setengah*
first *pertama*   third *ketiga*
second *kedua*   fourth *ke'empat*

Time
minute *menit*   Sunday *Hari Minggu*
hour *jam*   Monday *Hari Senin*

Pronunciation and Grammar

Vowels
a As in f**a**ther
e Three forms:
  1) Schwa, like th**e**
  2) Like **é** in touch**é**
  3) Short **è**; as in b**e**t
i Usually like long **e** (as in Bali); when bounded by consonants, like short **i** (h**i**t)
o Long **o**, like g**o**
u Long **u**, like y**ou**
ai Long **i**, like cr**i**me
au Like **ow** in **ow**l

Consonants
c Always like **ch** in **ch**urch
g Always hard, like **g**uard
h Usually soft, almost unpronounced. It is hard between like vowels, e.g. *mahal* (expensive).
k Like **k** in **k**ind; at end of word, unvoiced stop.
kh Like **k**ind, but harder
r Rolled, like Spanish **r**
ng Soft, like fli**ng**
ngg Hard, like ti**ngle**
ny Like **ny** in So**ny**a

Grammar
Grammatically, Indonesian is in many ways far simpler than English. There are no articles (a, an, the).
The verb form "to be" is usually not used. There is no ending for plurals; sometimes the word is doubled, but often number comes from context. And Indonesian verbs are not conjugated. Tense is communicated by context or with specific words for time.

(also clock/watch)　Tuesday　*Hari Selasa*
day　*hari*　Wednesday　*Hari Rabu*
week　*minggu*　Thursday　*Hari Kamis*
month　*bulan*　Friday　*Hari Jum'at*
year　*tahun*　Saturday　*Hari Sabtu*
today　*hari ini*　later　*nanti*
tomorrow　*besok*　yesterday　*kemarin*
What time is it?　*Jam berapa?*
(It is) eight thirty.　*Jam setengah sembilan*
　(Literally: "half nine")
How many hours?　*Berapa jam?*
When did you arrive?　*Kapan datang?*
Four days ago.　*Empat hari yang lalu.*
When are you leaving?
　Kapan berangkat?
In a short while.　*Sebentar lagi.*

Useful words

yes　*ya*　no, not　*tidak, bukan*
Note: *Tidak* is used with verbs or adverbs; *bukan* with nouns.

and　*dan*　better　*lebih baik*
with　*dengan*　worse　*kurang baik*
for　*untuk*　this/these　*ini*
from　*dari*　that/those　*itu*
good　*baik*　same　*sama*
very good　*bagus*　different　*lain*
more　*lebih*　here　*di sini*
less　*kurang*　there　*di sana*
to be　*ada*　to be able to　*bisa*
to buy　*membeli*　correct　*betul*
to know　*tahu*　wrong　*salah*
big　*besar*　small　*kecil*
to need　*perlu*　to want　*ingin*
to go　*pergi*　to stop　*berhenti*
slow　*pelan*　fast　*cepat*
to wait　*tunggu*　to continue　*terus*
to　*ke*　at　*di*
old　*tua, lama*　new　*baru*
full　*penuh*　empty　*kosong*
quiet　*sepi*　crowded, noisy　*ramai*
few　*sedikit*　many　*banyak*
cold　*dingin*　hot　*panas*
clean　*bersih*　dirty　*kotor*
entrance　*masuk*　exit　*keluar*

Small talk

Where are you from?　*Dari mana?*
I'm from the US.　*Saya dari Amerika.*
How old are you?　*Umurnya berapa?*
I'm 31 years old.
　Umur saya tiga pulu satu tahun.
Are you married?　*Sudah kawin belum?*
Yes, I am.　*Yah, sudah.*
Not yet.　*Belum.*
Do you have children?　*Sudah punya anak?*
What is your religion?　*Agama apa?*
Where are you going?　*Mau ke mana?*
I'm just taking a walk.　*Jalan-jalan saja.*
Please come in.　*Silahkan masuk.*
Please sit down.　*Silahkan duduk.*

Hotels

room　*kamar*　bed　*tempat tidur*
towel　*handuk*　bedsheet　*sprei*
bathe　*mandi*　bathroom　*kamar mandi*

hot water　*air panas*
Where's a losmen?　*Di mana ada losmen?*
cheap losmen　*losmen yang murah*
good hotel　*hotel yang baik*
Please take me to…　*Tolong antar saya ke…*
Are there any empty rooms?
　Ada kamar kosong?
Sorry there aren't any.　*Ma'af, tidak ada.*
How much for one night?
　Berapa untuk satu malam?
One room for two people.
　Dua orang, satu kamar.
I'd like to stay for 3 days.
　Saya mau tinggal tiga hari.
Here's the key to the room.
　Ini kunci kamar.
Please call a taxi.
　Tolong panggilkan taksi.
Please wash these clothes.
　Tolong cucikan pakaian ini.

Restaurants

to eat　*makan*　to drink　*minum*
drinking water　*air putih, air mimun*
breakfast　*makan pagi, sarapan*
lunch　*makan siang*　dinner　*makan malam*
Where's a good restaurant?
　Di mana ada rumah makan yang baik?
Let's have lunch.　*Mari kita makan siang.*
May I see the menu?
　Boleh saya lihat daftar makanan?
I want to wash my hands.
　Saya mau cuci tangan.
Where is the toilet?　*Di mana kamar kecil?*
fish, squid, goat, beef, chicken
　ikan, cumi-cumi, kambing, sapi, ayam
salty, sour, sweet, spicy (hot)
　asin, asam, manis, pedas

Shopping

cheap　*murah*　expensive　*mahal*
Please, speak slowly.
　Tolong, berbicara lebih pelan.
I want to buy…　*Saya mau beli…*
Where can I buy…　*Di mana saya bisa beli…*
How much does this cost?　*Berapa harga ini?*
2,500 Rupiah.　*Dua ribu, lima ratus rupiah.*
That cannot be true!　*Masa!*
That's still a bit expensive.　*Masih agak mahal*
May I bargain?　*Boleh tawar?*
Is there a discount?　*Ada diskon?*
Thanks, I already have one/some…
　Terima kasih, saya sudah punya …

Directions

here　*di sini*　there　*di sana*
near　*dekat*　far　*jauh*
inside　*di dalam*　outside　*di luar*
map　*peta*　street　*jalan*
north　*utara*　south　*selatan*
east　*timur*　west　*barat*
central　*pusat*　middle　*tengah*
left　*kiri*　right　*kanan*
straight　*terus*　turn　*belok*
I am looking for this address.
　Saya cari alamat ini.

Ambon PRACTICALITIES

Once referred to as "The Queen of the East," Ambon is now the political and transportation center of Maluku province. It is the essential stopping-off and stocking-up place before and after trips to the other islands in the province.

Prices in US $. Telephone code is 0911. AC=Airconditioning. S=Single, D=Double, T=Triple.

ORIENTATION

Most of the activity in Ambon Town takes place in a compact area of downtown, between the Wai Tomu and the Wai Batu Gajah Rivers, formerly the city limits. Jalan Raya Pattimura, one of two principal streets, starts at the sports field and heads inland at right angles to the harbor. The governor's office is located in a large white building at the begining of this street.

TOURIST INFORMATION

Maluku Government Tourist Office Jl. Raya Pattimura, ☎ 52471. The *Kantor Pariwisata*, is on the ground floor of the governor's office building in the center of town. Use the entrance in front of Harlim and Tip Top restaurants. The staff is helpful and dedicated. Maps and leaflets are distributed free of charge.

P.T. Daya Patal Tour and Travel Jl. Said Perintah SK II/27A, Ambon, Maluku, Indonesia. ☎ 53529, 53344, 52498. Fax: 44709. Telex: 73140 DPAB IA. This quality outfit will provide you with information without forcing you to buy tours or tickets. Contact Hans Rijoly or Salomon—they speak excellent English and know heaps about Ambon.

GETTING THERE

Air travel to Maluku usually involves at least one transit through Ujung Pandang; usually to tranfer from larger jets coming from Jakarta and elsewhere onto smaller ones heading to Ambon. The Ujung Pandang airport is normally chaotic enough, but the place becomes a virtual madhouse during Indonesian holidays.

Arriving in Ambon

Pattimura Airport is on Ambon Island's Hitu Peninsula across the bay from Ambon City—37 kilometers and 45 minutes by road. Vehicle and passenger ferries run every few minutes between Poka and Galela, where the bay narrows, which cuts the traveling distance in half. The airport taxis charge $9 (AC cars) for the trip.

You can also get to town cheaply by taking public transport. Stop a public minibus on the road in front of the airport area and ask for the ferry. Get out at the ferry terminal and take the ferry across to Galela. Here minibuses will be waiting for passengers going to Ambon Town. The whole trip will cost 50¢ or a little more if your luggage takes up seats in the minibuses.

GETTING AROUND

In general, the public transportation system in Ambon works well. Minibuses radiate out around the island from the Mardeka bus terminal which is situated along the waterfront. They leave for their destinations only when they are full. For nearby destinations during the day, the wait is normally just a couple of minutes, but may be a half hour or more at night. Further destinations often require a wait of up to 20 minutes.

The fare for rides of less than 5 km from the terminal is 15¢; 10 km, 25¢. The 80 km trip to Wakasihu costs $1.25. Returning to Ambon can be difficult at times in the afternoon and evening.

The easiest solution is, of course, to take one of Ambon's few taxis. Let your hotel arrange one for you or just go to one of only two taxi stands in Ambon (one in front of the city police post) to bargain for fares. Expect to pay about $5/hour.

Within the city, take a minibus (15¢). They stop only a marked bus stops within the town. If the *kenek* (the conductor of sorts who hangs out the door, shoves passengers in and collects the fares) is shouting "*pasar*" or "*Mardeka*", the bus is headed for the Mardeka bus terminal.

Short distances in Ambon are covered by *becak* or walking. There are over 2,000 *becaks* in Ambon town, peddling everywhere. Too many, in fact. The local government has divided the *becaks* into three equal groups, one painted red, one white, and one yellow. Only *becaks* of one of these colors can seek passengers on any given day, followed by two days of rest. A *becak* trip costs Rp500–Rp2,500 (22¢–$1), depending on the distance and your bargaining skills.

ACCOMMODATIONS

There are no really cheap accommodations on Ambon. The **Mutiara** is highly recommended. For a middle priced, clean hotel with airconditioning, try **Hero**. On the budget side, **Beta** is the backpackers' favorite, followed by **Wisma Game**.

Nearly all hotels will have vacant rooms if you arrive during the day. Many get full at night. A good place to start, if arriving without reservation, is Jl. Wem Reawaru. Four hotels sit in a row and there are many other hotels nearby.

Abdulalie Jl. Sultan Babullah, ☎ 52057, 52058. Fax: 52796. 34 rooms of different standards. $6S without bath, $27S with TV, AC. $8–$32D, $11–$30T.

Amboina Jl. Kapt. Ulupaha 51, ☎ 41725, 41641, 41712. 44 rooms with TV, video, AC. $30S, $39–$42D.

Ambon Manise Jl. Pantai Mardeka 53, ☎ 53888, 54888, 55888. Fax: 54492, 54493. A new hotel with 99 rooms with TV, AC. Facilities include restaurant, swimming pool, tennis court, squash, money changer. $54–$90S, $114–$210 suites.

Baliwerti Jl. Wem Reawaru 9, ☎ 55996. 9 rooms with TV, AC. $23S, $30D.

Beta Jl. Wim Reawaru, ☎ 53463. 26 rooms. One of the bargain favorites. $7S, $9–$10D.

Carlo Jl. Philips Latumahina, ☎ 42220. 11 rooms with AC. $10S, $12–$18D.

Cendrawasih Jl. Tulukabessy 39, ☎ 52487, 41653. 18 rooms with TV. $23S, $30–$36D, $31T.

Eleonor Jl. Anthony Rhebok, ☎ 52834. $7–$8S with fan, $10–$12 S with AC, $10–$13D with fan, $18D with AC.

Hero Jl. Wem Reawaru 7, ☎ 42978, 55973. Fax: 52493. 34 rooms all with TV, AC. $18–$34D. 10% discount if staying more than one night.

Josiba Jl. Tulukabessy 27, ☎ 41280. 12 rooms. $16–$33S.

Manise Jl. W.R. Spratman 1, ☎ 41445, 51553, 42713. 59 rooms, all with TV, video, AC. A businessman's hotel. $25–$30S, $65 executive, $90 VIP.

Mutiara Jl. Pattimura 12, ☎ 53075, 53873, 53874, 53879. Fax: 52171. 30 rooms, all with TV, video, and AC. Pleasant staff. $48–$54S, $54–$60D.

Rezfanny Jl. Wem Reawaru, ☎ 42300. 17 rooms. $6–$10D, $16 AC.

Wisata Jl. Mutiara 3/15, ☎ 53292, 53293, 53567, 53577. Fax: 53592. 26 rooms. $16S, $21–$38D.

Wisma Game Jl. Jend. A. Yani 35, ☎ 53525,

41284. 17 rooms. One of the best of the cheaper hotels. $5–$8S with fan, $10–$18S with AC, $7–$8D with fan, $10–$18D with AC.

Amahusu

Tirta Kencana Jl. Raya Amahusu, ☎ 42324. 20 rooms with TV, AC. Right on the shore, 4 km south of Ambon Town. $40D, $45–$55 VIP, $40 cottage.

Latuhalat

Lelisa Beach Jl. Latuhalat, ☎ 51989, 51988, 51990. 18 rooms with TV, video, AC. $25–$30S, $30–$35D.

Santai Beach Resort Book through Ambon Dive Centre, Pantai Namalatu, Latuhalat, ☎ 62101. Fax: 62104. Quiet, relaxing resort overlooking sandy beach. $26 standard (AC, *mandi*-style bathroom), $42 deluxe (AC, hot water, private bathroom). Airport transfer can be arranged.

Passo

Miranda Beach Jl. Netsepa. ☎ 61244. 10 rooms. Near a good beach 17 km from town. $10–$15.

Vaneysa Natsepa Beach, ☎ 61651. Three bungalows and a restaurant near a good beach.

Hila/Kaitetu

Hila and Kaitetu are two old villages on the north coast of Ambon which have grown together. One of the most interesting places to visit on Ambon, it is very peaceful; where the Christians help to repair the mosque and the Muslims help to repair the church. The beautiful Fort Amsterdam, which was finally rebuilt in 1994, is here, as well as the oldest church and the oldest mosque on Ambon. Half a kilometer from the villages is Manuala Beach Hotel. A bridge leads out to a small restaurant built on poles 30 meters from the coast—the perfect place to sit with a cold fruit juice, looking at the fish swimming among corals in azure blue water. In the background, the island of Seram stretches over the entire horizon. The mountains inland from Hila/Kaitetu have some of the best forests on Ambon where one can see wild parrots.

Manuala Beach Jl. Kaitetu, ☎ 61666. 18 rooms. The closest to a tropical island paradise you can get on Ambon. Sometimes full on weekends. If full, families near the old church will be able to provide homestays $10–$12.

DINING

The traditional cuisine of Ambon is not one of the archipelago's most exciting. The staples, such as sago cakes, are generally bland. The fruits, however, are excellent. Bananas and papayas are available year-round and durian, mangosteens, rambutans and other tropical delights can be found in season. Unfortunately, local palates seem attached to liberal doses of Aji-no-moto (*monosodium glutamate*).

Ambon's claim to culinary fame rests on two dishes. *Colo-colo* is a spicy-sweet, soy-based sauce—with chopped onions, chillies, and tomatoes—served over fresh roasted fish. *Kohu-kohu* is a hot-spicy shredded tuna fish salad, which comes with bean sprouts, onions and cabbage. A bit dry, but still nice if your palate can handle the chilies.

One of the most exotic local dishes is *laor*, a kind of seaworm that wriggles ashore to breed for several days each year, usually in March or April. The special flavor seems to come more from the spice mixture than the worms.

When available, lobster is priced at $6–$10 each. Check first at the Hotel Manise—this restaurant actually takes pains to present the lobster properly and fills the empty portion of the head with goodies. Around town, one can't go wrong by sticking to the wide variety of local fish, or the usually delicious standard Chinese dishes. On the average, meals run $2–$5 per person, plus beverages.

Amboina Jl. A. Y. Patty 63. Best bakery in town, locally-made ice cream. A nice place for a quick meal. Makes a good *roti saucise*, a hot dog in a bun.

Harlim Jl. Sultan Hairun 14, ☎ 52177, 55046. Seafood, Chinese and Indonesian. A tourists' favorite. There is an outdoor dining patio.

Jakarta Jl. Jend. A. Yani, ☎ 52591. Chinese and Indonesian.

Kupu-kupu Ambon Plaza, third floor. European food (pizza). Situated amongst many other small self-service food stands.

Mirasa Jl. Diponegoro 28, ☎ 41702. Chinese. Clean.

Nelayan Jl. Dr. Sutomo 22, ☎ 53070. Sea food, Chinese and Korean.

Nelayan II Jl. Yan Paays 2, ☎ 44550 Seafood.

Pondok Asri Jl. Kapt. Ulupaha, ☎ 42216. Features Chinese and Indonesian dishes as well as Japanese meals, imported US beef, and lots of seafood. Nice decor and quiet setting.

Ujung Pandang Jl. Said Perintah. Chinese and Indonesian. Tables set in backyard garden.

Yang-yang Jl. Wem Reawaru 9, ☎ 44992. Chinese and Indonesian; nearly always has duck. A tourists' favorite.

Dog meat

If you want to try dog meat (usually quite spicy, but not unbearably so), try the roadside stalls in Amahusu and Poka. Obviously, these places are not geared to tourists. Local chefs say that the younger the dog, the more tender the meat, but actually, the secret to a succulent dish lies in the sauce.

BANKS AND MONEY CHANGING

There are plenty of banks around Ambon for money changing, including Bank Central Asia (Jl. Sultan Hairun 24, ☎ 44315), Bank Bumi Daya, Bank Dagang Negara, Bank Expor-Impor, and Bank Negara Indonesia. All exchange U.S. dollars and other major currencies at competetive rates. Credit cards are becoming more popular—the best are Visa and the card issued by Bank Central Asia. Although American Express is also accepted, it takes a long time for merchants to get their money, so there is some reluctance to accept it.

MEDICAL

Rumah Sakit Hative Kecil (Ottokuyk) Jl. Tantui (3 km from town), ☎ 52711, 52712, 52715. The best hospital in Ambon. Contact English speaking Dr. Krisna. VIP rooms (hot water, TV, refrigerator, and an extra bed for visitors) costs $35/day.

Rumah Sakit GPM Jl. Anthoni Rhebok, ☎ 51654.

Rumah Sakit Umum (Public Hospital) Jl. Dr. Kayadoe, ☎ 51933.

Pelita Farma Apotik (pharmacy) Jl. Dr. Setia Budi, ☎ 42014. Open 24-hours.

Meitty Bessy Jl. Mutiara, ☎ 51372. Best dentist in town.

COMMUNICATIONS

Post Office. Jl. Raya Pattimura. ☎ 52165. Fax: 54488.

Telephone Office Jl. Raya Pattimura. In general, phone connections are good, both nationally and internationally. Fax and telex machines are available as well as IDD telephones.

BOOKSTORES

Dian Pertiwi Bookstore Jl. Diponegoro 25, ☎ 42342. Books on Maluku in English.

Nobel Bookstore Jl. Sam Ratulangi 69, ☎ 42983.

Matahari department store, second floor in Ambon Plaza, has a large bookstore with many books in English.

SHOPPING

There is not a great diversity of souvenirs to buy in Ambon. Try the following shops: **Rinamakana**, Jl. Pattimura; **Sulawesi**, Jl. A.Y. Patty, **Kole-kole**, Jl. Said Perintah.

Matahari in Ambon Plaza is the largest supermarket in the city. **Robin's** is on Jl. Sam Ratulangi and **Citra** is on Jl. Tulukabessy.

PHOTOGRAPHY

Bella Vista Ambon Plaza, 45390. Fuji film only. Fastest print processing (half an hour, when not too busy).
Sempurna Jl. A.Y.Patty 40, ☎ 41049. Good quality print processing.
Union Photo Jl. A.Y. Patty 3, ☎ 53569. Largest stock of cameras and binoculars.
All three shops, as well as Citra supermarket, usually have some slide film to sell.

AGENCIES AND TOURS

Travel agencies offer a wide variety of tours from a half-day city tour to several days in the islands: Saparua, Seram, Ternate, Banda, and the Tanimbars. Some tours concentrate on history, others on local culture, still others on diving or wildlife. Tours can also be tailored to your interests and schedules.
Natrabu Tours and Travel Jl. Rijail 53, SK 8/1, ☎ 53537. Contact: Mrs. Tanasaleh.
P.T. Daya Patal Tour and Travel Jl. Said Perintah, SK II/27A, Ambon, Maluku, Indonesia. ☎ 53529, 53344, 52498. Fax: 44709. Contact: Tony Tomasoa.
Sumber Budi Tour and Travel Jl. Mardika II/16, ☎ 53205. Contact: Bruce Nanloh. (After hours: 52625.)
Only the Daya Patal agency runs tours to Banda, Tanimbar and Misool, an island off western Irian Jaya. They also offer dive packages. (See below.) Some typical offerings:
Ambon Island tour 3 days, 2 nights. For a group of 2, $185/person. For a group of 5–9, $166/person.
Ambon Island tour 6 days, 5 nights. For a group of 2, $256/person. For a group of 5–9, $244/person.
Ambon Island tour with traditional dancing 4 days, 3 nights. For a group of 2, $360/person. For a group of 5–9, $305/person.
Ambon, Saparua and Seram 5 days, 4 nights. For a group of 2, $275. For a group of 5–9, $257.
Banda Islands tour 4 days, 3 nights. For a group of 2, $212/person. For a group of 5–9, $200/person.
Tanimbar Islands 5 days, 5 nights. For a group of 2, $450/person.

Guides

While travel agencies provide guides, you may want to hire one yourself. The government has licensed local freelance guides. Their rates run $7–$10 for a half day, or $10–$17 for a full day, on Ambon Island. Off the island, the price goes up, $12–$23/day, plus expenses. Rates depend on the guide's experience and language skills. The better hotels can help you find a licensed guide, or ask at the tourism office (*Kantor Pari-*

wisata) at the governor's office building. One can also find unlicensed guides of varying degrees of competence at equally varying rates.

SCUBA DIVING

P.T. Daya Patal Tour and Travel Jl. Said Perintah, SK II/27A, ☎ 53529, 53344, 52498, 41136, 41821. Fax: 44709. Contact: Tony Tomasoa. P.T. Daya Patal can arrange boats, tanks, guides, food, and, if needed, a compressor. For rent: Regulators $14/day, BCD's $10/day.
While there are no certified dive guides yet, staff members can show you where the good spots are located. We had superb diving with this outfit, with all arrangements running like clockwork. Try to have Hentje, a pleasant young man and good diver, as your guide. He will look after your gear and be generally quite helpful. One day, all-inclusive, two-tank tours in Ambon/Saparua area run $125/person (group of 1) to $55/person (group of 4). All-inclusive packages:
Ambon 3D/2N $225/person (2–4 persons), $217/person (5–9 persons)
Saparua 5D/4N, $325/person (2–4 persons), $313/person (5–9 persons)
Misool 12D/11N, $650/person, only groups of 5–9 persons.
Ambon Dive Centre Pantai Namalatu, Latulahat, Ambon, Maluku 97118, ☎ 62101. Fax: 62104. Offers daily dive tours, all-inclusive ($70), as well as NAUI scuba courses. Airport pick-up can be arranged for 1 hour journey from airport. Open all year, except May.

NIGHTLIFE

Hotels like **Manise, Mutiara**, and **Tirta Kencana** have *karaoke* singing or professional artists performing. **Top Ten Discotheque** is much like discos all over the world, except that you are expected to keep in row when you dance and that half-an-hour, perhaps, will be with local music and *yospan* dancing imported from Irian Jaya. Little happens before midnight at Top Ten. **Regent Discotheque**, Jl. Said Perintah, is hottest on Sunday afternoon. This is the only place university girls can go without starting rumors.
English language films are always playing at Ambon's two theaters: **21** in Ambon Plaza and **Ambonia**, close-by on Jl. Raya Pattimura.

Lease PRACTICALITIES

INCLUDES HARUKU, SAPARUA, NUSA LAUT

2 Lease

Idyllic white sand beaches, living local traditions and spectacular underwater scenery lie quietly in the Lease Islands; ideal for a quick by relaxing trip from Ambon.
Prices in US $. Telephone code for Saparua is 0931. S=Single, D=Double.

GETTING THERE

To Haruku and Saparua. It is easiest to reach Haruku and Kailolo by speedboat from Tulehu (20 minutes). Pay $1 for a public speedboat or charter one for $10–$30, depending on the size of the boat and how long you will need it. Other villages on Haruku and Saparua can also be reached by speedboat from Tulehu, but it is drier and safer to take a ferry or a passenger (motor) boat. Pelau on Haruku and Kulur on Saparua can be reached by ferry from Tulehu daily ($1.50–$2). Passenger boats leave twice daily from Tulehu for larger villages on Saparua (Porto Haria, Ihamahu and Tuhaha), $2–$2.50.

GETTING AROUND

Mini-buses will be waiting at the dock when ferries and passenger boats arrive in Saparua. Most villages can be reached easily by mini-bus. There are few buses on Haruku and the wait between runs can be hours. Walking to isolated villages is actually quite pleasant, as long as you avoid the mid-day heat.

ACCOMMODATIONS

Losmen Siri Sori In Sirisori Islam, on the east shore of Saparua Bay. 12 rooms. $12–14S; $13–18D.
Mahu Village Resort Near Kampung Mahu on Saparua's north coast, on the east shore of Tuhaha Bay. 4 bungalows. $25S, $35D.
   Note: There are losmens in Saparua Town and in Ihamahu. Elsewhere in the Lease Islands where there are no lodgings, you will have to depend on local hospitality. Arrangements should be made through the village head (*kepala desa*). Pay $6 for room and meals.

PLACES OF INTEREST

Haruku village is an old Christian village with many local traditions. One of which, the **Sasi Kian Lompa** (one day between November to February) attracts many visitors. Catching of the lompa fish is banned except for one day out of the year. Ceremonies to call the fish begin in the evening and continue throughout the night. Beginning at 8 am, upon signal, everybody jumps in the river to catch the fish. About 20–35 tons of lompa are caught in a single day with the use of nets, buckets or just hands.
Kailolo is a village famous as the world's largest nesting ground for the Moluccan Scrubfowl (called *maleo* in Maluku). The birds spend the day in the forests on Seram, then bury their large eggs in the sand at night in the area around the graveyard just south of the village. The heat from the sand hatches the eggs. The chicks must dig themselves free out of more than half a meter of sand. More than 200 birds can be seen on full moon nights. Expect to pay $5 to watch the birds from small hiding places near the nesting grounds.
Saparua. Many good beaches and possibilities for snorkeling. Visit Duursteede Fort or see pottery making in Ouw.
Nusa Laut is the smallest and most isolated of the Lease Islands. It can be reached by passenger speedboat from Saparua Town on Wednesdays or Saturdays. Or, ask around to get a ride with a small boat, or charter one ($25–$50).
Pombo Island between Ambon and Haruku is a very small inhabited island. Pombo and the surrounding coral reefs is a nature reserve. Hundreds of pied imperial pigeons breed on Pombo and many egrets and other water birds visit the island. It is a good place for swimming and snorkeling. If you want to visit Pombo you must obtain permission from PHPA *sub-balai* in Passo before chartering a speedboat from Tulehu.

WEATHER

During the southeast monsoon, June–August, the seas are roughest and underwater visibility is reduced. Things are fine the rest of the year, although the seas get a bit rough during the northwest monsoon, January–February, but this does not affect diving.

3 Seram PRACTICALITIES

INCLUDING MANUSELA NATIONAL PARK

Few tourists find their way to Seram, Maluku's second largest island. Yet thanks to lumber operations, particularly the plywood factory at Waissarisa, roads and communications, at least in the southwest, are quite well developed. Manusela National Park is home to traditional Naulu villages and offers spectacular bird watching.

Prices in US $. Telephone code is 0914. S=Single, D=Double.

TOURIST INFORMATION

A tourism office (*Kantor Pariwisata*) is scheduled to open at the district head (*bupati)* 's complex in Masohi, with information on the central Maluku district. Try to find John Lisapeli there; he speaks English well and is quite knowledgeable, especially on Naulu culture.

GETTING THERE

There are frequent ferry and boat connections between Ambon and Seram. It is possible to leave for Seram in the morning and return to Ambon the same evening. However, at least a week is needed for visiting the more interesting parts of the islands, including the Manusela National Park.

By air

There is a weekly flight between Ambon and Amahai (Saturday, $25), but there is little reason for flying, as the ferry connections are so frequent and inexpensive.
Merpati Jl. Pemda, Amahai, Kab. Masohi, Maluku Tengah.

By sea

Hitu to Piru Vessels make this regular run from Hitu on Ambon Island's north coast to Piru, at the head of a deep bay on Seram's southwest coast. The trip, which usually starts around noon, takes four hours and costs $3.
Liang to Kairatu A ferry makes this daily two-hour run from Liang (2 pm) on Ambon's northeast coast to Kairatu on Seram. Kairatu is a the site of a plywood factory and a transmigration area, $1.
Tulehu to Amahai A fast boat, *Lailai* sails every day from Tulehu, 8 am and 2 pm, and from Amahai 10 am and 4 pm. The trip only takes one-and-one-half hours, and costs $7.

Motor vessels connect Tulehu and Amahai twice daily (7 am and 9 pm from Tulehu). This trip takes 3.5 hours, $3.50. A last possibility is to hire a speedboat for $32–$45.

There are connecting buses between Amahai and Masohi.

By land

The easiest solution is to go by bus from Ambon to a town in Seram (Masohi, Tehoru, Piru, Saleman, etc). Buses leave from Ambon's Batu Merah bus terminal every morning at 6 am. Tickets, which can be bought in any of the many small stalls in the terminal, include the price of the ferry and a meal: $ 6 for Masohi, $10 for Tehoru or Saleman.

GETTING AROUND

Public minibuses ply the road network in southwestern Seram, mainly between Kairatu, Piru and Masohi, but also connect the western part of the north coast between Asaudi and Hulung. The stretch of road along the central and western north coast (Wahai–Bula) also has roads and minibuses. The roads to Tehoru and Saleman are often in such poor condition that only larger buses can manage them.

ACCOMMODATIONS

There is one hotel and a number of *losmen*-type accommodations in Masohi.
Belohy Indah Jl. Abd. Soulissa, ☎ 21251. 6 rooms. $5 w/o meals, $7.50 w/meals.
Lelemuku Jl. Abd. Soulissa 12. Small rooms. $5 w/o meals, $7 w/meals.
Masohi Manise Jl. Abd. Soulissa. Scheduled to open in late 1996.
Nusa Ina Jl. Banda 2. $5 w/o meals, $7.50 w/ meals; $9 w/indoor toilet and ladle bath.
Nusantara Jl. Abd. Sulaiman 15, ☎ 21339. Restaurant next door. $5S; $10D.
Sri Lestari Jl. Abd. Said 5. This is the best of the *losmen*. Meals included. $10 S; $18D.

Outside of Masohi, there are a few *losmen*, including one at Wahai on Seram's north coast

(**Sinar Indah**, 8 rooms, $7.50 without meals) and in Tehoru (**Penginapan Susi**, Jl. Pelabuan 299, 5 rooms, $3.50 without meals, and **Penginapan Manusela**, Jl. Pelabuan, 6 rooms, $3.50–$5 without meals). The government runs a small *losmen* in Waipirit (Kairatu).

Manusela National Park

At least a week is needed for a hike through the Manusela National Park. First, you need to obtain permission from the Directorate General of Forest Protection and Nature Conservation (PHPA, Sub-Balai Konservasi Sumberdaya Alam Maluku) office in Passo to visit the park. Passo is 12 km from Ambon town by red minibus, towards Hunut.

Before you enter the park, you must report to PHPA's office in Mosso, on the south coast (Pak Alexander) or in Wahai on the north coast (Pak Edi). The trail from Mosso is unbelievably steep. You must also report in at the local police offices.

Mosso is reached by public speedboat from Tehoru ($1.50) and Wahai by public speedboat from Saleman ($4). You can also hire a speedboat for 10–20 times higher prices.

Pak Alexander and Pak Edi will provide you with a guide/porter (which is absolutely necessary) and tell you how much rice, noodles and canned fish you should take with you. You need to take cooking equipment, camping gear, worn-in walking boots, a compass, and raingear. Expect to pay $7–$10/day for the guide; $5/day per porter, plus their food and cigarettes. It will take most of a day before you really get inside the park from either Mosso or Wahai.

This park, which is not yet developed for large-scale tourism, includes large areas of virgin forest and mountains reaching above 3,000 m. The park is very rich in bird life. Ten of the bird species which can be seen here live only on Seram. Three of these are parrots, with the large white salmon-crested cockatoo as the favorite of most visitors.

Several isolated villages are situated in an enclave in the central part of the park. Accommodations can always be arranged. Expect to pay $5 to your hostess and another $5 to the village chief (*kepala desa*).

The best time to visit the park is during the dry season, between August to October.

If you are returning to Ambon via Wahai, this can be done in a single day by speedboat from Wahai to Saleman leaving at 5:30 am and connecting with a bus from Saleman to Ambon leaving at 9 am.

Banda PRACTICALITIES

4

Perhaps the most beautiful of the islands scattered throughout Maluku, the tiny Bandas sparkle like gems in the vast Banda Sea. The one-time center of the world's nutmeg production, these islands boast fabulous diving and snorkeling and breathtaking scenery.

Prices are in US $. Telephone code is 0910. AC= Airconditioning. S=Single, D=Double.

GETTING THERE

You can fly to Bandaneira from Ambon by Merpati on Monday, Wednesday, Saturday, and Sunday, by 18-passenger Twin Otter, $42. The flight takes 65 minutes and leaves at 7 am. (Divers note: baggage limit on this flight is 10 kilos, with 63¢/kilo for overweight. This regulation, however, is not always religiously enforced.) You can easily walk from the airstrip to the Bandaneira hotels, or hop in a minibus.

Pelni's *Rinjani* makes a stop between Ambon and Banda every two weeks, as does the smaller *Daya Nusantara*. Inter-island mixed freighters also make the trip about every three weeks.

ACCOMMODATIONS

Des Alwi's three hotels offer the only watersports facilties. For reservations, contact: Hotel Maulana, P.O. Box 3193, Jakarta, Indonesia. ☎ (021) 360372, Fax: 360308. In Banda: ☎ (0910) 21022, 21023, Fax: 21024.
Maulana The best rooms in Bandaneira are in the 50-room Maulana Inn, and offer a nice view of Gunung Api across the lagoon. Three meals $16/person +10%. Cold beer $1.75. Bottle of arak $3. Separate meals: breakfast $3, lunch $5, supper $8. A big plate of sashimi, $4.50 extra (subject to availability, must be ordered one day ahead). Sea front rooms, $35S, $45D; other rooms, $30S, $40D; bungalows $45. All plus 10% tax.
Laguna Inn Jl. Pelabuhan. 12 rooms. $25S, $30D. Three meals $12, all plus 10% tax.
Rumah Budaya Jl. Nusantara. Four rooms in the back for budget travelers. Try to get a room with a view of Gunung Api. $11–$14, including tax and breakfast.

Aside from Des Alwi's places, there are three simple *losmen*: The **Delfika** (Jl. Nusantara, ☎ 21027), 8 rooms, all enclosed facilities, $14; the **Selecta** (Jl. Nusantara), 7 rooms, offers full board, $10 with attached toilet, $8.50 for rooms with shared facilities; the **Likes Homestay**, just past the Maulana Hotel, 6 rooms, $4.

These are quite close to the main mosque and its blaring loudspeakers. All accommodations on Banda tend to fill during October and the last two weeks of December—reserve ahead. There are no banks here, so bring your rupiahs.

DINING

Best at the **Maulana** and the **Laguna**, where you usually are served two kinds of fish and a vegetable. Fresh sushi is a specialty at the Maulana—order one day ahead. There are many little restaurants in Bandaneira town where the simple meals of rice or noodles with chicken cost about 75c. We found the **Selecta II** the most pleasant of these—there is cold beer available here (sometimes) for a $1.50 per can. Generally, fresh vegetables, eggs, and other produce are often hard to come by, so when they are available, they're expensive.

DIVING

Diving is available to guests at any of Des Alwi's three hotels. Contact them for reservations. A day dive tour (2 tanks), including equipment rental, works out to about $80.

BOAT RENTAL

Des Alwi's boats can run divers to Hatta Island ($25) and to Ai and/or Run ($30) with a 5 person minimum. The cost is less for closer spots, such as Sjahrir. You can also rent the boats by the hour, for example for night dives: speedboat (4–6 people) $30/hr; diesel-powered boat (8 people) $25/hr; or a bigger diesel-powered boat (12 people) $35/hr. The largest boat, the *Boi Kherang*, can accommodate 20 people and goes for $40/hr. The rental fees for the larger boats include a Zodiac with a small outboard.

For snorkeling off Banda Neira, the near coast of Lontar and Gunung Api, a boat can drop you off and pick up at a predetermined time for $6/person (6 persons or more). The same arrangement to Sjahrir Island and the far side of Lontar, $10/person.

For a special trip to Manukang (Suangi) Island ($160–$350) or far-away Manuk Island, with lots of birds ($880), contact the manager of the Maulana Hotel.

OTHER WATERSPORTS

Windsurfing, mid June to September, January to March, $2/hr; waterskiing $30/hr; fishing is included in the boat rental. May–September, the yellowtail tuna, sailfish, swordfish, and Spanish mackerel run; from October–June, it's barracuda. Jacks are caught all year round.

EXCURSIONS

Sunset cruise Two-hour cruise around Gunung Api by boat, and a stop at Sambayang to visit a cinnamon plantation, to snorkel, and to sit in hot water springs. $6 (6 person minimum).
Climbing Gunung Api It takes one–three hours to climb the 656-meter-high volcano. (See page

99.) One day's notice required. Guide $5.50 per trekker, plus round-trip boat, $6.
Lontar Village This is a trip to Lontar island to see a nutmeg plantation, sacred wells and Fort Hollandia. The tour starts at 4 pm, and takes about two hours. $6/person, minimum of two; if guide needed, extra $5.

CULTURAL EVENTS

In April and October, 37-man *kora-kora* (war canoe) races are held. During the rest of the year, you can commission a demonstration: $150 for one *kora-kora* and crew. A *cakalele* war dance costs $350, and requires 10-day's notice.

WEATHER

The rainy season is from mid-June through August (southeast monsoon). High winds often blow from mid-January through February. The very best for sun and calm seas: April, and late September–early November.

PERIPLUS LANGUAGE GUIDES

Practical Indonesia

ISBN: 0-945971-52-4

As any seasoned traveler knows, the ability to communicate in the language of the country you are visiting makes a very big difference in the experiences you have. With this guide, and a few hours of practice, you can begin to communicate in Indonesian and Malay easily and effectively. Get where you want to go, pay the right prices, relate to the locals! A handy glossary and the Malay appendix complete the guide.

The Practical Indonesia *is available in English, French, German and Dutch editions.*

PRACTICAL INDONESIAN
a communication guide
JOHN BARKER

BAGUS!

English Edition

Distributed by:

Berkeley Books Pte. Ltd. (Singapore & Malaysia)
5 Little Road, #08-01, Singapore 536983   Tel: (65) 280 3320   Fax: (65) 280 6290

C.V. Java Books (Indonesia)
Jl. Kelapa Gading Kirana, Blok A14 No. 17, Jakarta 14240 Tel: (62-21) 451 5351   Fax: (62-21) 453 4987

5 Ternate PRACTICALITIES

INCLUDES TIDORE

Ternate and Tidore rise majestically out of the depths of the Maluku Sea. The twin volcanoes—Ternate's Gamalama and Tidore's Kiematubu—dominate the once famous clove islands. Ternate is the departure point for all travels to northern Maluku.
Prices in US $. Telephone code is 0921. AC= Airconditioning. S=Single, D=Double.

TOURIST INFORMATION

The Ternate tourism bureau, located in the district head's office complex on Jl. Pahlawan Revolusi, can help with most arrangements. They can find an English-speaking guide (don't expect perfection) for $10 a day, plus expenses. The tourism office can also arrange a demonstration of traditional dances.

GETTING THERE

By Air

Ternate is connected by air to Ambon and Manado, and from Ternate one can reach several small airstrips in North and Central Maluku. Ternate's Babullah airport services daily flights to Ambon (which connect to larger cities in the western archipelago), Manado, and Gorontalo on Merpati, and Bouraq. From Ternate, flights connect to Labuha, Langgur, Namlea, Namrole, Sanana, Jayapura, Sorong, and Timika. From the airport, a taxi to town costs about $5–$7.
Merpati. PT Eterna Raya, Jl. Busoiri 81. ☎ 21314, 21648, 21649.

Manado	Daily	$38
Denpasar	WThSu,	
	via Ambon, U.P.	$225
Ambon	Daily	$63
Galela	TuThSu	$25
Gebe	MWF	$43
Kao	Sa	$16
Morotai	Sa	$35
Labuha	TuF	$28
Sanana	TuF	$52

(**Note**: You need permission from the nickel mining company, Aneka Tambang, to visit tiny Gebe Island. Their office in Ternate is on Jl. Kayu Merah, ☎ 21689.)
Bouraq Jl. Sultan Babullah, ☎ 21042. Daily flights to Ambon and Manado; connections to Jakarta, Surabaya, Denpasar, and Ujung Pandang four times/week.

By Sea

Ternate is an important shipping center, connected by large passenger ships of the national Pelni Line to Java, Sulawesi and Irian Jaya, and by mixed freighters and passenger ships to Halmahera, Mangole, Sula, Sanana, Obi and Buru, and by lots of smaller boats to points within a day or so of motoring.
Pelni Lines. Two ships of the Pelayaran Nasional Indonesia (Pelni) line stop in Ternate: the *Kerinci* and the *Ceremai*. Pelni is located in the harbor complex (Komplex Pelabuhan), at ☎ 21434, Fax: 21276. See the Transportation section for their respective routes (page 181).

GETTING AROUND

Sea Travel

Mixed cargo/deck passage boats. Two ships run out of Ternate, chiefly freighters but with deck passage available. Passenger fares are dirt cheap, but it's no love boat luxury cruise. They are extremely crowded, not at all clean, and the few toilets are in horrible shape. We strongly suggest bargaining with the crew for one of their berths—say $7.50/day for up to 3 days, $5 a day for longer.

1) To Halmahera. Every 28 days a mixed cargo with deck passengers leaves Bitung in North Sulawesi, stops at Mayoa Island and then goes on to Ternate and Soa-Siu on Tidore. From Tidore, it circles Halmahera counter-clockwise on the following route: Gita, Payahe, Saketa, Besui, Mafa, Weda, Patani, Gebe Island, Bicoli, Akelamo, Wasile, Subaim, Tobelo, Daruba (Morotai Island) , Berebere (Morotai), Dama, Loloda, and then back to Ternate and Bitung.

2) To Bacan, Obi and the Sulas. A similar ship makes a run every 20 days from Ternate, to Babang (on Bacan), Laiwui and Wailoar (both on Obi), Mangole, Bobong, Sanana (the Sula Islands), Bara, Leksula, Namrole and Namlea (on Buru Island), and then Ambon and back.

Local passenger boats. There are also frequent boats—often several a week—to Bitung, Tobelo, Bacan, Obi, Kayoa, Sanana and, once a week, direct to Manado. There are two places to check up on departure. Small offices at the entrance to the main harbor handle the better passenger ships. Unfortunately these ships travel mostly (but not always) at night, so you miss the scenery. The fares are according to distance: Bacan ($5); Obi ($7.50); Tobelo/ Daruba ($5); Bitung ($6.50). For about $1.75 you can rent a mattress or about $5 (after perhaps a bit of bargaining) should get you one of the crew's bunks for the night.

Small craft. From Bastiong's small-craft harbor, small wood motor boats travel frequently to the islands south of Ternate, as well as to ports on Halmahera's west coast. These are not at all pleasant in rough seas. A special harbor near Bastiong serves a passenger–vehicle ferry to Sidangoli, due to the activities of the large lumber mill located there. You can also charter a small 25–40 Hp outboard-powered, covered boat out of Tidore, which can sleep 4–6 in very basic levels of comfort, for $40–$50 a day, all included. Don't do this in December, January or February, however, when the waves are strong.

Land Travel

There are plenty of minibuses around Ternate town and nearby villages, but it is harder to find them in the further out places. Chartering a bemo/taxi costs about $3 an hour. The regular bemo routes, all beginning at Ternate Town, run 10¢–35¢.

ACCOMMODATIONS

Ternate has many hotels in various price categories. Price corresponds closely to quality. Of the better hotels, we recommend the **Neraca**, the best, and the **Nirwana**. Among the medium priced ones, the **Sejahtera** and in the low-budget category, the **Sentosa**.

Anda Baru Jl. Ketilang, ☎ 21262. 16 rooms. AC rooms $8 with meals, $7 without; fan-cooled rooms $6 with meals, $3.50 without.

Chrysant Jl. Jend. A. Yani, ☎ 21288.13 AC rooms. Regular room $10; VIP room $15. Add $2.50 for board.

El Shinta Jl. Pahlawan Revolusi, ☎ 22216, 23633. 13 AC rooms, $15; 10 fan-cooled rooms, $5. Add $3 for board.

Indah Jl. Boesoiri, ☎ 21334. 10 rooms. Very helpful staff, especially Saiful. Excellent meals. AC rooms $17.50 with food, $12.50 without; fancooled, $12.50 with meals, $9 without.

Merdeka Jl. Merdeka, ☎ 21120. 10 rooms. Clean. AC rooms with meals $12.50, without $10; fan-cooled with food $7, without $5.

Nauli Jl. Nuku, ☎ 21353. 10 rooms. Economy $8, Standard $11.

Neraca Jl. Pahlawan Revolusi, ☎ 22534. 28 rooms, all AC. Meals available. $15 per person.

Nirwana Jl. Pahlawan Revolusi, ☎ 21787. 24 rooms. $12S, $18D, $24VIP.

Nusantara Jl. Salim Fabanyo, ☎ 21086. 10 rooms. $6S, $9D.

Rahmat Jl. Pahlawan Revolusi. 10 rooms. $5–$6.50.

Sejahtera Jl. Salim Fabanyo. ☎ 21139. 12 rooms. $6.50S, $10.50D.

Sentosa Jl. Pahlawan Revolusi. 10 rooms. $5–$6.50.

Ternate City Hotel Jl. Nuku I. ☎ 22555, 22777. Fax: 22630. 36 rooms. Restaurant, hot water, AC. New. $20–$35S, $30–$45D.

DINING

Most of the better hotels have restaurants and several places in Ternate town serve good Indonesian and Chinese dishes for some $3 to $5 per meal.

Gamalama Jl. Pahlawan Revolusi, ☎ 21712. Indonesian.

Garuda Jl. Pahlawan Revolusi, ☎ 21090. Chinese, Indonesian.

LaBamba Jl. Salim Fabanyo. Excellent Chinese cooking. Karaoke.

Nikmat Jl. Pahlawan Revolusi, ☎ 21491. Middle Eastern, saté.

Nirwana At the Hotel of same name, Chinese, Indonesian.

Pondok Katu Jl. Baranjangan, for all kinds of excellent fish, prepared various ways.

Roda Baru Jl. Pahlawan Revolusi, ☎ 21513. Padang.

Siola Jl. Stadion, ☎ 21377. Generally considered the best in town. Try their speciality, coconut crab, $8 for the whole beast, $5 for enough to fill a hungry traveler. The hard shell is well cracked before serving. It's one huge crab. The dish is prepared with hot chili peppers, so tell them to hold the little red ones if your palate is delicate. Make sure they serve the rear part of the body; some people don't like it—but we did. This is the part which makes the coconut crab different from any other crab. They also serve Chinese and Indonesian style fish, lobsters, prawns, chicken, steak, rice and noodle dishes, $1.50–$5. Cold beer, $2. Attached disco is open on Friday and Saturday, 10pm–2am, $3 door.

BANKS AND MONEY CHANGING

It's better to have all the rupiahs you will need before you get to Ternate. Should you run short, try the Bank Expor-Impor (Exim) or the Bank Negara Indonesia (BNI) for travelers checks or cash. Both banks are on Jl. Pahlawan Revolusi, near each other.

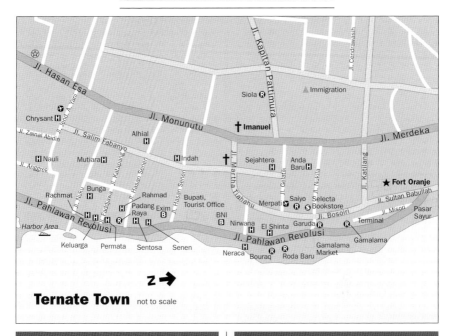

Ternate Town not to scale

CRAFTS AND SOUVENIRS

There are no shops where you can obtain a selection of local craft. There are traveling salesmen flogging lobsters or coconut crabs mounted on a board covered with red felt ($5–$10). The coffee shop at the airport sells the locally famous *batu Bacan* (Bacan stones), hard, polished, semi-precious stones, some mounted, some not, for $2–$4.

It is much better to go to Koloncucu compound in Ternate town, where women still weave cloth in the traditional fashion. Local weaving techniques were imported from Buton Island in the 15th century, using patterns that may have come from Palembang, Sumatra. The women weave *sarong*s usually on order, so there may not be any for sale. If there are any spare cloths around, the price is about $20–$30.

More practical local objects include heavy earthenware pottery from Mare Island, just south of Tidore, including sago molds, incense burners and mortars for mixing traditional medicines. These can be found at Soa Siu's market. You might also find hats resembling Dutch helmets made from orchid fibers and woven leaf mats from Halmahera.

Villages in back of Ternate town make bamboo chairs, sometimes sold in the market. The distinctive funnel-shaped baskets—the smaller *saloi* for women and larger *peludi* for men (as well as miniature ones), are the speciality of Dowora village, north of Soa Siu on Tidore. Usually made from strips of rotan, these baskets are found throughout northern Maluku.

TRAVEL AGENCIES

Travel agencies can arrange a circle Ternate tour. Many downtown agencies sell airplane tickets for Merpati, Bouraq and Sempati.

Indo Gama Jl. Jend. A. Yani 131 (next to Crysant Hotel), P.O. Box 21, ☎ 21288, 21580, 22873. Fax: 21165.

Pelita Express Jl. A. Yani, ☎ 21580.

An alternative to travel agents, we suggest that you have Pak Haji Umar Ammari, a professional photographer, set up tours for you and serve as your guide. He speaks English and Dutch, and can be contacted at home. He can make all the necessary arrangements for climbing Gamalama, as well as homestays with honest, friendly people for $3–$5, room and board. He can also set up basic round-Ternate tours, $12.50/person for two, $10/person for 3–4, and $7.50/person for 5–6. It would be even better to take a longer tour with him, for which he charges a very reasonable $7.50/day, plus his expenses.

Pak Haji Umar Ammari. Jl. Pahlawan Revolusi, Falajawa, Ternate. ☎ 21197.

Some of his suggestions:

1) **Kayoa Island**. Two days, one night (sleep in a local home) to explore the beautiful coral reefs. It takes 6 hours each way from Ternate on a local passenger boat. $15–$20/person.

2) **Widi archipelago**. Off the southernmost tip of Halmahera, this little-visited group of islands offers great fishing, snorkeling and panoramas.

3) **Sayafi Island**. Near Buli in eastern Halmahera, this island is the home of a bird he says is black at night and turns to a golden color in the day,

Ternate 5

hence its Indonesian name, *burung mas*, or "gold bird". Mating season, when the birds' colors are best, is in September or March.

Pak Haji also knows the whereabouts of the yearly June migration of hundreds of lobsters in the shallow waters off Hamahera's southwest peninsula, accessible from the town of Patani.

Guides

Be very selective of guides, particularly if you are doing something tricky like climbing Gamalama. Make sure you get someone with experience. We highly recommend Bakri Ali, but if you can't get him, Hanafi or Yusman are also good.

DIVING

Qualified scuba divers should contact the local tourism office (see above) for information on the Ternate diving club. This club has tanks and often plans group dives on the weekends. The best scuba diving spots are said to be off Maitara Island, between Ternate and Tidore.

TERNATE EVENTS

There are two noteworthy events in the Ternate area—one very modern, one traditional. Both are named for Ternate's most famous sultan.
Babullah Motor Rally This motorcycle race takes place in the first week of October and covers 460 km from Sidangole (the site of the huge Barito lumber mill) to Galela and back, over a two-day period, with an overnight in Tobelo.
Babullah Kaloli Kie This one sounds like a spectacle worthy of the days when the Sultanate of Ternate was at its prime. The son of the last Sultan leads a canoe procession around the island from the gayly decorated *Kaguna,* a 10 ton, 15 m craft, followed by 40 *kora-kora* canoes, each 2 ton and 9 m. There are songs, dances and feasting too. This week-long event takes place on the Muslim holiday of Idhul Adha.

SCENIC BOAT RIDE SOUTH

Unsurpassed scenery awaits boat passengers traveling between Ternate and Bacan. (Check at Bastiong Dock for times and prices.) Island after island glides by, each bright green and beautiful. Looking back towards Ternate, the slopes of Gamalama seem to leave no room for humans as they rise out of the blue and emerald seas. Wisps of cloud decorate the volcano's peak and an occasional discreet belch of smoke reminds you that it is still active.

A bit further along, Kiematubu's peak rises from the lower ridges until the whole mountain is revealed, with tree-shaded Soa Siu at its base. A few small canoes out on a fishing jaunt sail or paddle by. By then, the small island of

Mare, a low hill peaking out of the sea, is already slipping by on port side. Two pottery making villages cling to Mare's shores. Then the cone of Moti, fully clad in vegetation, rears up over seaside mosques and villages.

Makian at first seems like just another volcano, but then you see a huge gash running from the central crests to the sea–the remains of a fierce explosion that nearly split the island in two on July 17, 1988. Ejecta from the crater flew up 11,000 meters! Makian's previous great explosions occurred in 1646, when all villages on its flanks were destroyed, and again in 1862. There should be an added bonus when cruising by Makian. On one of our trips, at this very spot, our ship was "assaulted" by dozens of dolphins, performing gracefully arched jumps and exhuberant flips.

The scenery is less noteworthy as you cruise past long, fairly flat Kayoa Island, smack on the equator and boasting of sea gardens off its western side, especially in the Guriaci mini-archipelago. The second half of the trip to Bacan from Kayoa to the port of Babang on Bacan's east coast is anti-climactic.

Tidore

Motor launches ferry passengers back and forth between the docks at Bastiong on Ternate and Rum on Tidore. Service runs from 7 am to 6 pm and the 5 minute ride costs 30¢. The frequency of departure depends on the traffic—anything from a few minutes to a couple of hours or more. The boats are covered, but once underway it's pleasant on the roof. Both sea and land transportation are much more frequent on market days—Tuesday, Friday and Saturday.

GETTING AROUND

Minibus/taxi charter runs $2/hour or $20 for a full day. Public transport on Tidore covers all the passable roads; fares range from 6¢–30¢.

ACCOMMODATIONS

Penginapan Jangi Soa Siu. ☎ 21131. 12 rooms, $9/day, including breakfast and supper.

SUGGESTED ITINERARIES

1) **Telaga**. A visit to the village of Telaga, perched near a crater lake requires a four to five hour climb and a local guide—a splended jaunt.
2) **Mare Island.** Boats from Tidore run regularly to Mare island, where the people make simple, utilitarian pottery, sold throughout the north Maluku area.

6 Halmahera PRACTICALITIES

INCLUDES MOROTAI AND BACAN

Rugged, densely forested and thinly populated, Halmahera, Maluku's second largest island, is way off the beaten track. Morotai offers potentially exciting diving, undisturbed reefs for snokeling, and white sand beaches for sunbathing.

Prices in US $. Telephone code for Tobelo 0924, Labuha is 0927, Sanana 0929. AC= Airconditioning.

GETTING THERE

There are four ways to reach Halmahera: by air from Ambon or Ternate to Galela, by air from Ternate to Kao, by motor launch to Jailolo, and by various sea carriers to Tobelo.

By air

To Galela. Merpati's flights from Ambon land at the airstrip about 14 kms from Galela. There are often more passengers than the planes can handle, so waiting lists can stretch. And, after a particularly heavy rainfall, the grass strip can become too soggy for a safe landing.

There are no accommodations at Galela, so you have to take a public minibus to Tobelo ($3/person), some 50 kilometers south on Halmahera's east coast. Don't fall asleep during the trip, as the minibus passes beautiful lagoons and village scenery.

From Galela, Merpati flies once a week to Ambon, Denpasar, Langgur, and Ujung Pandang, all through Ternate. It also flies to Manado, also through Ternate, on Tuesday, Thursday and Sunday.

Merpati Cabang PT Eterna Galela, Jl. Kampung Soa Sio, Galela.

To Kao. Merpati flies to Kao from Ternate on Saturday, landing on a restored section of the former World War II Japanese airfield. It is not unusual for this flight to be cancelled. You can catch a ride to town in the Merpati agent's minibus.

By sea

To Kao. A combination sea and overland operation provides twice weekly service to Kao (and other points on the east coast of Halmahera's northern peninsula). On Mondays and Thursdays, a motorboat leaves Ternate and lands three hours later at Dodinga, on Halmahera's west coast. A truck meets the boat and hauls the passengers across the 5 km-wide neck of land at the base of the northern peninsula. Passengers then transfer to another motorboat at Bobaneigu,

and the ride from there to Kao takes 2–3 hours. The fare is $4. The operation runs the reverse route on Tuesdays and Fridays. (A similar odyssey connects Ternate to points on Kao Bay's southwestern coast, providing transport for 2,500 transmigrant families there.)

One can also take the regular motorboat to Jailolo from Ternate (2 hours, $1.50), then take a public minibus to Bobaneigu (less than 1 hour, 33¢). From there, catch a coastal motorboat for the 2–3 hour ride to Kao.

To Jailolo. Small boats make the run daily from Ternate Town to Jailolo, just 2 hours each way. $1.50 one-way.

To Tobelo. An efficient ferry service connects Ternate to Tobelo via Daruba on Morotai. Three passenger boats, the 80-ton *Garuda*, the 60-ton *Tobelo Star* and the 45-ton *Super Star* ply the route. The capacities of these three ships vary from 75 to 200, but everyone manages to squeeze in. The Ternate–Daruba leg takes 13 hours, and after a several-hour stopover on Morotai, the Daruba–Tobelo leg takes another 3 hours.

Fares run about $5 for the Ternate–Daruba leg, another $1.50 to Tobelo. Mattresses are provided; a short bed in a mini-cabin costs an extra $6. Departures average three times a week. These boats plough through all but the worst storms. There's no food to purchase on board, so bring your own. Only one toilet per boat, so waiting lines can be desperately long.

At the Tobelo wharf, there will be lots of *becaks* at quay-side, eager for your body and luggage. The drivers charge Rp500–Rp1,000 to the hotels; agree on a price before you get in.

GETTING AROUND

Jailolo region. Minibuses ply the roads around Jailolo; the fares range from 15¢–40¢.

East coast of the north peninsula. Crowded minibuses connect Galela, Tobelo and Kao on the partially paved road running along Halmahera's east coast. You can charter these minibuses, but prices vary widely depending on distances, time and operator. Let your hotel arrange this unless your Indonesian is up to snuff. Ordinary fares on these "taxis" range from 7¢–45¢.

ACCOMMODATIONS

Tobelo

The owners of Tobelo's three hotels are most helpful in providing information on rituals and events in the area. Almost no English is spoken here; communication is strictly in Indonesian. The hotels can help make bookings on Merpati or find an outboard-powered outrigger to hire to offshore islands for swimming and snorkeling.

We recommend the **Pantai Indah Hotel**. Ask for one of the upstairs rooms which gives an excellent view over the bay. Great sunrises with paddled outriggers, mini-sailed canoes, and coconut islands. Repeat performance at sunset. **Pantai Indah Hotel** Jl. Imam Sideba Gamsungi, ☎ 21068, 21064. 10 rooms, all with attached toilet bath. $18 non-AC, $20 AC, with meals. **Hotel Megaria** Jl. Gamsungi, across from the movie house on the coastal road. 10 rooms, half with attached toilet/bath. $3–6 w/o meals; $5–$8 w/meals. **Hotel Karunia** Jl. Kemakmuran. ☎ 21202. 6 rooms, 2 with attached bath/toilet. $8 w/meals.

Kao

There are two decent losmen in town, inexpensive and with full board, quick laundry service, and tea and coffee all day. There are no restaurants in town. Dirgahayu is by far the better of the two. Prices include meals. **Dirgahayu** 8 rooms, 2 w/ attached bath. The owner, Pak Tungabalin, can help arrange activities, including diving, boat rentals, traditional music and dances, all at reasonable prices. His oldest son speaks English. His hotel averages 8 foreigners a year, just about the total number of visitors to Kao. $7. **Sejahtera** 6 rooms w/o attached bath. $6.

Jailolo

There is one small *losmen* in Jailolo. It charges $3/day, without board.

SOUVENIRS

The Tobelorese are known for finely woven pandanus leaf *tikar* sleeping mats, rice winnowers and handsome, funnel-shaped backpack baskets called *saloi*. Occasionally, huge coconut crabs or lobsters mounted on red felt are offered for sale, although these items usually have to be specially ordered. Shell collectors should ask around for local varieties.

DIVING

Tobelo

With a bit of advance warning, your hotel can help you arrange the rental of an outboard powered outrigger canoe, called a "Johnson" in the local idiom. Depending on the engine and boat size, a half day costs $10–$20. You can reach Pulau Tagalaya in a half hour. A white-sand beach, Pantai Leleboto, faces the bay and a shallow, coral-strewn bottom perfect for swimming and snorkeling. About 50 m out, the bottom drops off steeply and here you can see a variety of fish, including an occasional reef shark. Serious scuba divers are better off on the other side of Tagalaya, which faces the open sea, where there is a more impressive collection of coral and marine life than the bayside.

Another small island south of Tagalaya, Pulau Tuputupu, also offers good swimming, snorkeling and diving. (This island is said to be haunted by dwarf ghosts.) Remember hats, sunscreen and plenty of drinking water.

Kao

There is no diving equipment in Kao, but qualified divers can rent equipment from either of two pearl diving teams on Bobale island, off Daru village between Kao and Tobelo. The pearl divers have a boat, a compressor, tanks, and regulators, which they will rent for $30–$50 a day. To accompany them on one dive, $13–$15.

WEATHER

It rains every month, with February, May, September, and December receiving the most, over 300 mm a month. January, March, April, June, and October get about 100–200 mm of rain. Generally, the drier season is during the southwest monsoon (May–October), and the wetter one during the northeast monsoon (December–March).

The strongest winds are in January and July, while the quietest seas are during the transition periods between monsoons, April and November. But winds and weather change so much that no one should plan on a trip based solely on the seasonal forecast.

Morotai

Every Saturday Merpati flies from Ternate to the U.S.-built airfield near Daruba ($35), where there is a ferry that makes a run from Ternate to Daruba to Tobelo and then back.

There is one *losmen* in Daruba, Losmen Tonggak, with 4 rooms renting for $6–$10.

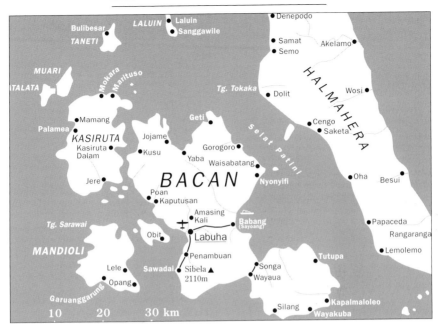

Bacan

GETTING THERE

By air

Merpati flies from Ternate to Labuha (Tuesday and Friday) and from Ambon via Sanana in the Sula Islands (Monday and Thursday). The landing strip is 3 km from Labuha.

Merpati P.T. Sibela Mega Jaya, Labuha, Bacan ☎ (0927) 21006.

By sea

The boats call daily (almost) at Bacan's Babang harbor, then go on to Obi Island's two ports, Laiwui on the north coast and Wailower on the southern shore. It takes about 9 hours, $6 for passage, plus $5.50 if you want a berth in one of the crew's cabins.

The boats return to Ternate via Bacan. From Babang, it's 16 km on a paved but narrow road (45 min) to Labuha, 50¢ by public transport, or free if you stay at the *losmen* Borero Indah, whose minibus meets all boats and flights. Tickets for ship passage from Bacan are sold at Babang, usually on the day of departure.

ACCOMMODATIONS

Pondok Indah Jl. Usman Shah, ☎ 48. 11 rooms. Clean and pleasant. $17.50 for one person in one of the two AC rooms, with meals; two persons sharing AC room, with meals, $28. Fan-cooled rooms, $8.50, with meals.

Borero Indah Jl. Tanah Abang, ☎ 24. 11 rooms. Clean and pleasant. They can put a minibus at your disposal, with driver $3 per hour. 3 AC rooms, $14 with meals; fan-cooled rooms, $8.50 with meals.

Harmonis Jl. Molon Junga, ☎ 20. 12 rooms, all fan cooled. A bit seedy. $8.50 per person, with meals.

DINING

Best to take your meals at the hotels, but if you want to step out, there are two restaurants featuring *karaoke* sing-alongs.

At the **Caffetaria Sibela**, you can eat rice or noodle-based dishes for $1, chicken dishes $1.50, gado-gado 50¢, beer $1/can or $1.75/bottle. About the same fare and prices at the **Ekaria**, plus *pangsit* (a kind of Chinese noodle or ravioli), 50¢. At both places, each *karaoke* song (Indonesian or American) costs 50¢.

BOAT CHARTER

A speed boat with 40 Hp outboard will cost about $70 for round-trip to Kasiruta, 3–4 passengers. For a canoe with small outboard, round trip to nearby Nusadeket and Nusara islands, $14 including waiting around while you snorkel and lie on the beach.

7 Southeast PRACTICALITIES

INCLUDES KEI, ARU, AND TANIMBAR ISLANDS

The tiny islands scattered between Wetar (near Timor), and the Aru group (next to Papua New Guinea), are probably the more remote islands of Indonesia. The beaches of the Kei Islands are unsurpassed, the wooden ancestral figures and gold jewelry of the Tanimbars is famous, and the birds of paradise of the Aru Islands spectacular.

Prices are in US $. Telephone code for Tual (Kei) is 0916, Dobo (Aru) is 0917, Saumlaki (Tanimbar) is 0918. AC=Airconditioning. S=Single, D=Double.

Kei Islands

ORIENTATION

The Kei Islands are the gateway to the entire southeast Maluku province, and all flights into the region must be via Dumatubun airport, at Langgur on Kei Kecil, which is connected to Dullah Island by a bridge. Tual, the capital of southeast Maluku province, is on Dullah Island.

GETTING THERE

By air

Merpati flies to Langgur from Ambon on Monday, Tuesday, Thursday, Friday, and Saturday. The 2-hour flight, in an 18-seat Twin Otter, costs $71. The planes look somewhat old, but their safety record is excellent. The flights are often either cancelled or overbooked.

Minibus/taxis wait at the airport, ready to whisk you and your luggage off. Rip-offs are standard operating procedure. About $7 should get you to Tual, or walk out to the main road and take a *bemo* for Rp350.

Merpati. C.V.Rahmat Jaya Maira. ☎ (0916) 21376, 21353. Open (in theory) 9am–2pm.

By sea

The Pelni liners are still the surest way to get to and from the southeast islands. The *Rinjani* leaves Ambon every second Friday for Tual and arrives there on Saturday morning. Two weeks later, it leaves Tual on Saturday morning for Fakfak, Banda and Ambon. Ambon-Tual $20 (economy), $30 (4th class); Tual-Ambon $30 (economy). *Tatamilau*, stops at Tual four times during its 28-day route. See the Transportation section (page 181) for the routes.

The mixed freighters, Daya Nusantara and

Dharma Wisata, also make Tual a regular stop. Other mixed freighters swing by occasionally.

Motor launches to Dobo in the Arus make the trip about once or twice a month. This 12-hour run is usually made at night (about $3).

Boat traffic throughout Southeast Maluku increases around Christmas, when ships bring civil servants home from southern Irian Jaya.

GETTING AROUND

Ferry

A daily morning and afternoon ferry links Tual to Banda Elat on Kei Besar, a 2–3 hour trip ($1.50). Other than this, all other boat links are extremely unreliable. Check with your hotel proprietor or look for free-lancers at the docks to visit nearby islands. Or try going by "Motor" for $1.

Taxi/minibuses

Public minibuses within Tual and from Tual to Langgur are easy to find and run about 15¢. Short trips to nearby villages (say 15 km) cost about 25¢ and to the tip of Kei Kecil costs about $1.25. These buses are not for the impatient, however, and they only run when full, so they're always crowded. Chartering a minibus costs $4.50–$6 an hour, including waiting time.

ACCOMMODATIONS

Accommodations in the Tual–Langgur area are fairly standard. Everywhere the TV lulls you to sleep, sometimes with English language programs relayed by satellite from Jakarta. Rooms with attached bath and toilet cost about $10 a day with meals, $8 without food. The friendliest of the small lot, with a good hilltop location, is the **Linda Mas**, although it is a bit far from the "downtown."

Closest to the harbor and market, the Arab-owned **Mirah** is also close to the mosque, whose blaring call makes a very effective alarm clock—permanently set for 4:30 am. The **Rosemgen** is decent enough, but the food here, as elsewhere, could improve greatly. Only Padang-style mini-restaurants and *warung*s are available for eating out.

Tual

Tual is the biggest town south of Ambon and is the district capital of Southeast Maluku. Tual: 12,500 people, Langgur: 7,500. This urban sprawl almost makes up 10% of the district of the southeast Maluku. There's not much to do in Tual or Langgur, except to wait for a boat or minibus to visit the surrounding countryside and beaches.
Rosemgen Jl. Aipda KS Tuban. ☎ 21045. On a short but steep hill, just off the main street through town. 10 rooms, 4 with attached bath. $8, $10 with meals.
Nini Gerhana Jl. Raya Pattimura. ☎ 21343. 12 rooms, 4 with attached bath. $6 with meals.
Mirah Jl. Mayor Abdullah, ☎ 21172. Conveniently located for harbor, market, taxi terminal and mosque. 6 rooms, 3 with attached bath, $4 without meals.
Linda Mas Jl. Anthony Rhebok (the area is better known as "Komplek Kantor Bupati"), ☎ 21271. 10 rooms, all with attached bath. The friendliest joint, but far from the little bit of downtown Tual action. The local high school English teacher often hangs out here. $6.50, meals available.

Langgur

Rosemgen II Jl. Merdeka, near the Jembatan Watdek bridge to Tual. ☎ 21477. 26 good-sized rooms. This is the newest, best and most expensive hotel in town. There are plans for a restaurant and conference room as well as seaside cottages. All AC, $15S, $21D.
Rama Indah Jl. Pahlawan Revolusi, near the airport in Langgur, ☎ 21232. 9 rooms, some with facilities. $4.50 bare room, $6 room with facilities. Add $3 for board.

Aru Islands

Getting to the Aru Islands is, to put it mildly, difficult. Ships average once or twice a month out of Ambon, or you could get on the *Dharma Wisata*'s Tual–Dobo leg. From Tual, motor launches make the trip much more quickly—about 12 hours, overnight. The run costs only $3, but again, the boats run once, maybe twice a month. If you don't have the patience to wait two weeks or more, you can charter a boat—$125 to $185, each way. If you can find some friends with whom to split the cost, this might be the way to go. Merpati runs a pioneer flight from Ambon via Langgur on Tuesday and Sunday ($30), but don't count on this.

Tanimbar Islands

GETTING THERE

Merpati flies directly from Ambon to Saumlaki on Yamdena twice a week, Thursday and Saturdays ($80). The flight reveals a stupendous view of the Kei islands on the way. As with flights to Tual, cancellations and overbookings are frequent. Plenty of minibuses greet arriving passengers, and you might as well hop into one sent by either of the two hotels, which will give you a free ride. Otherwise, bargain and expect to settle at Rp1,000–2,000 for the short ride to town.
 Sea transport from Ambon is handled by Pelni Lines' *Tatamailau* on its way to and from Denpasar via Tual; other ships also (see above) make the trip from Tual. The surest way to get to the Tanimbars is by ferry from Tual to Saumlaki. The ferry leaves Tual every Monday and arrives in Saumlaki on Tuesday, then back to Tual, on Wednesday night. This gives you one full week in the Tanimbars.

GETTING AROUND

Public buses, also available for charter, carry full loads of passengers, chickens and ducks to all villages within reach. A 30 km stretch of paved road snakes north, and it is planned to extend this artery the length of Yamdena Island. Because of the swampy coasts, this main thoroughfare swings inland as it roughly parallels the east coast, so all the seaside villages require access roads. There are no interior villages.
To Sanglia Dol From Saumlaki, a "speedboat" can be chartered for the 4-hour round trip to the traditional village of Sanglia Dol ($30–$60). For those with more time and less money, there are buses to Ilnge (about 18 km from Saumlaki, 50¢) from where outboard canoes ply a regular route along the coast—it's about $1 to Sanglia Dol. Theoretically, service is once or twice a day, but plan to spend the night if you take this route. Alternately, you might be able to hire one of the outboard canoes at Ilnge to Sanglia Dol, about $25–$35 for the 4–6 hour round trip.

ACCOMMODATIONS

You have two to choose from, both close to each other on the main street in town, Jalan Bhineka. The hotels come with full board, and if you don't want food, knock off about 40% of the room rental. In that case you can eat out at one of Saumlaki's two Padang-style restaurants. We recommend the hotel food.

Harapan Indah 10 rooms, some with AC. ☎ 21019. The best in town. The hotel rents boats, for use nearby, $30/day. Minibus, $6/day. $12S, $35D with AC. Includes food.
Pantai Indah Jl. Kp. Babar. ☎ 21059. Same prices as above.

DIVING

The most spectacular diving spots in the Tanimbars are off the coasts of Nustabun Island, a half-hour by launch from Saumlaki. Several speedboats (25–40 HP) are available in Saumlaki for charter, about $10–$15 per hour. One of the town's local Indonesian-Chinese merchants runs a small-scale, seasonal pearling operation. He will rent scuba gear—including a full tank—to qualified divers for $8 a day.

CANOE RENTAL

Sailing canoes can be rented in Saumlaki. Bring a local man along as the sails can be difficult to handle. A paddle and a pole for shallow water are both recommended. About $8 should cover an afternoon's outing with sail and a crew of two. Protect your camera equipment as well as your head and skin from the sun.

MONEY CHANGING

Toko Selatan. At this shop on Jl. Bhineka, the proprietor will change cash (no travelers checks) from most countries. He charges a slight commission over the rates in the money-exchange list in the Jakarta newspapers. Still, it's best to bring all necessary cash from Ambon or Tual. The banks in town don't handle foreign exchange.

WEATHER

The weather is warm and pleasant year-round. The northwest monsoon, from May or June to November, brings short rains while the hot southeast monsoon, brings dry air from Australia, and lots of sunshine.

PERIPLUS LANGUAGE GUIDES

These handy pocket dictionaries are a must for travelers to Indonesia and Malaysia. Each book contains the 2,000 most commonly-used words and is bidirectional, giving definitions from the language to English and vice versa.

English-Indonesian / Indonesian-English
Pocket Dictionary

ISBN 0-945971-66-4

The Indonesian Pocket Dictionary *is available in English, French, German and Dutch editions.*

English-Malay / Malay-English
Pocket Dictionary

ISBN 0-945971-99-0

Distributed by:
Berkeley Books Pte. Ltd. (Singapore & Malaysia)
5 Little Road, #08-01, Singapore 536983 Tel: (65) 280 3320 Fax: (65) 280 6290

C.V. Java Books (Indonesia)
Jl. Kelapa Gading Kirana, Blok A14 No. 17, Jakarta 14240 Tel: (62-21) 451 5351 Fax: (62-21) 453 4987

Further Reading

Shirley Deane's excellent *Ambon, Island of Spices,* about her stay as an English schoolteacher in Ambon, offers glimpses into a strange, and supernatural world.

Maria Dermôut plunges into this world of magic in *The Ten Thousand Things.* A best-seller translated into 11 languages, her novel is based on 30 years' experience in Indonesia. The spellbinding narrative is woven through a haunting setting.

Dermôut owes much of her inspiration to a previous description of the exquisite treasure trove of Ambon's tropical ecology. Her mentor was Rumphius, the "blind seer of Ambon," who appears as a moving force in Dermôut's work.

Rumphius arrived in Ambon in 1652 and died there 50 years later. Starting in the military, he then worked his way up to the prestigious position of chief merchant in the Dutch East Indies Company. His hobby — more like a consuming passion, really — was to write superb desciptions of Ambon's tropical plants and "curiosities": unusual shells, fish, animals, minerals, and stones.

Rumphius' *Ambonese Herbal* described and illustrated some 8,000 species of tropical plants. He pioneered an improved method for processing sago, a staple food in much of eastern Indonesia. The main species of sago now bears his name: *Metroxylon rumphii.* His name is also familiar to shell collectors, for the elegant descriptions of many beautiful shells found in Ambon's rich waters.

English-speaking readers can now examine a part of Rumphius' writings. *The Poison Tree,* edited and translated by E.M. Beekman, offers selected passages, along with fascinating biographical notes.

Banner, H.S. *A Tropical Tapestry.* London, 1929.

Barbosa, D. *The Book of Duarte Barbosa.* Hakluyt Society, 1918.

Bartels, D. *Guarding the Invisible Mountain Wall.* Unpubl. PhD thesis, Cornell University, 1977.

Beekman, E.M. *The Poison Tree: Selected Writings of Rumphius on the Natural History of the Indies.* Amherst, MA: University of Massachusetts Press, 1981.

Bickmore, A.S. *Travels in the East Indian Archipelago.* London, 1868.

Boxer, C.R. *The Dutch Seaborne Empire, 1600-1800.* London, 1973.

——. *The Portuguese Seaborne Empire, 1415-1825.* New York, 1969.

Burhamzah. "An Economic Survey of Maluku" in *Bulletin of Indonesian Economic Studies 6* (1970) 2:31–45.

Chauvel, Richard. *The Rising Sun in the Spice Islands.* Monash University, 1985.

Cooley, F. *Altar and Throne in Central Moluccan Societies.* 1967.

——. *Ambonese Adat.* New Haven, 1962.

Coolhaas, W.Ph. *A Critical Survey of Studies on Dutch Colonial History.* The Hague, 1980.

Crofton, R.H. *A Pageant of the Spice Islands.* London, 1936.

Deane, Shirley. *Ambon, Island of Spices.* London, 1979.

Defranca, Pinto. *Portuguese Influences in Indonesia.* Jakarta, 1970.

de Jonge, Nico & Toos van Dijk. *Forgotten Islands of Indonesia: The Art & Culture of the Southeast Moluccas.* Singapore, 1995.

Dermôut, Maria. *The Ten Thousand Things.* Amherst, MA: University of Massachusetts Press, 1983.

Drake, F. *The World Encompassed.* London, 1854.

Earl, G.W. *The Native Races of the Indian Archipelago.* London, 1853.

Ellen, R.F. *Nualu Settlement and Ecology.* The Hague, 1978.

Fairchild, D. *Garden Islands of the Great East.* New York, 1943.

Forbes, Anna. *Unbeaten Tracks in the Islands of the Far East.* Singapore: Graham Brash, 1987.

Forbes, Henry O. *A Naturalist's Wanderings in the Eastern Archipelago.* New York, 1940.

Forrest, Thomas. *A Voyage to New Guinea and the Moluccas 1774-6.* Kuala Lumpur, Oxford in Asia Reprints, 1969.

Foster, W. *The Journal of John Kourdain 1608-1617.* Cambridge, 1905.

Glamann, K. *Dutch-Asiatic Trade 1620-1740.* The Hague, 1958.

Hanbury-Tenison, R. *A Pattern of Peoples.* New York, 1975.

——. *A Slice of Spice.* London 1974.

Hanna, Willard A. *Indonesian Banda.* Phila., 1978.

LeBar, Frank. *Ethnic Groups of Insular South-East Asia.* New Haven, 1972.

Masinambon, E.K.M. *Halmehera and Raja Empat.* Leknas LIPI, Jakarta, 1980.

Masselman, George. *The Cradle of Colonialism.* New Haven, 1963.

Masselman, George. *The Money Trees.* New York, 1967.

McKinnon, Susan. *Hierachy, Alliance and Exchange in the Tanimbar Islands.* Unpubl. PhD Thesis. Chicago, 1983.

Middleton, H. *The Voyage of Sir Henry Middleton.* Hakluyt reprint, 1980.

Pigafetta, A. *The First Voyage around the World by Magellan.* London, 1874.

Pires, Tome. *Summa Oriental.* London, 1944.

Polman, Katrien. *The Central Moluccas: an Annotated Bibliography.* Leiden, 1983.

Thomlinson, C.M. *Tidemarks.* London: Cassell, 1945 (last printing). Originally published in 1924, first paperback in 1928.

Glossary

adat tradition; customs
agama religion
agar-agar seaweed
air belanda lit. "Dutch water"; creek on Bacan
Alfur original inhabitants of the region, of Papuan stock; live on Seram and other islands; souce of much of Ambon's adat
alus refined, smooth; polar opposite of *kasar*
andong horsecart with four wheels
apotik pharmacy
arak palm brandy
atap roof

bahar weight measurement; approx. 11.1 lbs.
bahasa language
bahasa Indonesia Indonesian language; national language of Indonesia
baileo commual meeting hall (Ambon)
bakmi/bakmie noodles
bakmi/bakmie goreng fried noodles
bakmi/bakmie godong noodle soup
batik process of "lost-wax" dye technique for printing cloth; done primarily in Java
batu Bacan semi-precious stones found on Bacan; believed to hold magical powers
batu pamali sacred stones vested with supernatural powers (Ambon)
bemo mini-bus; public transport, some can be chartered for private use
bendé horsecart with two wheels
beras hulled, uncooked rice
bulan month

cakalélé war dances
camat head government official of the district
cengkeh cloves
cuci negeri village cleansing/purification; annual event

danau lake
dati corporation of patrilineally related kinsmen (Ambon)
delman horsecart with two wheels
desa village
desa adat "traditional village"; lowest administrative level of the state
diskon discount

fam localized patrilineal clan group (Ambon)

gaba-gaba central spine of the sago palm leaf
gaharu aloes wood, valuable incense resin (Bacan)
gunung mountain

harga mati lit. "dead price"; fixed price
harga pas fixed price
hongi sea-going war expedition to collect tributes

ikat woven cloth from Flores, Timor

jam karet "rubber time"
jeruk citrus fruit
jeruk nipis lime

kabupaten regency, headed by the bupati; second level administrative unit under the province
kain material; fabric
kain sinun special woven cloth, features tree of life motif, man with upraised arms.
kampung neighborhood
kanari canari tree or its nuts
kasar rough, uncouth; polar opposite to *alus*
kebaya women's long-sleeved blouse; often made of brocade or light voile
kecamatan district, headed by the camat
kedaton palace; place of the *datu* (ruler)
kelapa muda young coconut
kepala desa village head
keris daggers, some considered magically powerful; may have eiter straight or wavy blade; part of formal male attire; worn in the back, handle tipped to the right
keroncong popular music; mixes indigenous, Malay, and Portuguese musical elements
ketan glutinous ("sticky") rice
ketang kenari coconut crab
KNIL Koninklijk Nederlands Indisch Leger, Royal Dutch Army; consisted entirely of Moluccan soldiers, formed in 1830
koli lontar palm; provides palm wine
komo small tuna, usually smoked, served as a snack (Saparua)
kora-kora traditional warship of the Maluku
kretek clove-filled cigaret
KSDA (Kehutanan Sumber Daya Alam) Natural Resources office of the Department of Forestry
kupu-kupu butterfly
kupu-kupu raja "king butterflies"; some with wing span of 1.5 m, sporting 12 colors

lalosi herring, usually smoked, served as a snack (Saparua)

mahkota crown
maleo megapode which lays eggs in vegetation heaps on certain beaches
manusia mamole spirits on Gamalama Moun-

tain (Tidore)
massoi variety of tree bark; used for medicinal purposes; highly prized trade item
mata rumah lit. "eye of the house"; localized patrilineal clan group (Ambon)
mauwen traditional animist priesthood (Ambon)
Mel-Mel aristocrats of the Kei islands
minyak kayu putih lit "white wood oil"; oil extracted from leaves of a kind of myrtle; external medicinal uses, including alleviating muscle ache, nausea

nasi cooked rice
nasi campur rice with varied condiments
nasi goreng fried rice
natar boat-shaped stone altar/platform (Tanimbar)
negeri one or more *soa*; village (Ambon)
NGO non-government organization; promotes community self-reliance activities
nonok large, black tailless monkeys found on Bacan island, also called *yakis*

obat medicine
orang kaya lit. "rich people"; local aristocracy
orang Sirani term used for Christians in Maluku in mid-1850's; thought to be of Portuguese descent

pahlawan national hero/heroine
pala nutmeg
parang machete
pariwisata tourism
pasar daily market for food, clothing, flowers, utensils, etc.; bargaining is the way of life
pasar malam night market
pela complicated set of inter-village alliances (Ambon)
penginapan lodging
perken parcels of land 1.2 hectares each
perkenier licensed Dutch plantation owners
pesantren traditional Moslem school
PHPA Perlindungan Hutan dan Pelestarian Alam, Forest Protection and Nature Conservation; division of Department of Forestry
pondok little shelter
prahu large boats, may be motorized
pusaka sacred heirloom
puskesmas Pusat Kesehatan Masyarakat, community health center

raja king, ruler
rijstaffel "rice table," full meal of rice with various side dishes
RMS Republik Maluku Selatan, South Moluccan Republic; independent country promised to Dutch Moluccans by Dutch government
rujak raw fruits mixed with sauce of shrimp paste, chilies and sometimes palm sugar
rumah makan restaurant
rumah sakit hospital

sagero palm wine (Tanimbar)

sago gummy starch from the pith of a tall palm tree (*Metroxylon rumphii*)
sakuda snapper, usually smoked, served as a snack (Saparua)
sambal hot chili sauce
saloi rattan/reed baskets made by Makian islanders
saniri negeri central committee of elders who assist the ruler (Ambon)
sapu lidi broom made of split coconut midribs, used for sweeping yards; also used in ritual dance during which dancers are flogged with this broom
sarong 2 meter piece of fabric sewn into a tube, worn as a wrapped skirt by men
sawah irrigated rice field
siput oyster; snail
soa political unit consisting of several united clan groups (Ambon)
sopi local palm wine
stampal royal crown
suane village ritual house where sacred heirlooms are stored (Seram)

Tenggara Jauh distant southeast; refers to islands between the Tanimbar islands and Timor
toko obat store which sells medicine without prescriptions
tongkat cane, stick
trepang dried sea cucumbers, Chinese delicacy; prime trade item

ubi sweet potato
uli lit. "brotherhood"; division of villages into several federations (Ambon)

warung food stall, small eatery
WWF World Wide Fund for Nature; assisting in conservation projects throughout Indonesia

yakis large, black, tailless monkeys found on Bacan island, also called *nonok*

Index

Map Index